Innovative Methods in Korean Language Teaching

Innovative Methods in Korean Language Teaching showcases research-based and experience-based contributions and reflections on the potential of adopting technological and non-technological innovations to promote Korean language students' learning.

The chapters included in this book consider a wide range of innovative technologies and approaches, such as large language models, virtual reality solutions, metaverse platforms, multimodal teaching, and critical pedagogy, and represent a variety of geographical learning contexts from North America to Europe, from Korea to the broader Asia-Pacific region. Overall, these contributions make the case for embracing new technologies instead of banning them and for accepting pedagogical shifts that take into consideration contemporary understandings of the communication, teaching, and learning processes.

This book will be of interest to graduate students, researchers, and practitioners of Korean language education and to those working on language teaching and learning in general, to inform future teaching practices through careful consideration of contemporary technologies and teaching approaches.

Nicola Fraschini is a senior lecturer at the University of Melbourne Asia Institute, where he is convener of the Korean Studies program and director of the Global Korea Research Hub. His research interests are the psychology of language learners and teachers and Q methodology.

Jieun Kiaer is the YBMK KF Professor of Korean Linguistics in the University of Oxford's Asian and Middle Eastern Studies Faculty. She publishes widely on linguistics, Asian studies, and translation. Her recent research covers the future of human language, social media behaviors, big data, and AI linguistics. Wearing the hats of linguist, pragmatist, and Asian specialist, she is uniquely positioned to respond to the recent developments in AI.

The Korean Wave in Translation
Series Editor: Jieun Kiaer
University of Oxford, UK

The Korean Wave in Translation series will aim to discuss issues of translation, invisibility, and the meanings of 'K-ness' in conjunction with the cultural phenomenon, the Korean Wave.

Following the explosion of K-Wave products into the global mainstream, this series comes at an opportune moment. Though there has been study into the difficulties and nuances of translation of Korean into English, recent smash hit films, record breaking TV shows, and successful bands – i.e. *Parasite* (2019), *Squid Game* (2021), and BTS, to name a few – demonstrate that the K-Wave is influential on such a scale that specific attention must be paid to the translation of K-Wave media. This series will consider how K-media is being translated for the global audience and how depth of meaning has thereby been limited. This study is both a linguistic and cultural study, examining the process of translation and meaning-making engendered by the ever-successful K-Wave, with specific focus on the role of consumers in crowd-sourced meaning-making.

The series will primarily consist of monographs dedicated to discussing the following issues:

- Dialogue translation for K-Film and K-Dramas
- Lyric translation for K-Pop
- Narrative translation for K-Literature
- How to tackle translating the 'invisibles' of Korean language
- Crowd-sourced meaning-making
- Social media and its impact on translation
- The K-Wave as a harbinger of diversity and the desire for diversity in Western-centric popular culture
- The K-Wave as a model for other Asian countries to export popular culture products
- The role of Hangeul in K-media translation

Innovative Methods in Korean Language Teaching
Edited by Nicola Fraschini and Jieun Kiaer

www.routledge.com/languages/book-series/KWT

Innovative Methods in Korean Language Teaching

Edited by Nicola Fraschini and Jieun Kiaer

LONDON AND NEW YORK

Designed cover image: elenabs via Getty Images

First published 2025
by Routledge
4 Park Square, Milton Park, Abingdon, Oxon OX14 4RN

and by Routledge
605 Third Avenue, New York, NY 10158

Routledge is an imprint of the Taylor & Francis Group, an informa business

© 2025 selection and editorial matter, Nicola Fraschini and Jieun Kiaer; individual chapters, the contributors

The right of Nicola Fraschini and Jieun Kiaer to be identified as the authors of the editorial material, and of the authors for their individual chapters, has been asserted in accordance with sections 77 and 78 of the Copyright, Designs and Patents Act 1988.

All rights reserved. No part of this book may be reprinted or reproduced or utilised in any form or by any electronic, mechanical, or other means, now known or hereafter invented, including photocopying and recording, or in any information storage or retrieval system, without permission in writing from the publishers.

Trademark notice: Product or corporate names may be trademarks or registered trademarks, and are used only for identification and explanation without intent to infringe.

British Library Cataloguing-in-Publication Data
A catalogue record for this book is available from the British Library

ISBN: 978-1-032-72528-4 (hbk)
ISBN: 978-1-032-72526-0 (pbk)
ISBN: 978-1-003-46348-1 (ebk)

DOI: 10.4324/9781032725307

Typeset in Times New Roman
by Apex CoVantage, LLC

Contents

Acknowledgments	*vii*
List of contributors	*viii*
AI declaration	*xi*

Introduction: Innovative methods for global Korean language teaching 1
NICOLA FRASCHINI AND JIEUN KIAER

PART I
Large language models and Korean language education 11

1 **AI-powered writing assistance: Korean language students' and teachers' views and experiences** 13
   INHYE LEE

2 **Students' perceptions of utilizing AI chatbots as conversation partners for Korean speaking practice: acceptance, benefits, and challenges** 28
   NA-YOUNG RYU

3 **Large language models for Korean grammar and spelling corrections: comparative evaluation of Bard, Bing, ChatGPT, CLOVA X, and Perplexity AI** 46
   NARAE JUNG

4 **The potential of generative AI in writing feedback for Korean L2 learners: an analysis on grammar error correction by ChatGPT-3.5 for TOPIK II writing tasks** 64
   KUKJIN KIM

PART II
VR, metaverse, and other technology-based approaches to Korean language teaching   77

5 Virtual interactions in Seoul: implementation of high-immersion virtual reality (HiVR) technology in a Korean language class   79
JIYOUNG KIM AND SOYEON KIM

6 Exploring the possibilities and limits of metaverse as a Korean teaching resource: the case of the Sejong Institute's metaverse proposal   100
ÁLVARO TRIGO MALDONADO

7 Using a YouTube channel as a supplementary language teaching and learning platform   115
MYOUNGHEE CHO

PART III
Moving beyond technology for innovation in Korean language teaching   131

8 Excitement and confusion: an emotion-based approach to Korean language teaching   133
NICOLA FRASCHINI AND YU TAO

9 Multimodal approaches to Korean language teaching   151
LUCIEN BROWN

10 Transformative learning through critical pedagogy in Korean language education   173
YOUNG-MEE YU CHO AND HEE CHUNG CHUN

Additional resources   *189*
Index   *193*

Acknowledgments

This work was supported by the Core University Program for Korean Studies of the Ministry of Education of the Republic of Korea and Korean Studies Promotion Service at the Academy of Korean Studies (AKS-2021-OLU-2250004).

Contributors

Lucien Brown is Korea Foundation Associate Professor in Korean Studies at Monash University. His research focuses on multimodal politeness in first and second language contexts. His book *Korean Honorifics and Politeness in Second Language Learning* is published by John Benjamins, as well as the co-authored edited volume *Multimodal Im/politeness*.

Myounghee Cho is Assistant Professor of instruction in Korean in the Department of Modern Languages and Cultures at the University of Rochester. She is interested in language pedagogy and the development of effective instructional methods and materials for Korean language education.

Young-mee Yu Cho is Professor of Korean Language and Culture in the Department of Asian Languages and Cultures at Rutgers, the State University of New Jersey. She is one of the three editors for the new series, DITTA: Korean Humanities in Translation (Rutgers University Press). Her publications include *Integrated Korean Textbook Series* (2000–2021), *Teaching Korean as a Foreign Language: Theories and Practices* (2021), *You Call That Music?!: Korean Popular Music Through the Generations* (2022), *Rereading Chang Lee Wook* (2022), *Korea Letters in the William Elliot Griffis Collection: An Annotated Selection* (2024), and many others.

Hee Chung Chun is Assistant Teaching Professor in the Department of Asian Languages and Cultures at Rutgers, the State University of New Jersey. Her research focuses on foreign language pedagogy, curriculum design, heritage language education, and conversation analysis. She has co-authored the workbooks accompanying the *Integrated Korean: Accelerated 1 & 2* (2020) textbook series tailored specifically for Korean heritage students and is also a co-author of the forthcoming *Integrated Korean: High Advanced 1 & 2* textbooks.

Nicola Fraschini is Senior Lecturer at the University of Melbourne Asia Institute, where he is convener of the Korean Studies program and Director of the Global Korea Research Hub. His research interests are the psychology of language teaching and learning and Q methodology. He is co-author of the textbook *Mission Accomplished: Korean 1& 2* (Hawoo, 2022/2023) and co-editor of *Advancing Language Research through Q Methodology* (Multilingual Matters, 2024).

Narae Jung is Senior Lecturer and Korean Language Coordinator at the Centre for Modern Languages in the School of Humanities at Nanyang Technological University, Singapore. Her publications include "Teaching Korean with BTS content" (2022), "Korean Learning Motivation and Demotivation of university students in Singapore" (2017), and "A Study on the Method of Designing a Korean for Hobby Purposes Course" (2016).

Jieun Kiaer is the YBMK KF Professor of Korean Linguistics in the University of Oxford's Asian and Middle Eastern Studies Faculty. She publishes widely on linguistics, Asian studies, and translation. Her recent research covers the future of human language, social media behaviors, big data, and AI linguistics. Wearing the hats of linguist, pragmatist, and Asian specialist, she is uniquely positioned to respond to the recent developments in AI. Her recent publications include *Emoji Speak* (Bloomsbury, 2023) and *Conversing in the Metaverse* (Bloomsbury, 2024).

Jiyoung Kim is an experienced language educator with a doctorate in curriculum and instruction from the University of Washington. She began her career teaching English in South Korean public elementary schools and has since taught the Korean language at a variety of skill levels and to both heritage and non-heritage learners. She is fascinated by the potential of technology in language learning, and she continually explores innovative approaches while teaching in the University of Michigan's Korean language program.

Kukjin Kim is Assistant Professor in Korean language and literature at the University for Foreigners of Siena. He obtained his PhD in history from the University of Pisa. Previously, he was a contract lecturer in Korean philology at the Sapienza University of Rome. His scholarly interests encompass cultural interactions between Korea and the Western world during both pre-modern and modern periods and the cultural and gender history of Korea. In tandem with his historical inquiries, he is fervently dedicated to the advancement of pedagogical methodologies for the effective teaching of Korean as a second language.

Soyeon Kim is Director of the Korean Language Program in the Department of Asian Languages and Cultures at the University of Michigan. Her research areas include interactional linguistics, discourse analysis, and second language pedagogy.

Inhye Lee is Associate Professor at Chonnam National University in South Korea. She earned her PhD in Korean language and cultural education from Korea University. With a passion for language education, her research has been published in peer-reviewed journals, covering diverse areas such as writing, L2 motivation, teacher education, and curriculum development. Currently, her research focus lies in exploring how AI technology influences the writing process for Korean language learners.

Álvaro Trigo Maldonado is Adjunct Professor and coordinator of Korean Studies at the Department of Modern Philology at the University of Salamanca.

He obtained his PhD from the University of Salamanca. In 2017, he won the prize for new translators awarded by the Literary Translation Institute of Korea (LTI) after spending two years at the LTI specializing in Korean–Spanish literary translation. He has translated novels by authors such as Kim Kyeong-uk, Chang Kang-myoung, O Jeonghui, Kim Aeran, and Kim Hoon, among others. His main areas of research are modern Korean language, literature, and history.

Na-Young Ryu is Assistant Teaching Professor in the Department of Asian Studies at Penn State University. Her research focuses on computer-assisted language learning and Korean phonology. Recently, she has expanded her interests to include the impact of AI-powered tools on language education. In this rapidly evolving field, she investigates how both learners and educators perceive AI chatbots for improving Korean speaking skills. With a keen eye for integrating innovative technologies into education, Na-Young is dedicated to enhancing language learning experiences and outcomes through her research and teaching.

Yu Tao is Associate Professor at the University of Western Australia (UWA), where he designs, coordinates, and teaches Chinese and Asian studies courses and served as the Discipline Chair of Asian Studies. A multiple-award-winning educator, he is passionate about conducting research into evidence-based pedagogical innovations and broader teaching and learning matters. His research interests in pedagogy and education include teaching methods in language and language-based area studies, international student mobility, and the internationalization of higher education.

AI declaration

Chapter 1 (Lee)

Tool used: ChatGPT 4.0
Link to the tool: https://openai.com/chatgpt/
Link to the terms of service: https://openai.com/policies/terms-of-use/
Purpose: Grammar and spelling corrections
Version: Paid
Output modified Y/N: Y
Percentage: about 2~3%.
No tool was used to generate parts of the text.

Tool used: CLOVA Note
Link to the tool: https://clovanote.naver.com
Link to the terms of service: https://clovanote.naver.com/terms/conditions
Purpose: Transcription of Korean interviews
Version: Free
Output modified Y/N: Y
Percentage: 0%
The tool was used only for the purpose of transcribing Korean interviews, not to generate/edit parts of the text.

Chapter 2 (Ryu)

Tool used in Figure 2.2: Sejong Hakdang AI teacher App
Link to the tool: https://app.ksif.or.kr/kor/study/aiTeacher.do
Purpose: Illustrate the tool used to conduct the study
Version of the tool represented in the screenshot: Sejong AI Auto 1.3.5
Prompt used: No prompt was used for the screenshot. The capture represents the basic homepage and its functionalities.
No tool was used to generate parts of the text.

xii *AI declaration*

Chapter 3 (Jung)

Tools used:

- ChatGPT 3.5 and 4.0 (https://chat.openai.com); (https://openai.com/policies/terms-of-use/); Free version (3.5) and paid version (4.0)
- Bard (https://bard.google.com); (https://ai.google.dev/gemini-api/terms); free version
- Bing (www.bing.com/chat), (www.microsoft.com/en-au/servicesagreement), free version
- ClovaX (https://clova-x.naver.com), (https://clova-x.naver.com/terms-of-use), free version
- Perplexity AI (www.perplexity.ai), (www.perplexity.ai/hub/legal/terms-of-service), free version

Purpose: Conducting the research (comparing the efficacy of different AI tools in identifying and correcting errors in Korean language)
Output modified Y/N: N (because of the need to show the original output of each tool)
Percentage: About 5%
No tool was used to generate parts of the text; output of the AI tools was used to support the discussion through illustrative examples.

Chapter 4 (Kim)

Tool used: ChatGPT 3.5
Link to the tool: https://openai.com/chatgpt/
Link to the terms of service: https://openai.com/policies/terms-of-use/
Purpose: Grammar and spelling corrections
Version: Free
Output modified Y/N: Y
Percentage: About 15%, including the output used in the appendix to illustrate the focus of the research, which was Chat-GPT's ability to correct text produced by the students.
No tool was used to generate parts of the text.

Chapter 5 (Kim and Kim)

Tool used: ChatGPT 3.5
Link to the tool: https://openai.com/chatgpt/
Link to the terms of service: https://openai.com/policies/terms-of-use/
Purpose: Grammar and spelling corrections
Version: Free
Output modified Y/N: Y
Percentage: About 1.5~2%
No tool was used to generate parts of the text.

Chapter 6 (Trigo Maldonado)

Tool used: ChatGPT 3.5
Link to the tool: https://openai.com/chatgpt/
Link to the terms of service: https://openai.com/policies/terms-of-use/
Purpose: Grammar and spelling corrections
Version: Free
Output modified Y/N: Y
Percentage: About 2%
No tool was used to generate parts of the text.

Chapter 7 (Cho)

Tool used: ChatGPT 3.5
Link to the tool: https://openai.com/chatgpt/
Link to the terms of service: https://openai.com/policies/terms-of-use/
Purpose: Grammar and spelling corrections
Version: Free
Output modified Y/N: Y
Percentage: About 3~4%
No tool was used to generate parts of the text.

Chapter 8 (Fraschini and Tao)

Tool used: Grammarly
Link to the tool: https://app.grammarly.com/
Link to the terms of service: www.grammarly.com/terms
Purpose: Grammar and spelling corrections
Version: Premium
Output modified Y/N: Y
Percentage: About 1.5~2%
No tool was used to generate parts of the text.

Chapter 9 (Brown)

- No AI tool used to generate and/or edit the manuscript.

Chapter 10 (Cho and Chun)

- No AI tool used to generate and/or edit the manuscript.

Introduction

Innovative methods for global Korean language teaching

Nicola Fraschini and Jieun Kiaer

1. Global Korean language learning in a post-pandemic world

The growth of Korean language learners is a global reality. Students of Korean have increased at all levels and on all continents, to the point that in 2023, CNN predicted that after K-pop and dramas, the Korean language could be the next global trend. The reality is that it is already a global trend within language learning.

At the tertiary level, the most recent report published by the Modern Language Association shows that in US universities, Korean language learners have grown 38% in the period 2016–2021. To put things in perspective, Korean is only one of the three major languages examined in the report showing an increase in enrolment and the only language displaying double-digit growth (Lusin et al., 2023). Several European universities, such as those in Italy and France, have introduced admission caps to Korean studies degree courses. In Australia, where enrolments in language subjects at the tertiary level swing from periods of concern to periods of cautious optimism (Kinder et al., 2024), Korean is still preserving its steady upward thrust (Fraschini et al., 2024).

At the secondary level, the number of high schools in Europe that have introduced a Korean course has almost doubled during the pandemic years (MOE, 2023), while in the 2023 Thai university entrance examination, Korean has been elected by nearly one out of five students sitting a second foreign language subject, increasing from the previous year (KOCIS, 2023). The past few years have also observed growth in countries that have developed, adopted, or introduced guidelines for secondary Korean language. The state government of Western Australia introduced its brand-new Korean language curriculum in 2023, making Australia the only country in the world where a Korean language curriculum has been independently developed and introduced by the government of four states or territories. In 2020, India announced that Korean will be offered as an elective for a second foreign language in the public education system, highlighting its importance and ranking it as the top choice among eight options (KBS, 2020). In the Indian case, the Korean Embassy and the Korean Cultural Centre actively advocated for including Korean as an official subject due to a rise in demand for Korean language learning in India.

DOI: 10.4324/9781032725307-1

The popularity of Korean extends well beyond the traditional formal offline classroom. Over the past ten years, the Sejong Institute has benefitted from and supported the global interest in Korean language learning. Over 580,000 students worldwide have completed the Sejong Institute courses, with 80,000 new students joining annually. As of May 2024, the Sejong Institute operates 258 locations across 85 countries, offering more than 150,000 foreign learners the possibility to engage in Korean language and cultural studies using online and offline platforms (Sejong Institute Foundation, n.d.). What is worth noting regarding the range of offers of the Sejong Institute is the number of registered users of its online learning platform, 444,019 learners as of 2022, and the fact that the Sejong Institute Foundation developed and runs an online metaverse campus (see Chapter 6), along with ten applications for online and mobile learning, including one AI-based application. The growth of Korean language learners in the online learning space is also highlighted by the 2023 annual Duolingo report, showing that Korean ranked sixth as the most-studied language on the learning platform and the most popular Asian language among younger learners (Duolingo, 2023).

It is possible to make two important remarks by considering the numbers illustrated so far. The first is that Korean language learner have grown through the pandemic years, and the second is that expanding Korean language learning opportunities through the online space and with remote solutions is the way forward in the coming years. This brings us to consider newly developed technologies and approaches, such as, but not limited to, large language models, virtual reality solutions, metaverse platforms, and multimodal teaching, as innovative methods to support the future development of Korean language teaching.

2. A watershed moment in language teaching

The disruption caused by the COVID-19 pandemic raised awareness regarding an impending paradigm shift, where language educators see technological tools not as accessories but as necessities. As if the change in perspective brought by the COVID-19 pandemic had not been enough to prompt a change of pace at which educators embrace technology, the equally disruptive emergence of artificial intelligence (AI) is now pushing language teachers and educational administrators alike even further, prompting them to reconsider their teaching practices from upside down. We are living, educationally speaking, in a watershed moment, and this volume is born out of the need to acknowledge this watershed moment, that is, to recognize that the way we teach and learn languages must adapt to our times, characterized by global mobility and interconnectivity, digital-native young learners, and rapid technological advances. The contributions contained in this book aim to provide research- and experience-based insights into how language educators can adopt and adapt the most recent technological advances and pedagogical approaches to improve their teaching efficacy.

The reader may have been attracted by the word "innovative" in the book's title. It is, therefore, essential to illustrate how the contributions included in this volume propose reflections on pedagogical innovations. The Oxford English Dictionary defines "innovate" as "to bring in or introduce novelties; to make changes in something established". Nevertheless, when speaking in educational terms, just making changes to something established does not guarantee increased teaching efficacy and better learning outcomes. For this reason, De Lano et al. (1994) pointed out that, in the field of language teaching and learning, innovation is usually characterized, at the same time, not only by change, development, and novelty but also by improvement. This last aspect, improvement, is at the core of the volume, insofar as the chapters included in this book provide an invaluable reflection on whether the innovation considered could lead to actual improvement to help educators navigate the risks and the possibilities of this watershed moment.

Markee (1993) pointed out several aspects affecting the introduction and, ultimately, the definitive adoption of pedagogical innovations. A key role among these important aspects is played by the teachers. Markee (1993) observed that accepting and adopting an innovation comes with a change of pedagogical values, and it is in this respect that the teacher figure is fundamental in the successful introduction of an innovation. Teachers who tend to challenge old pedagogical values will likely facilitate the introduction of new approaches, while teachers relying on established pedagogical practices may resist the introduction of new tools, techniques, and teaching approaches. Kennedy (1988) shows different nested systems through which an innovation is introduced, from the classroom, the inner system, to the political and cultural, the outer systems, through the administrative and institutional systems in the middle. The teachers are tasked with embracing, accepting, and adopting innovation within the inner systems of the classroom.

In this volume, the contributors draw from empirical research as well as first-hand teaching experience, and by presenting their reflections and findings regarding the introduction of innovative tools and approaches, they posit themselves as a facilitator of the introduction of innovations, leading the way for other educators to follow. Of course, the acritical adoption of an innovation for the sake of change does not lead to any improvement. Waters (2009) stressed that evaluating an innovation, that is, monitoring the effects of changes, is fundamental to considering its efficacy, whether the innovation should be refined, and ultimately, whether it can contribute to the curriculum. From this perspective, the chapters included in this volume also evaluate the effectiveness of new pedagogical tools or innovative educational programs and practices grounded on new pedagogical approaches.

The chapters exploring large language models deal with the disruptive introduction of new AI-based chatbots in Korean language education, which prompts teachers to reconsider educational practices and assessment approaches to use these tools to benefit learners' progress. These chapters want to assess the impact of AI on Korean language education while arguing for the need to embrace this new reality and pushing teachers, policymakers, and educational administrators to proactively reimagine language education alongside AI instead of advocating for bans. Overall, this volume argues that the integration of AI into language teaching has considerable potential to affect in a positive way future pedagogical practices, and it constitutes an invitation to the reader to redesign future teaching approaches

4 *Innovative Methods in Korean Language Teaching*

and tools by providing insights and guidance to educators navigating the complexities of AI integration.

Similarly, the chapters dealing with virtual reality (VR) and the metaverse analyze the potential of these new technologies in opening new (virtual) spaces, thus expanding the opportunities to communicate in the target language and providing the reader with the necessary information on whether and how to implement these tools into their teaching. The pandemic has accelerated the pace at which people communicate and interact in virtual environments, affecting verbal and nonverbal communication with important repercussions on language learning (Kiaer, 2024).

This book also includes chapters not focused on technology-based innovations, instead dealing with new understandings of the communication, teaching, and learning processes. These chapters are focused on learners' emotions, multimodal language teaching, and critical pedagogy and want to be innovative in suggesting a pedagogical shift. This volume, therefore, presents both new technology-based and non-technology–based innovations. However, we do not claim a mutually exclusive distinction between technology- and non-technology–based pedagogies. On the contrary, we want to stress that being "innovative" does not necessarily involve adopting new technological tools. This volume reminds us that considerations of emotion, multimodal teaching and learning, and education for critical consciousness are essential in the realm of Korean language teaching, independently of the tools used for instruction delivery. This is clear, for example, when arguing that using AI-based chatbots may affect learners' anxiety (Chapter 2) or when showing that constraints in VR technologies, which are inherently multimodal, may inadvertently contribute to students' frustration (Chapter 5). Therefore, the contributions dealing with emotions, multimodal teaching, and critical pedagogies do not want to suggest alternatives to technology-based approaches but are proponents of pedagogical considerations that cut across technology- and non-technology–based approaches.

3. Structure of the book and summary of the chapters

The ten chapters in this book explore non-traditional, contemporary, and cutting-edge approaches to Korean language teaching and want to become "food for thought". In other words, we hope that the reader will find these accounts helpful in evaluating and considering pedagogical innovations for Korean language teaching and will use them to reflect on whether and how to implement the suggested approaches into their own practice.

The four chapters in Part I are focused on the topic of large language models and explore the applications of AI tools to Korean language teaching by investigating stakeholders' perceptions and the use of such tools for teaching productive skills. The four chapters in Part II focus on other technology-based teaching resources, such as virtual reality, the Korean language metaverse, and the YouTube platform. Therefore, the chapters in Parts 1 and 2 offer an overview of technology and resources still underexplored in the context of Korean language teaching and, thus, provide substantial evidence and research-based considerations for the future adoption of such technologies.

The three chapters in Part III present non-technology–based considerations for the future advancement of Korean language teaching. These chapters conclude the volume by dealing with epistemic emotions in Korean language learning, multimodal Korean language activities, and instructional programs designed to increase students' critical awareness and sense of social justice.

In Chapter 1, Inhye Lee investigates the perceptions of Korean language educators and international students regarding AI-powered writing assistance, therefore setting the context regarding AI and education through the opinion of the main stakeholders, that is, learners and educators. Thanks to a series of qualitative interviews with three advanced-level Korean language learners and three educators, this chapter examines the potential and challenges of AI in writing education as seen from the perspective of the main stakeholders. Both teachers and learners appreciated AI's role in facilitating idea generation and information sourcing in the context of writing education but expressed concerns about plagiarism and the possible undermining of critical thinking skills. Lee's contribution underscores AI's capacity to assist in the language learning process by reducing communication barriers yet highlights the call of both instructors and students for the need to foster foundational writing skills without over-relying on technology. By exploring the implications of AI across different knowledge domains, this chapter contributes to the discourse on writing pedagogy in the digital age, advocating for a balanced approach to using AI in Korean writing education and recognizing its benefits and limitations in enhancing students' learning experience.

Chapter 2, by Na-Young Ryu, explores the acceptance and impact of AI chatbots in the context of Korean language acquisition. The chapter assesses Korean language students' acceptance of chatbots and examines the benefits and challenges students experience when interacting with chatbots as language-learning partners. The quantitative results suggest a strong positive association between high chatbot acceptance and perceived ease of use, perceived usefulness, attitude, and self-efficacy. Additionally, the students reported several advantages of chatbots, including increased flexibility, reduced language anxiety, and an enjoyable learning experience. Nevertheless, they also identified challenges, such as frustration with speech recognition and limited creativity. These findings suggest that AI chatbots can enhance learners' confidence and motivation in speaking Korean but also highlight that advanced speech recognition, meaningful conversations, and customized feedback are essential for successfully implementing AI-based instructional tools in teaching productive oral skills. Therefore, the practical implications of the findings of Ryu's chapter extend to L2 teachers, students, and technology developers seeking to optimize AI chatbots for language learning.

Narae Jung, in Chapter 3, focuses on evaluating different large language model (LLM)–based chatbots to support Korean language teachers in the feedback process. In particular, she tests the efficacy of Bard, Bing, ChatGPT-3.5, ChatGPT-4, CLOVA X, and Perplexity AI in correcting grammatical and spelling errors in Korean texts. Utilizing nine Korean texts containing 100 deliberate errors, the chapter measures the accuracy of each model in error correction. The findings reveal that while ChatGPT-4 and CLOVA X demonstrate superior performance, there is a notable variety in the responses of these LLMs. The chapter identifies limitations of current LLMs, including instances of inaccuracies and the necessity for specific prompts to obtain accurate responses. It sheds light on the evolving nature of LLMs and their significant role in language learning, especially in providing immediate feedback crucial for enhancing writing skills. The chapter also raises concerns about the appropriateness of vocabulary for different learner levels and the variability in LLM responses. While advocating for an integrated learning approach, the findings suggest combining LLMs with human instruction to leverage the strengths of both AI and human expertise, thereby fostering a more balanced educational environment. The research underscores the importance of thoughtfully integrating LLMs into language education, acknowledging their potential benefits and limitations while anticipating future advancements.

Chapter 4, by Kukjin Kim, instead of comparing feedback provided by various LLM-based tools, sets out to understand and compare differences in error marking by one LLM-based tool and human instructors. The chapter argues that conversational AI chatbots, such as OpenAI's ChatGPT, demonstrate considerable promise in Korean writing education. A possible benefit of such technology lies in its ability to deliver grammatical accuracy, therefore supporting the development of writing skills in Korean language learners who have yet to fully become acquainted with the process of writing in Korean. In other words, Kim assumes that learners can use AI-based chatbots to refine their writing. The comparison between ChatGPT-3.5 and two human raters shows that this AI-based tool has considerable proficiency in identifying and correcting basic orthographic and grammatical inaccuracies, underscoring its potential use as a support tool for self-directed learning. However, Kim warns that ChatGPT-3.5's performance is weak when addressing more advanced grammatical structures, such as subject-predicate agreement, revealing a limited ability to deal with Korean grammatical complexities.

Chapter 5, by Jiyoung Kim and Soyeon Kim, opens the part of the book dedicated to other technology-based approaches to Korean language teaching not focused on using AI chatbots. Kim and Kim note that VR has recently gained significant attention in language education and, therefore, is set to examine the use of high-immersion VR (HiVR) technology in the context of Korean language instruction. The authors designed and deployed two HiVR videos to enhance students' language proficiency by providing an immersive cultural experience. Their contribution investigates students' perceptions of HiVR for Korean language learning and documents the challenges faced by the instructors/researchers during the design and implementation process of the HiVR-based classes. This chapter, through the analysis of open-ended questionnaires, interviews, and other documents, shows that while the concrete effects of HiVR on language acquisition are not definitively established, the technology harbors considerable promise for enhancing educational outcomes. Nevertheless, the authors recognize the existence of several obstacles, concluding that further technological advancements are needed to harness the full educational potential of HiVR.

In Chapter 6, Álvaro Trigo Maldonado critically analyzes a metaverse platform developed specifically for Korean language learning by the King Sejong Institute

Foundation. Trigo Maldonado remarks that metaverse platforms have attracted attention over the past few years as learning tools that can offer more immersive experiences than traditional learning settings. This chapter sets out to explore the possibilities and limits of the King Sejong Institute metaverse, a ZEP (Zettaverse Expansion Platform)-based project launched in 2022, in which users can create avatars and freely explore digital environments simulating a Korean village while completing a series of language learning tasks.

Chapter 7, by Myunghee Cho, considers YouTube not as a platform where instructors can find learning content but as a platform allowing instructors to be creators, that is, active users instead of passive users. In doing so, Cho demonstrates the potential utility of using a YouTube channel as a supplementary platform for language teaching and learning. While many studies discuss the benefits of incorporating YouTube videos into language classrooms, there are fewer descriptions of how Korean language teachers can be YouTube creators and integrate audio-visual language resources to supplement material already available to students through traditional channels. In this contribution, Cho describes her first-hand experience of providing students with additional assistance by creating video tutorials that students could use for self-directed learning and explains how, over time, she expanded the channel to include various content on the Korean language and culture. This chapter shows how the instructor, acting as a content creator, can provide opportunities for active, self-directed learning, expanding the limited class time available in overseas Korean language learning contexts.

Chapter 8, by Nicola Fraschini and Yu Tao, opens Part III. This part is dedicated to overarching approaches and provides important considerations that stretch far beyond the technology used in the classroom. Fraschini and Tao's chapter focused on learners' emotions and points out that so far, the focus of emotion research in second language teaching has been predominantly on how emotions affect learners' communicative performance and that, consequently, what is needed at the moment is a deeper understanding of epistemic emotions and their interaction with the language learning process. This chapter illustrates the result of a large-scale longitudinal survey conducted on epistemic emotions in Korean language learning. The results, analyzed through structural equation modeling, illustrate two epistemic emotions, excitement and confusion; their relationship with teacher friendliness and strictness; and their effect on students' learning efforts. The results argue for introducing a research-based, emotion-based approach to teacher/student interaction.

In Chapter 9, Lucien Brown makes a case for teaching Korean as an embodied and multimodal system rather than merely spoken or written words and grammar. By adopting a systemic functional approach to language as a social semiotic system, Brown proposes a model of communication that includes gesture, bodily movements, emojis and visual components of written texts, all as integral parts of multimodal communicative competence, and discusses how pedagogies based on the principles of multiliteracies have been proposed as methods for teaching critical knowledge of multimodal texts in language classrooms, equipping learners with the ability to interpret various semiotic cues. This chapter also presents three ideas for incorporating multimodality in Korean language teaching. Whereas the first of these ideas involves using a multiliteracies approach for analyzing Korean visual texts, specifically adverts, the second idea is about teaching politeness as a multimodal phenomenon, and the third is an idea for project work using multimodal ethnography. The chapter aims to move Korean language education towards adopting multimodal pedagogies.

Chapter 10, by Young-mee Yu Cho and Hee Chung Chun, examines Korean as a foreign language practice through the lens of critical pedagogy. The authors argue that adopting critical pedagogy is a way of dealing with the challenges of the open-ended nature of advanced learning and the superdiversity of the learner population while sustaining students' motivation through multi-year Korean language learning by introducing socially responsible transformative learning. The chapters, drawing on rich data on learners' sociolinguistic acquisition, metalinguistic insights, and awareness of social justice as collected among participants in an internship course and a Korean for career pursuit course, reveal that students' perception of learning Korean goes beyond the acquisition of language/cultural competences. Some students reported that critical pedagogy had an immediate influence on their professional careers, a serendipitous development brought on by the learning experience and the acquired skill sets that gradually modified their initial career goals. The chapter concludes by making a call for adopting a critical pedagogy lens in KSL, which supports the resolution of local problems within a globalized intercultural framework while opening the door to reach local and global Korean-speaking communities.

The reader can find at the end of the volume a section with additional resources. These resources are briefly commented upon and have been curated by the editors and the contributors. The reader may use these resources to deepen their knowledge of the topics dealt with in the volume and to experiment themselves with innovative approaches to teaching the Korean language.

References

CNN. (2023, January). *South Korea brought K-pop and K-dramas to the world. The Korean language could be next*. Retrieved May 2024, from https://edition.cnn.com/2023/01/17/asia/korean-language-learning-rise-hallyu-intl-hnk-dst/index.html

De Lano, L., Riley, L., & Crookes, G. (1994). The meaning of innovation for ESL teachers. *System, 22*(4), 487–496.

Duolingo. (2023). *2023 Duolingo language report*. Retrieved May 2023, from https://blog.duolingo.com/2023-duolingo-language-report/

Fraschini, N., Cho, H. E., & Kim, H. (2024). *Report on fostering the provision of Korean language education in Victoria (2024)*. Zenodo. http://doi.org/10.5281/zenodo.11114713

KBS. (2020, August). *India, Korean adopted as second foreign language subject . . . Chinese excluded*. Retrieved May 2024, from https://news.kbs.co.kr/news/pc/view/view.do?ncd=4507860

Kennedy, C. (1988). Evaluation of the management of change in ELT projects. *Applied Linguistics, 9*(4), 329–342.

Kiaer, J. (2024). *Conversing in the metaverse*. Bloomsbury.

Kinder, J., Fraschini, N., & Caruso, M. (2024). Resilience, renewal, revival: Language teaching in the 2020s. In J. Kinder, N. Fraschini, & M. Caruso (Eds.), *Enabling learning: Language teaching for Australian universities*. ANU Press.

KOCIS (Korean Culture and Information Service). (2023). *Korean second foreign language chosen by 20% [of test takers] in the Thai university entrance examination . . . second for the second consecutive year*. www.kocis.go.kr/koreanet/view.do?seq=1044949

Lusin, N., Peterson, T., Sulewski, C., & Zafer, R. (2023). *Enrollments in languages other than English in US institutions of higher education, Fall 2021*. The Modern Language Association.

Markee, N. (1993). The diffusion of innovation in language teaching. *Annual Review of Applied Linguistics, 13*, 229–243.

MOE (Ministry of Education) (2023). *Overseas Korean education portal*. http://okep.moe.go.kr

Sejong Institute Foundation. (n.d.). *Sejong Institute Foundation website*. www.ksif.or.kr/index.do

Waters, A. (2009). Managing innovations in English language education. *Language Teaching, 42*(4), 421–458.

Part I
Large language models and Korean language education

1 AI-powered writing assistance

Korean language students' and teachers' views and experiences

Inhye Lee

1. Introduction

The use of Artificial Intelligence (AI) in writing has seen a significant surge in interest with the rapid advancement of digital technology. The advent of generative AI, especially highlighted by the emergence of ChatGPT, has catalyzed a range of studies exploring its applications. Technological innovations have irrevocably altered the course of writing, from the advent of typewriters to the prevalence of computer-mediated composition. Moreover, the writing processes of second language learners show notable differences depending on the medium, whether traditional handwriting or computer-mediated text production. Writing not only goes beyond its role as a communication medium but also serves as a cognitive tool for introspection and thought refinement. In this process, authors often engage in complex mental re-evaluation crossing various cognitive activities. In this context, AI plays a critical role that goes beyond basic machine translation and extends to content generation and support. This is particularly relevant in academic Korean writing, which demands rigorous source evaluation and content synthesis, making the careful integration of AI tools like ChatGPT an urgent issue.

This chapter seeks to explore the views of both Korean language educators and international students on the use of AI in Korean writing, employing qualitative research methods and in-depth interviews as the primary mode of data collection.

2. Literature review

2.1 AI and writing in Korean language education

Atlas (2023) emphasizes the potential of AI in activating content schemas and providing valuable feedback, which is particularly advantageous for non-native learners aiming to improve their writing skills. Rahman et al. (2023) highlights its efficiency as a research support tool, facilitating the generation of ideas, integration of data, and summarization of comprehensive information. In some instances, AI has even supported the publication process of research papers (Kitamura, 2023). However, the application of AI in second language writing raises concerns, such as plagiarism and other ethical issues. Warschauer et al. (2023) critically highlight the necessity of sustaining a certain level of language proficiency when utilizing AI services, cautioning against over-reliance and the potential detrimental effects on writing skill development (Chan & Hu, 2023).

Within Korean language education, AI-related research has mainly focused on the development of educational programs using AI technologies. Recently, studies have investigated the design and application of AI-based chatbots for Korean language learning (Yan, 2022), the use of AI-powered instructional materials (Park, 2021; Kim & Ko, 2022), and the interactions with AI chatbots in educational contexts (Kim, 2023).

The focus within Korean writing education research regarding the use of digital technology has been mainly on machine translation. Research in this area has investigated Korean language learners' perspectives on machine translation (Nam, 2019; Quan, 2022), their usage patterns in writing (Lee, 2021), and the potential of machine translation to enhance Korean writing education (Kong & Baek, 2021). These studies collectively acknowledge a range of views on the use of machine translation by Korean learners and recognize the growing trend of incorporating such tools into second language writing practices. Korean learners frequently utilize machine translation for translating between their native languages and Korean, as well as for multilingual translation tasks, demonstrating the versatility of this approach. Despite this, a comprehensive body of research addressing the complexities of digital Korean writing education and its practices is still in its nascent stages.

2.2 Acceptance and perspectives on technology

Learners' perspectives significantly influence both their learning experiences and the pedagogical approaches adopted by educators (Marx, 1983). Their attitudes towards writing with digital technology not only shape the practices of language learners but also have implications for writing education methodologies. According to Davis (1986), the technology acceptance model (TAM) highlights how perceived usefulness and ease of use are critical in influencing learners' willingness to adopt a particular technology, affecting their actual usage patterns. Building on this foundation, Venkatesh and Davis (2000) introduced the technology acceptance model 2 (TAM2), an extension that explores the key factors affecting perceived usefulness and illustrates how subjective norms play a significant role in technology adoption, particularly in situations where the use of the system is compulsory.

In the field of Korean language education, Ryu (see Chapter 2) extends the insights from TAM2, demonstrating a strong correlation between the acceptance of chatbots and various factors affecting Korean as a Second Language (KSL) learners. This chapter observes that using chatbots for Korean education can alleviate language-related anxiety and create a more engaging learning environment while acknowledging some limitations such as reduced variety and creativity due to the nature of AI-generated responses.

Furthermore, Yoo and Yoo (2021) explored the perceptions of 55 KSL learners on the efficacy of the Sejong Institute AI Teacher chatbot, finding that learners considered the AI-enhanced education as effective as conventional methods. The chatbot was particularly useful for its ability to decrease learning anxiety and improve learning outcomes, with visual learners experiencing a notable reduction in anxiety levels. Similarly, Kim (2023) assessed the impact of ChatGPT on three advanced-level KSL learners, finding it beneficial for self-assessment, practice, and confidence building, indicating its beneficial potential for more advanced language learners.

Despite the increasing amount of research on digital technology in Korean language education, studies focusing specifically on the perceptions of international students and instructors regarding AI in writing remain limited. Considering the critical role of writing for Korean for academic purposes (KAP) and the significant impact that perceptions of digital technology can have on language learning, it is important to investigate how international students and instructors perceive the use of AI in writing.

3. Method

3.1 Participants

This chapter conducted interviews with six participants: three international students and three Korean language teachers in South Korea, all of whom had experience using interactive AI services like ChatGPT.

All three Korean language teachers held doctoral degrees in Korean language education and had extensive teaching experience at the undergraduate level ranging from 13 to 17 years. Their expertise spans teaching Korean culture, Korean language education courses, and introductory Korean language classes. Moreover, they have been teaching Korean writing courses and conducting writing tasks within their curriculum, underlining their practical experience in the area of study. These educators have also engaged in research related to Korean writing and literacy, with Teachers A and B specializing in literacy-related topics. Their selection for this chapter was based on their understanding of writing, literacy, and the pedagogical implications of AI in these fields, making them well equipped to provide insights into the relatively new and under-explored domains of AI-assisted writing and related perspectives.

The student participants are international students at universities in South Korea, one doctoral student, one master's student, and one bachelor's student, all majoring in Korean language and literature or Korean language. They exhibited advanced-level proficiency in Korean. The participant in the master's program, referred to as Student B, was in the process of writing their thesis, while Student A, from the doctoral program, had experience writing academic journal articles.

Table 1.1 Teacher participants

Name	Korean language teaching experience	L1	Department affiliation
Teacher A	17 years	Korean	Liberal Arts
Teacher B	13 years	Korean	Korean Language Education
Teacher C	13 years	Korean	Liberal Arts

Table 1.2 Student participants

Name	Korean language learning experience	L1	TOPIK[1]
Student A	9 years	Chinese	Level 6
Student B	5 years	Thai	Level 6
Student C	4 years and 6 months	Vietnamese	Level 5

These learners were selected for involvement in higher education within Korean language-related fields to ensure that they provided relevant insights into the use of AI in academic writing.

3.2 Korean universities' ethical considerations and responses on use of AI

Ethical challenges, notably plagiarism in assignments facilitated by AI tools, have received much attention in the recent years (Cotton et al., 202 4; Fyfe, 202 3; Jarrah et al., 2023; Meyer et al., 2023). In response to these challenges, Korean universities are exploring countermeasures, with a prevailing approach that favors granting instructors the discretion to manage AI's use in writing assignments over imposing strict regulations. Additionally, educational institutions are focusing on raising awareness about ethical practices by offering instructional videos and guidebooks. These resources are designed to educate both professors and students on proper AI usage in academic settings, including ethical writing guidelines and plagiarism detection methods. For example, Hanbat National University has introduced "AI Teaching and Learning Guidelines" featuring recommendations on how to cite AI-generated content (Go, 2024). Similarly, Sungkyunkwan University has established a "Comprehensive Guide Platform for Teachers and Lecturers on ChatGPT", aimed at curbing AI-related cheating in assignments and dissertations (Lim, 2023). The institutions attended by the participants of this study have adopted comparable guidelines for the academic use of AI tools.

3.3 Data collection and analysis

The interviews in this study included comprehensive discussions about the participants' experiences with interactive AI like ChatGPT, their perspectives on these tools, and the perceived impact of these tools on Korean language learning and teaching. Interviews were conducted using two methods: in-person meetings and virtual interviews via Zoom, each session lasting about one hour. Before each interview, the researcher provided a detailed explanation of the purpose of the study, the methodology employed, and the specific procedures involved. It was clearly communicated that any information gathered outside the research scope would not be utilized for different purposes. Informed consent was then obtained from each participant, with the understanding that the interviews would be recorded or video-recorded for analysis purposes only.

Following the interview sessions, the recorded audio content was transcribed into written text using CLOVA Note, a tool capable of converting audio recordings to text. The researcher reviewed the audio files while referencing the initial transcriptions to correct errors and discrepancies. The transcribed content underwent a thorough review process, wherein meaningful insights related to the use of AI technology in Korean writing were systematically extracted and categorized. Through this iterative process, distinct themes emerged and were organized according to various categories. This iterative analytical approach aimed to examine the impact of AI technology integration on the academic writing knowledge of KAP learners.

The qualitative data collected through interviews with KAP learners were analyzed based on the writing ability categories established by Tribble (1997), a seminal figure in writing ability research. Previously, Applebee (1982) identified the facets of writing ability as subject-related, reader-related, and language-related knowledge. Tribble (1997) further defined these categories, introducing content knowledge related to the subject matter, contextual knowledge related to the social context in which the text is read, and writing process knowledge offering insights into text construction suited to the context. Additionally, language system knowledge encompasses the understanding of vocabulary, grammar, spelling, and other linguistic elements. In this study, writing knowledge is categorized into content knowledge, contextual knowledge, language system knowledge, and process knowledge, with specific focus on Korean language learners pursuing academic objectives.

4. Results and discussion

4.1 Content knowledge: navigating the information landscape

In academic writing, students depend on their foundational knowledge to compare and synthesize information from diverse sources, a critical process for constructing cohesive arguments that integrate insights from various texts. Therefore, the ability to discern credible information from the vast array of sources and to distinguish suitable content is crucial. Participants in our study highlighted using ChatGPT as a significant advantage for sourcing and utilizing information. They particularly emphasized the capability of ChatGPT to generate ideas and act as a reference point for second language writers.

A common challenge for Korean learners is to identify critical information from the extensive resources available online and to determine the depth of their research. Some participants believed that AI services like ChatGPT are adept at organizing and presenting comprehensive summaries of online information. As Student C noted, "When you search on the internet, there's so much information, it's challenging. ChatGPT seems to organize a variety of internet information effectively". However, it is important to recognize that ChatGPT may not provide a complete overview of all available information, potentially leading to misconceptions among our study's participants.

Relying exclusively on ChatGPT without consulting additional sources, such as academic papers or books, might impede the development of intertextual content knowledge. Intertextuality suggests that a text is part of a network of texts, interconnected through various forms of reference, quotation, and adaptation. This concept includes understanding other relevant texts and the established concepts of audience, self, reality, and text. Overreliance on ChatGPT could limit learners' ability to integrate knowledge independently. Yet the ability to gauge the scope of information or assess the adequacy and generality of collected information can be advantageous. Teacher A stated, "When students research a topic for writing, ChatGPT's guidance on general information and the extent of research is often sufficient". Similarly, Student A remarked, "It's not about copying; it's about using the information as a kind of answer and a reference for my writing".

Most participants were aware of the limitations in the credibility of ChatGPT's information, primarily due to the difficulty in verifying its sources. They viewed ChatGPT as a tool for discovering materials or keywords and for verifying the scope of information, rather than as a direct and reliable source. Teacher B described it as "A tool to assist in searching for materials, useful for preliminary research". While recognizing that ChatGPT is useful for information retrieval, participants generally did not consider it a reliable source, especially due to the lack of proper citations. For example, Student C shared an experience from a course on understanding Korean society, where content provided by ChatGPT differed from the professor's materials. They decided to rely on the professor's materials instead, since those were properly referenced. Overall, participants saw ChatGPT as a valuable tool for exploring topics and deciding the scope of information for writing; however, they remained cautious about its reliability as a source for academic citations.

4.2 Context knowledge

Ethical considerations

In academic Korean writing, contextual knowledge is crucial because it involves understanding of research ethics within the sociocultural context and grasping the characteristics of texts within their specific environments. For international students, this knowledge includes adhering to academic writing conventions and the norms of discourse communities. The student participants in this study showed awareness of plagiarism risks when using ChatGPT.

Student B, who is working on a master's thesis, stopped using ChatGPT due to concerns over involuntary plagiarism, noting, "It's useful in non-academic situations, for example, when writing emails in Korean. However, using this for a thesis could be problematic because of the risk of unintentional plagiarism".

Similarly, teachers in our study expressed worries that students might inadvertently plagiarize using AI tools in their assignments. Teacher B shared concerns about assignments exceeding what students could typically produce, potentially indicating plagiarism. They mentioned,

> For final papers, I've used plagiarism detection programs. With the advent of ChatGPT, there might be a need for tools that specifically detect GPT-generated content. I also demonstrate to students how professors can

detect if an assignment is written by ChatGPT by using the assignment topic as a prompt in ChatGPT.

On the other hand, Teacher C, who teaches intermediate-level Korean, observed that plagiarism concerns are less pronounced in courses focusing on grammar and vocabulary. Nonetheless, the strategic incorporation of newly learned grammatical structures and expressions post-ChatGPT use remains an essential consideration.

Enhancing sociocultural communication in university life

Beyond the ethics of academic writing, such as avoiding plagiarism, academic Korean writing also plays an important role in the broader context of university life, including email correspondences with professors and university staff. The development of generative machine translation tools like ChatGPT and Google Translate has been instrumental in aiding learners with academic Korean writing, facilitating a smoother integration into university life and reducing communication apprehensions.

Teacher A highlighted the importance of maintaining formality in written communications within the sociocultural context, particularly in email exchanges.

> In past communications with international students via email or text, the use of sentence-by-sentence translation often resulted in awkward Korean. While I understood the messages, they sometimes came across as impolite, occasionally causing offense. However, with the advancements in translation technology, these tools now provide translations or compose messages that preserve formality, improving communication significantly.

Thus, generative translation tools can enhance the appropriateness of communication across various sociocultural contexts within university life.

4.3 *Writing process knowledge*

Students' strategies and adaptations in integrating AI into academic writing

Writing process knowledge covers familiarity with the distinct characteristics of each writing stage, including idea generation, outlining, drafting, and revising, along with strategies that can be employed at each phase. Proficient second-language writers skillfully navigate these stages, demonstrating metacognitive abilities to evaluate their writing process. The integration of AI technologies, such as ChatGPT or machine translation, into their strategies may influence their writing process knowledge.

Student C chose to stop using ChatGPT, believing that it hindered the improvement of writing skills and promoted dependency and intellectual passivity. They provided comments such as "I deleted ChatGPT. Continuous use makes people reliant and unreflective. Engaging with your own thoughts, especially in assignments, is important". Similarly, Student A, who is enrolled in a doctoral program, highlighted the significance of crafting an outline as a fundamental part of the learning journey, noting, "Creating an outline is the most challenging and vital learning process. Using outlines by ChatGPT skips essential steps". These perspectives underline that students tailor their use of AI based on the nature of the writing task, including academic contexts.

Nevertheless, they acknowledged its usefulness in scenarios like summarizing academic work, including coursework. Campbell (1990) categorizes quoting, paraphrasing, summarizing, and explaining the original text as types of writing derived from sources. Therefore, summarizing can be seen not just as a form of reading but also as a distinct writing activity. This process helps international students integrate reading materials and lectures into their academic studies. University students, as noted by Keck (2006), often need to draw from source texts for assignments or exams. The task of summarizing, a common skill for Korean for academic purpose students wishing to synthesize various materials for literature reviews or exam responses, requires substantial cognitive effort and poses challenges, consuming significant time. AI-based chatbots offer the ability to instantly generate summaries from provided prompts and materials. This feature can save KAP students considerable time that would otherwise be dedicated to reading all materials in Korean, thereby allowing them to devote more effort to other aspects of writing, such as critique or creative writing. These insights highlight that learners tailor their AI usage to fit the specific demands of the writing task at hand, even within academic writing.

However, this convenience poses a potential drawback, as it might deter learners from engaging deeply with the material through direct reading and comprehension, or from exploring various related materials to uncover intertextuality and weave these insights into their summaries. This highlights the learners' awareness of the importance of adapting AI tool use to suit specific writing tasks. When using ChatGPT for summaries, Student B emphasized the critical need to verify the accuracy of the summarized content and rephrase it personally, underlining the importance of active engagement in the learning process.

Pedagogical adaptations in integrating AI into academic writing

Teacher A shed light on the evolving dynamics within Korean universities, where an increasing number of international students face difficulties in understanding textbooks and producing presentation materials due to limited Korean proficiency. This challenge persists even at the graduate level, where many students struggle to create academic materials unaided by translation tools. In this context, tools like ChatGPT can offer essential support, acting as supplementary aids that help students meet their academic obligations. However, reliance on such tools might impede the development of summarization skills. Teacher A highlighted the growing influx of international students as a factor that complicates efforts to reduce ChatGPT dependency. This situation calls for educators to innovate their teaching approaches by breaking down assignments into smaller, skill-focused segments, thereby nurturing specific writing competencies.

Teacher C introduced a pedagogical method involving the comparison of student-generated writings with content produced by ChatGPT across different stages of the writing process. This approach encourages a thorough examination of the variances and improvements in idea generation, outlining, drafting, and finalizing texts, fostering a collaborative and iterative learning experience. The emphasis on discussion and refinement plays a crucial role in enriching the content, making it more comprehensive. Teacher A also pointed to the potential emergence of new student strategies as a response to the integration of AI in writing tasks. For instance, while using AI for summarization might bypass traditional writing steps, it could also lead to the development of innovative strategies appropriate for the digital age, like cross-referencing various online sources. Such evolving strategies have the capacity to transform academic writing practices significantly.

The students participating in this study expressed concerns about potential inadvertent plagiarism with ChatGPT and worried about not improving their academic writing skills, making them hesitant to use the tool. The teachers recognized the inevitable integration of ChatGPT in universities as an ongoing trend and anticipated the need for students to adapt new strategies in the age of AI, similarly to adjustments made in the internet era. This necessitates language teachers to evolve their instructional methods to address these challenges.

4.4 Language system knowledge

Determining the best time for AI integration in language learning

Participants shared varied views on the most suitable stages for learners to begin incorporating AI technology for writing assistance. There was agreement that introducing AI at the initial stages of language learning, where basic sentence construction skills related to the language system knowledge are being developed, might not be advisable. However, opinions on when to start using AI varied widely, from the intermediate levels to more advanced stages of proficiency. Student B suggested, "From around level 3,[2] learners likely have sufficient understanding to decide if AI-generated text is suitable, making it a feasible point to begin its use". Conversely, Student A recommended waiting until the more advanced stages of learning Korean writing, emphasizing the importance of manual writing practice before integrating AI tools.

Using AI for translation

Regarding translation, most participants had a positive view of using AI tools, seeing them as a means to "express one's own thoughts", according to Student A, rather than as plagiarism. Teacher A acknowledged the growing reliance on translation tools in current L2 classroom as an expected development. Teacher B, however, highlighted concerns over using ChatGPT to organize content for academic writing, which demands a deep understanding and original knowledge creation. The debate extends to whether employing AI for translation might be considered plagiarism. Moreover, Teacher A noted the improved quality of translations with AI but cautioned against starting AI use at the very beginning of language learning. Translating requires significant linguistic knowledge, and the use of translation tools can hinder the development of such skills. This applies not only to high-level translation but also to writing abilities at the beginner level.

The teacher participants agreed that early reliance on translation tools could hinder the acquisition of fundamental Korean language skills. Teacher B argued, "In this digital age, the attitude towards AI-based translation tools in language classes is seen as dependent on the learners' effort. Excessive dependence on these tools for Korean language assignments might suggest a diminished dedication to mastering the language". Teacher A also contended that completely prohibiting their use is impractical; therefore, it is preferable to instruct on how to utilize them effectively.

5. Discussion

5.1 The unique context of using AI in academic writing at Korean universities

The present study investigates Korean language educators' and international students' perceptions of AI-powered writing assistance. Graduating from universities in Korea typically requires achieving a TOPIK Level 4,[3] motivating students to enhance their Korean language skills. However, students' need for learning Korean for academic purposes varies depending on the university and major. For instance, in universities specializing in science and engineering, most classes, except for some electives, are conducted in English.[4] Furthermore, on August 16, 2023, the Ministry of Education of the Republic of Korea announced the Study Korea 300K Project, aiming to attract 300,000 international students by 2027. This plan allows for the creation of departments customized to international students, facilitating academic departments that operate exclusively with international student bodies. To attract international students, an increase in colleges and majors specifically designed for them has been observed, with entire curriculums conducted in English. Recently, many universities, including Korea University and Seoul National University of Science and Technology, have established colleges exclusively for international students under names like College of International Studies. There is also a growing trend of converting departments that used to admit both domestic and international students into ones exclusively for international students to alleviate difficulties in student recruitment and to facilitate the attraction of foreign students.

In cases where Korean and international students are mixed, universities invest in Korean language education for international students. However, departments primarily for international students often opt to conduct English-medium instruction (EMI) courses rather than promoting Korean language proficiency adequate for academic tasks. Teacher B stated that for these students, acquiring a deep understanding of Korean for academic purposes might not be necessary; learning Korean for daily communication in Korea could be adequate. They anticipate that the level of Korean proficiency needed for academic purposes will differ depending on the academic context of the learner, suggesting that the approach to using AI will also vary for international students at Korean universities. Should these students engage in academic writing, AI technology could be a resource. This viewpoint indicates a shift in Korean language teachers' attitudes in response to the evolving strategies and changes implemented to attract international students at Korean universities.

When it comes to teaching and learning Korean writing for international students with the aid of AI, adopting a differentiated approach that aligns with the learners' Korean proficiency levels is needed. Additionally, the instructional and learning environment, including the language of instruction at Korean universities, must be carefully considered.

5.2 The extent of AI use in academic writing contexts at Korean universities

As discussed earlier, receiving AI assistance when writing at universities helps international students adapt to studying in Korea. Currently, due to the government and university policies for attracting international students, there is an increasing number of international students on the so-called English-track who are admitted to universities based on their English proficiency rather than their proficiency in Korean. The previously required Korean language entry scores of TOPIK levels 3 to 4 are being replaced with more basic levels, such as TOPIK level 2 or completion of level 2 at King Sejong Institutes[5] or language institutes of Korean universities. In this context, international students inevitably face significant challenges in academic writing at universities. At this juncture, AI assistance helps students understand the materials and adapt academically, thereby facilitating access to data-based writing tasks such as paper writing.

Furthermore, as mentioned earlier, the use of AI technology assists in email exchanges with university members such as professors and staff, and in preparing various documents. Communicating with Korean native speakers within the university, such as professors and seniors, can be burdensome for international students, and such interactions may contribute to the academic stress experienced by international students (Lee, 2014, 2020). Compared to low-context societies, Korea is hierarchical, traditional, and places great importance on saving face, making it a high-context society (Cohen, 1997). In Korean communication situations, maintaining face against the threat of losing face takes on a more significant role. Therefore, in the context of communication among international students at Korean universities, AI-assisted communication could potentially play a role in facilitating smooth adaptation within a high-context society.

However, not only positive aspects exist. Even though the participants in this study generally held favorable views on using ChatGPT for translation or communication, when it does not involve content creation, previous research has raised concerns that AI use in academic writing, such as scholarly research and university education, could lead to plagiarism issues. Rane et al. (2023) expressed concerns about ChatGPT's lack of critical thinking, limited creativity, restricted access to current research, and the presence of incomplete or inaccurate information, along with ethical and bias issues. However, as Wang et al. (2022) observed that if the public has confidence in its use and finds it user friendly, then this technology could aid in disseminating research findings by translating them into simple language accessible to the wider public. In essence, ChatGPT enables smooth translation, potentially broadening the reach of new ideas, discoveries, and academic achievements beyond linguistic barriers. Naturally, this necessitates ongoing discussions within academia, including universities, about the definition of plagiarism in translation and its boundaries. For example, there needs to be a dialogue on the extent to which its use is permissible and recognized, such as whether it constitutes plagiarism if someone writes the content themselves but uses ChatGPT for translation or if it is considered plagiarism when one organizes the content, translates it with ChatGPT, and then paraphrases that translation.

While there is no clear research yet on how the use of AI will affect the expected gradual development of Korean language skills, both previous studies and participants in this study have expressed concerns about reliance on AI in foreign language learning. However, it may be unrealistic to completely prohibit the use of such tools for international students who enter Korean universities without sufficient Korean proficiency and need to quickly adapt to unfamiliar environments. In this context, it would be advisable to actively discuss to what extent AI can be used in academic contexts and how it can be positively utilized for one's academic adaptation and the development of Korean language skills. While ChatGPT excels at reproducing knowledge, it cannot generate original knowledge, which is essential to academic writing. Thus, while ChatGPT's utility as a tool in teaching and learning academic writing is worth exploring, caution must be exercised to prevent its overuse from undermining the ethics of academic writing, bypassing the academic writing process, and neglecting the critical thinking that learners are expected to develop.

Additionally, in a broader writing context, Korean academic writing inherently involves cognitive and social processes. Writing theories must address cognitive strategies that investigate writers' active mental processes and social strategies that recognize the influence of readers' social and cognitive processes on text interpretation. The adoption of AI in writing significantly impacts the social-cognitive dynamics of writers, with outcomes varying based on its application.

6. Conclusion

This chapter investigates the perspectives of Korean language educators and international students within South Korean universities on the use of AI-powered writing tools. The findings were organized into four areas of writing knowledge: content knowledge, context knowledge, writing process knowledge, and language system knowledge. Content knowledge discussions revealed a general appreciation for idea generation and information gathering, whereas context knowledge brought to light concerns over ethical issues, notably plagiarism. There was an acknowledgment of role of AI in reducing communication anxiety and aiding adaptation in academic settings. Concerns were noted regarding AI's potential to sidestep critical thinking in the domain of writing process knowledge, underlining the importance of developing core writing skills alongside AI usage. Educators recognized AI's potential to support international students in their academic writing endeavors, while the discussion on language system knowledge reflected a cautious stance towards AI usage at beginner levels, despite a broader acceptance of AI for translation purposes not being seen as plagiarism.

This study has limitations, as it was conducted among members of a limited number of majors within Korean universities and could not utilize a variety of qualitative research tools. Nevertheless, this study pioneers in exploring the implications of AI on the social-cognitive aspects of Korean writing, laying the groundwork for further research in this evolving field.

Notes

1 The Test of Proficiency in Korean (TOPIK) is the most recognized Korean language proficiency test, graded from Level 1, the lowest, to Level 6, the highest. South Korean universities typically require a TOPIK Level 3 or 4 for graduation, corresponding to the B1 or B2 levels of the Common European Framework of Reference for Languages (CEFR), respectively.
2 See content of note 1.
3 See content of note 1.
4 Examples of such specialized universities in Korea include the Gwangju Institute of Science and Technology (GIST), the Daegu Gyeongbuk Institute of Science and Technology (DGIST), the Ulsan National Institute of Science and Technology (UNIST), Pohang University of Science and Technology (POSTECH), the Korea Advanced Institute of Science and Technology (KAIST), and the Korea Institute of Energy Technology (KENTECH).
5 King Sejong Institutes, also known as *Sejong Hakdang*, are a global network of educational centers dedicated to promoting and teaching the Korean language and culture around the world. Named after King Sejong the Great, who is credited with the creation of the Korean alphabet, Hangul, in the 15th century, these institutes serve as official, government-supported entities aimed at spreading Korean language education globally. The King Sejong Institute Foundation, under the South Korean government, oversees the operation and quality control of these institutes, ensuring they meet educational standards and effectively foster global Korean language learning and cultural exchange. As of March 2024, there are 258 King Sejong Institutes worldwide.

References

Applebee, A. N. (1982). Writing and learning in school settings. In M. Nystrand (Ed.), *What writers know: The language, process, and structure of written discourse*. Academic Press.
Atlas, S. (2023). *ChatGPT for higher education and professional development: A guide to conversational AI*. https://digitalcommons.uri.edu/cba_facpubs/548
Campbell, C. (1990). Writing with others' words: Using background reading text in academic compositions. In B. Kroll (Ed.), *Second language writing: Research insights for the classroom* (pp. 211–230). Cambridge University Press.
Chan, C. K. Y., & Hu, W. (2023). Students' voices on generative AI: Perceptions, benefits, and challenges in higher education. *International Journal of Educational Technology in Higher Education, 20*, 1–18.
Cohen, R. (1997). *Negotiating across cultures: International communication in an interdependent world*. US Institute of Peace Press.

Cotton, D. R., Cotton, P. A., & Shipway, J. R. (2024). Chatting and cheating: Ensuring academic integrity in the era of ChatGPT. *Innovations in Education and Teaching International*, *61*(2), 228–239.
Davis, F. D. (1986). *A technology acceptance model for empirically testing new end-user information systems: Theory and results* [Doctoral dissertation, Massachusetts Institute of Technology].
Fyfe, P. (2023). How to cheat on your final paper assigning AI for student writing. *AI & Society*, *38*(4), 1395–1405.
Go, M. (2024, January 15). Professor, should we use ChatGPT? Universities explore smart usage strategies. *Joongdoilbo*. https://m.joongdo.co.kr/view.php?key=20240114010004040
Jarrah, A. M., Wardat, Y., & Fidalgo, P. (2023). Using ChatGPT in academic writing is (not) a form of plagiarism: What does the literature say. *Online Journal of Communication and Media Technologies*, *13*(4), e202346.
Keck, C. (2006). The use of paraphrase in summary writing: A comparison of L1 and L2 writers. *Journal of Second Language Writing*, *15*(4), 261–278.
Kim, H. (2023). Exploring the potential application of a conversational AI chatbot in Korean language education – an interaction analysis between advanced learners and ChatGPT. *The Study of Korean Language and literature*, *76*, 261–292.
Kim, H., & Ko, H. (2022). Performance evaluation of open source AI technology for Korean reading text classification. *Journal of Korean Language Education*, *33*(2), 115–135.
Kitamura, F. C. (2023). ChatGPT is shaping the future of medical writing but still requires human judgment. *Radiology*, *307*(2), e230171.
Kong, T. S., & Baek, J. P. (2021). The effectiveness of Korean writing education using machine translation: Development of MTPE teaching method and its application. *Journal of Korean Language Education*, *32*(2), 1–30.
Lee, I. (2020). Mixed methods research on international students' adjustment to college. *Journal of Korean Language Education*, *31*(4), 275–308.
Lee, S. (2021). A study on the machine translation and post-editing behavior in Korean writing by Chinese learners. *Bilingual Research*, *83*, 159–179.
Lee, Y. (2014). A study about acculturation of amongst foreign exchange student's Korean culture and graduate school. *Bilingual Research*, *55*, 249–284.
Lim, J. (2023, September 4). The era of ChatGPT has arrived . . . education using 'generative AI' is "not a choice, but a necessity". *University News Network*. https://news.unn.net/news/articleView.html?idxno=551792
Marx, R. W. (1983). Student perspective in classrooms. *Educational Psychologist*, *18*(3), 145–164.
Meyer, J. G., Urbanowicz, R. J., Martin, P. C., O'Connor, K., Li, R., Peng, P. C., Bright, T. J., Tatonetti, N., Won, K. J., Gonzalez-Hernandez, G., & Moore, J. H. (2023). ChatGPT and large language models in academia: Opportunities and challenges. *BioData Mining*, *16*(20), 1–11.
Nam, S. (2019). A Study on the experience and attitude of Korean learners using online machine translation tools. *The Language and Culture*, *15*(2), 55–81.
Park, J. (2021). A study on the production of Korean listening education materials utilization of artificial intelligence (AI): Focusing on using speech synthesis program (TTS). *Bilingual Research*, *82*, 61–84.
Quan, M. (2022). A study on experience in using a machine translation and perception of Korean language learners at a Chinese university. *The Journal of Humanities and Social Sciences*, *13*(4), 953–962.
Rahman, M. M., Terano, H. J., Rahman, M. N., Salamzadeh, A., & Rahaman, M. S. (2023). ChatGPT and academic research: A review and recommendations based on practical examples. *Journal of Education, Management and Development Studies*, *3*(1), 1–12.
Rane, N. L., Choudhary, S. P., Tawde, A., & Rane, J. (2023). ChatGPT is not capable of serving as an author: Ethical concerns and challenges of large language models in education.

International Research Journal of Modernization in Engineering Technology and Science, 5(10), 851–874.
Tribble, C. (1997). *Writing*. Oxford University Press.
Venkatesh, V., & Davis, F. D. (2000). A theoretical extension of the technology acceptance model: Four longitudinal field studies. *Management Science, 46*(2), 186–204.
Wang, X., Lin, X., & Shao, B. (2022). Artificial intelligence changes the way we work: A close look at innovating with chatbots. *Journal of the Association for Information Science and Technology, 74*(3), 339–353.
Warschauer, M., Tseng, W., Yim, S., Webster, T., Jacob, S., Du, Q., & Tate, T. (2023). The affordances and contradictions of AI-generated text for writers of English as a second or foreign language. *Journal of Second Language Writing, 62*, 1–24.
Yan, J. (2022). A Study on language intelligence education through case studies of AI-enhanced learning: Focusing on the online Sejong Institute's Korean AI tutor. In Korean Management Practice Association (Ed.), *Proceedings of the Korea-China Joint International Academic Conference* (pp. 111–120). Korean Management Practice Association.
Yoo, J. Y., & Yoo, H. S. (2021). The effects of smart-learning in Korean language education through chatbots: A focus on learner perception. *Multimedia-Assisted Language Learning, 24*(2), 82–105.

2 Students' perceptions of utilizing AI chatbots as conversation partners for Korean speaking practice

Acceptance, benefits, and challenges

Na-Young Ryu

1. Introduction

The educational landscape is undergoing a significant transformation due to the rapid integration of artificial intelligence (AI) technologies. One prominent area of impact is language education, where AI chatbots are emerging as valuable tools that offer unique advantages for language learners, particularly those facing limitations in practicing with native speakers. Studies have shown that chatbots can effectively address these limitations by providing accessible, location-independent practice opportunities (Huang et al., 2022) and by creating immersive conversational environments (Wang et al., 2017). Furthermore, chatbots demonstrate remarkable versatility, acting as peers, facilitators, or even expert figures to support student engagement (Kerry et al., 2008; Baylor, 2011; Kuhail et al., 2023).

This growing interest in AI chatbots within language learning has fueled a significant body of research. Existing studies have primarily focused on evaluating the effectiveness of chatbots (Hobert & Meyer von Wolff, 2019; Nghi et al., 2019; Hwang & Chang, 2023), their ability to enhance learning experiences (Winkler & Söllner, 2018; Thomas, 2020; Lee et al., 2022), and the evaluation of advantages and challenges (Okonkwo & Ade-Ibijola, 2021; Jeon, 2024; Kuleto et al., 2021; Lee, 2022). However, a critical gap remains in our understanding of how learners perceive these chatbots as conversation partners, particularly in the context of languages other than English.

To address this research gap, the study investigates L2 students' perceptions of integrating AI chatbots into Korean speaking practice. Understanding student perceptions is crucial as their acceptance of the technology directly impacts their motivation, engagement, and ultimately, their learning outcomes. This study's primary objective is to evaluate the receptiveness of L2 students towards chatbots through employing an extended version of the technology acceptance model (TAM2, Venkatesh & Davis, 2000). This study utilizes the TAM2 to explore L2 students' acceptance of AI chatbots for Korean language learning, as well as their perceptions of the benefits and limitations of chatbot use. By examining these perspectives, this chapter offers valuable insights for optimizing AI chatbot integration in language learning, enhancing accessibility for Korean language learners, and ultimately improving spoken Korean proficiency.

DOI: 10.4324/9781032725307-4

The chapter is structured as follows: Section 2 reviews existing research on integrating AI chatbots in language education, focusing on Korean language learning and the application of the TAM framework. Section 3 outlines the research methodology, including participants, the introduction of the Korean AI chatbot "Sejong AI Tutor", data collection procedures, and analysis. In Section 4, I will present the findings and discuss students' perceptions of using the AI chatbot in Korean speaking practice. Section 5 provides practical suggestions for integrating AI chatbots in Korean language education. Section 6 concludes the chapter, while Section 7 discusses limitations and future research directions.

2. Literature review

2.1 AI-based chatbots in language education

Previous research has predominantly concentrated on assessing the impact of AI chatbots in educational settings and examining the associated learning outcomes in the field of language education. Nevertheless, these investigations have generated diverse and sometimes contradictory findings (Fryer et al., 2017; Kim, 2018; Hobert & Meyer von Wolff, 2019; Nghi et al., 2019; Hwang & Chang, 2023; Okonkwo & Ade-Ibijola, 2021; Yin et al., 2021; Huang et al., 2022; Zhang et al., 2023).

Liu et al. (2022) conducted a study examining the potential of chatbots as companions for discussing books and their influence on students' engagement and interest in reading. The findings of this study revealed that students developed a profound sense of social connection with the chatbot. Notably, students who actively engaged in conversations with the chatbot maintained a consistent level of situational interest in the content, while those who did not partake in these interactions experienced a notable decline in their interest. These results imply a strong association between students' perceptions of their social connection with the chatbot and their level of engagement in the reading activity. Furthermore, this connection was found to correlate with both their initial interest and their sustained interest in the activity.

On the other hand, Fryer et al. (2017) conducted a comparative analysis, contrasting chatbot-human interactions with human-human interactions across various tasks to assess their impact on student engagement. Their findings indicated that tasks involving human partners were predictive of future course interest, while interest levels diminished under chatbot partner conditions. In essence, employing a chatbot had an adverse impact on students' long-term interest in tasks and their overall enthusiasm for the class when juxtaposed with using a human partner.

In the field of chatbot applications, studies have demonstrated considerable diversity, particularly in the context of L2 English education. It is noteworthy that research endeavors in chatbot applications have more recently broadened their focus to encompass the domain of Korean foreign language learning (Park & Lee, 2021; Yoo & Yoo, 2021; Lee, 2022; Suh, 2021, 2023).

Park and Lee (2021) demonstrated the potential of Korean chatbots as valuable tools in the context of Korean language learning. They achieved this by using four chatbot builders (Danbi AI, Closer, PingPong, and Dialogflow) to create a variety of Korean learning activities. Their findings underscored the importance of not only considering the chatbot's development objectives but also the intended use and language proficiency of the learners. Furthermore, their study noted that chatbots still face significant technological challenges in their pursuit of attaining human-level conversational abilities and the capacity to deliver adaptable knowledge that could potentially replace human educators.

In a study conducted by Lee (2022), an evaluation was performed on three AI-based Korean chatbot applications: Sejong AI tutor, TEUIDA, and Genie K. The study confirmed that these applications incorporate sound recognition technology and exhibit a notable degree of precision in evaluating Korean pronunciation. However, it is crucial to emphasize that, with regards to dialogue processing, these applications currently offer scripted conversations exclusively designed within predefined scenarios. The capacity for unrestricted, spontaneous interactions with an AI agent has not been implemented in these applications.

Kim and Su (2024) explored the effect of AI chatbots on L2 learners' willingness to communicate (WTC) in Korean. Their study consisted of 65 participants who were all Chinese L1 speakers, divided into an experimental group ($n = 20$) that used chatbots and a control group ($n = 45$) for communicative activities. Although the initial WTC levels were similar, the experimental group demonstrated significant improvement in WTC, reduced anxiety, and increased communication confidence after eight chatbot sessions, compared to the control group. Interviews with the experimental group confirmed that decreased anxiety led to enhanced WTC. These findings suggest that chatbots may create a learner-friendly environment that fosters WTC in Korean.

While research on Korean AI chatbots is on the rise, a crucial gap remains in understanding student perceptions, particularly regarding their acceptance of this technology. Student acceptance is a pivotal factor for successfully integrating AI chatbots into language learning as it directly influences motivation, engagement, and ultimately, learning outcomes. Students who find chatbots frustrating or unhelpful are less likely to use them consistently, hindering their language learning progress. Furthermore, if students do not perceive the chatbot as a valuable learning tool, they may not achieve the desired learning outcomes. Therefore, this study aims to address this critical gap and provide a comprehensive examination of student perceptions regarding their acceptance of AI chatbots in Korean language learning.

2.2 Technology acceptance model

The technology acceptance model (TAM), originally introduced by Davis (1985), is a widely recognized framework in technology adoption and human-computer interaction. TAM helps us explain and predict how users accept and adopt new information technology or applications into their routines. The fundamental concepts of TAM are composed of two essential factors.

First, perceived ease of use (PEU) assesses the user's perception of how easy it is to learn and use the technology. If users perceive a technology as user-friendly, they are more likely to accept and adopt it. In this context, PEU reflects students' willingness to use AI chatbots based on their confidence that the technology will improve their academic performance.

Second, perceived usefulness (PU) assesses users' confidence in the technology's potential to enhance their effectiveness and productivity. If users believe a technology will be useful in achieving their goals, they are more likely to accept and adopt it. In this study, PU is defined as students' perception of how AI chatbots can contribute to their academic performance. Figure 2.1 illustrates the original TAM model.

As shown in Figure 2.1, both PEU and PU significantly influence user attention (AT) towards the technology. Additionally, AT and PU play crucial roles in shaping users' behavioral intention (BI), which refers to their intention to use the technology in the future. A positive attitude toward the technology's usefulness and ease of use tends to result in a higher intention to adopt it.

Over the past decade, TAM has undergone significant extensions and adaptations by various researchers (Nikou & Economides, 2017; Hsieh et al., 2017; Venkatesh & Davis, 2000). As a result, TAM has received considerable attention in the field of language learning (Luan & Teo, 2009; Pindeh & Suki, 2016; Al-Emran et al., 2018; Alfadda & Mahdi, 2021; Belda-Medina & Calvo-Ferrer, 2022; Hsu & Lin, 2022). For example, Chocarro et al. (2023) conducted a study that examined the acceptance of chatbots among 225 primary and secondary education teachers using the TAM framework. This research explored the connection between chatbot conversational design, particularly the incorporation of social language and proactiveness, and the age and digital skills of teachers.

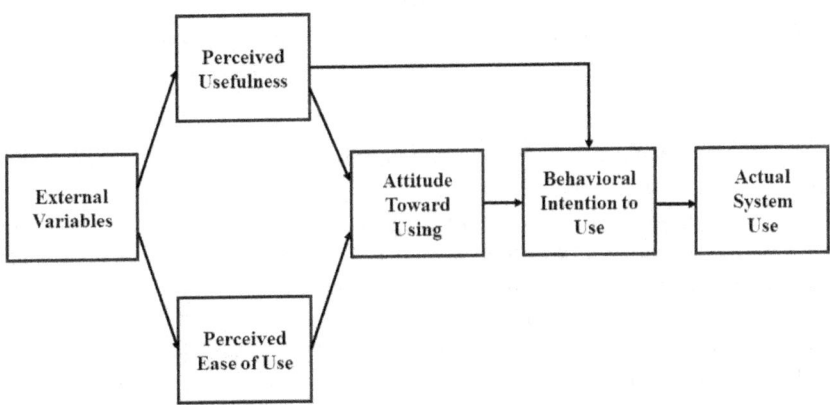

Figure 2.1 Technology acceptance model

The findings of the study revealed that PEU and PU played significant roles in enhancing chatbot acceptance. Additionally, Belda-Medina and Calvo-Ferrer (2022) explored educators' knowledge, satisfaction, and perceptions of integrating AI chatbots into English language learning, utilizing a modified TAM2 model (Venkatesh & Davis, 2000). This model consisted of 25 items across eight dimensions: perceived ease of use, perceived usefulness, usability (US), perceived behavior control (PBC), attitude, behavioral intention, self-efficacy (SE), and personal innovativeness (PI). Notably, their study revealed that educators held positive perceptions regarding the perceived usefulness, ease of use, and attitudes toward chatbot integration. However, there was moderate interest in future use.

This study builds upon Belda-Medina and Calvo-Ferrer's (2022) methodology, adapting it to investigate the perceptions of L2 learners of Korean using a Korean AI chatbot. By extending their research to a new language and learner population, this study aims to contribute to a more comprehensive understanding of the applicability and effectiveness of the TAM2 in language learning contexts, providing valuable insights into the potential of AI chatbots in language education.

3. Method

3.1 Participants

A total of 32 undergraduate students enrolled in an intermediate-level Korean language course at a university in the United States participated in this study. The participants had an average of 20 months of experience in learning Korean. Among the participants, seven were male, and 25 were female, with a mean age of 21.6 years old.

To investigate L2 learners' perceptions, this study employed the Sejong AI Tutor,[1] a popular language learning application widely used by Korean language learners. Due to its accessibility and familiarity among the target population, Sejong AI Tutor served as an ideal platform for the study. Participants accessed the application using their personal smartphones or tablet devices. They voluntarily downloaded and installed the application to ensure a seamless and familiar user experience.

3.2 Material: Sejong AI tutor application

The Sejong AI Tutor application was developed in 2020 by the King Sejong Institute Foundation, a government-supported South Korean institution dedicated to offering Korean language and cultural education programs for learners worldwide. This chatbot utilizes a scenario-based approach, offering discrete answer options that enable students to practice Korean conversation at various proficiency levels in diverse situational contexts. By simulating real-life conversations, the AI Tutor application aims to enhance learners' communication skills and cultural understanding.

The Sejong AI Tutor chatbot offers several features to support users in practicing Korean conversations. As illustrated in Figure 2.2, on the left, the chatbot presents

Students' perceptions of utilizing AI chatbots 33

Figure 2.2 Screenshots of the AI Tutor application
Source: (Sejong AI teacher app, v. Sejong AI Auto 1.3.5)

scenarios representative of daily conversations, allowing users to practice various situations in Korean. In the middle, the chatbot offers a "hint" option during conversations, providing users with guidance on employing appropriate expressions within the given scenario. Additionally, on the right, the chatbot encourages users to provide feedback, enabling an assessment of their satisfaction with the chatbot's performance and facilitating continuous improvement.

3.3 Procedures

The research procedure involved the following sequential steps for introducing and utilizing the AI chatbot to enhance oral performance in Korean:

Step 1: Introduction to the Sejong AI chatbot

Students were introduced to the AI chatbot, with a thorough explanation of its intended purpose and benefits for improving their Korean speaking skills.

Step 2: Installation and familiarization

Students installed the AI chatbot application on their electronic devices. The instructor guided them through the initial setup process, including creating accounts and familiarizing themselves with the interface.

Step 3: Instruction on chatbot utilization

Detailed instructions were provided to guide students in effectively utilizing the AI chatbot for practicing the designated topic of "Seeing a doctor" in Korean. This included information on:

(1) Getting started: Launching the application and accessing relevant features
(2) Learning objectives: Specific skills the chatbot would help them develop (e.g., vocabulary, sentence structure, pronunciation)
(3) Topics: Navigating the chatbot's topic selection and focusing on "Seeing a doctor"
(4) Proficiency levels: Choosing the appropriate difficulty level for their current Korean speaking ability
(5) Aiming sentence of the day: Selecting a daily target sentence to practice throughout their sessions

Step 4: Classroom practice program

Students participated in a conversation practice program, engaging with the AI chatbot for 10 minutes during each class session over a period of 2 weeks. This resulted in a total practice time of 80 minutes per student (40 minutes per week, with four classes per week, over 2 weeks).

The program employed role-playing scenarios where students practiced everyday conversations. The chatbot provided instant feedback to help students improve their pronunciation and fluency. Students had opportunities to repeat interactions, building confidence and proficiency. This daily practice aimed to enhance students' Korean speaking skills through focused conversation exercises, promoting consistent improvement and progress.

Step 5: Survey on chatbot perceptions

Upon completing the 2-week practice period, students participated in a survey designed to gather their perceptions and insights about utilizing the AI chatbot as a conversation partner. The survey was developed based on the TAM2 framework, following Belda-Medina and Calvo-Ferrer's (2022) methodology, with two additional questions exploring the advantages and disadvantages of the chatbot. The survey aimed to understand students' overall acceptance and experience with the AI chatbot, perceived improvements in their Korean speaking skills, any challenges or difficulties they faced while using the chatbot, and suggestions for further improvements or additional features that could enhance their learning experience.

3.4 Data collection and analysis

This study employed a mixed methods approach, combining quantitative and qualitative data collection methods through a survey. The quantitative section consisted of 25 questions using a 5-point Likert scale, organized into eight dimensions based on the TAM2 framework used by Belda-Medina and Calvo-Ferrer (2022). These dimensions included PEU, PU, US, PBC, AT, BI, SE, and PI. Additionally, the qualitative section featured two open-ended questions positioned at the end of the survey to gather insights on the benefits and challenges of using AI chatbots as conversational partners. Quantitative data were analyzed using R (R Core Team, 2017).

4. Results and discussion

4.1 Students' perceptions of using chatbots in Korean language learning

This section examines students' perceptions of using the Sejong AI Tutor chatbot in Korean language learning, based on the TAM2 framework. The results are presented in Table 2.1.

Table 2.1 Students' perceptions regarding the use of chatbots in Korean language learning in accordance with TAM2

Items and dimensions	Mean	SD
1. (PEU) I find chatbots easy to use.	3.59	1.00
2. (PEU) Learning how to use chatbots is easy for me.	4.24	0.75
3. (PEU) It is easy to become skillful at using chatbots in Korean language learning.	3.53	0.80
4. (PEU) I find chatbots in Korean language learning to be flexible to interact with.	2.94	0.90
5. (PEU) The interaction with chatbots in Korean language learning is clear and understandable.	3.35	0.93
6. (PU) Using chatbots in Korean language learning would increase the students' learning performance.	3.06	0.90
7. (PU) Using chatbots in Korean language learning would increase academic productivity.	3.18	0.88
8. (PU) Using chatbots would make Korean language learning easier.	2.94	1.03
9. (PU) Using chatbots in Korean language learning allows the learners to study outside of the classroom.	4.29	1.21
10. (PU) Using chatbots in Korean language learning is useful for context-based interactions as in real life.	3.65	1.22
11. (PU) Chatbots enable students to learn more quickly in Korean language learning.	3.18	0.95
12. (PU) Chatbots make it easier to innovate in Korean language learning.	3.35	1.00
13. (PU) The advantages of chatbots in Korean language learning outweigh the disadvantages.	3.06	1.09
14. (US) I believe that using chatbots will increase the quality of Korean language learning.	3.00	0.94
15. (PBC) I am completely satisfied in using chatbots for Korean language learning.	3.00	1.12
16. (PBC) I am very confident in using chatbots in Korean language learning.	3.00	1.27
17. (AT) Using chatbots in Korean language learning is a good idea.	3.47	1.07
18. (AT) I am positive towards using chatbots in Korean language learning.	3.29	1.16
19. (AT) Using chatbots in Korean language learning is fun.	3.53	1.18

(*Continued*)

Table 2.1 (Continued)

Items and dimensions	Mean	SD
20. (BI) I intend to use chatbots in Korean language learning frequently.	2.82	1.07
21. (BI) I intend to learn more about using chatbots in Korean language learning.	3.18	1.42
22. (SE) I feel confident in using chatbots in Korean language learning.	3.00	1.27
23. (SE) I have the necessary skills for using chatbots in Korean language learning.	3.76	1.15
24. (PI) I like to experiment with new technologies in Korean language learning.	3.71	1.40
25. (PI) Among my peers, I am usually the first to explore new technologies.	2.76	1.09
Total	3.32	1.13

Notes: Five-point scale: from 1 = not useful at all to 5 = very useful.

The internal consistency of the scales was evaluated using Cronbach's alpha, which exceeded the recommended threshold of 0.7 for all dimensions (PEU = 0.83, PU = 0.93, PBC = 0.76, AT = 0.88, BI = 0.81, SE = 0.83, PI = 0.73). These values indicate acceptable internal consistency, suggesting that the items within each scale effectively measure their respective constructs.

The findings presented in Table 2.1, along with the Cronbach's alpha values for each scale, offer insights into student perceptions of chatbot use in Korean language learning.

Perceived ease of use

Data from items 1–5 indicate a generally positive perception of ease of use. The average mean score is 3.53 on a 5-point scale (SD = 0.959). This result suggests that students, on average, find chatbots user friendly. Consistent with Chocarro et al. (2023) and Belda-Medina and Calvo-Ferrer (2022), this study confirms that PEU is a critical factor in chatbot acceptance.

Perceived usefulness and usability

While the mean scores for PU (items 6–13, mean = 3.34, SD = 1.1) and US (item 14, mean = 3.00, SD = 0.935) suggest that students perceive some value in chatbots for learning, the standard deviations indicate variability in these perceptions. Like the findings of both Chocarro et al. (2023) and Belda-Medina and Calvo-Ferrer (2022), PU is crucial for acceptance. However, this study highlights a need for further development to enhance perceived usefulness and address usability concerns.

Perceived behavioral control, attitude, and self-efficacy

The data present mixed findings regarding student confidence and control over their chatbot learning experience (PBC, items 15–16, mean = 3.00). Student attitudes towards chatbots (AT, items 17–19, mean = 3.43, SD = 1.12 and 1.27) appear generally positive, suggesting they view chatbots as a potentially beneficial addition. Students also report a moderate level of SE (items 22–23, mean = 3.00 and 3.76, SD = 1.27 and 1.15) regarding their ability to utilize chatbots for learning. These results align with Belda-Medina and Calvo-Ferrer (2022), indicating positive AT and SE towards chatbot use. However, lower PBC scores suggest students may feel limited in their control over using chatbots effectively.

Behavioral intention and personal innovativeness

While some students express a clear intention to use chatbots frequently (BI, items 20–21, mean = 2.82 and 3.18, SD = 1.07 and 1.42), the data reveal variability in this intention (BI). Similarly, scores for PI (items 24–25, mean = 3.71 and 2.76) suggest a moderate level of openness to new technologies, with some students more eager to experiment than others. Consistent with the findings of Chocarro et al. (2023) and Belda-Medina and Calvo-Ferrer (2022), these results highlight the importance of PI in technology acceptance. However, the moderate BI scores indicate that further work is needed to encourage consistent engagement.

These findings imply that chatbots designed with a focus on enhancing PEU and PU, fostering positive AT, and bolstering SE are likely to be embraced by L2 learners of Korean. Specifically, when learners perceive chatbots as user friendly, beneficial, enjoyable to interact with, and conducive to effective learning, they are more inclined to adopt them as a language learning tool. Moreover, learners who perceive chatbots as easy to navigate and interact with and who believe in their efficacy in facilitating language learning are more predisposed to accepting them as a valuable resource. This finding underscores the importance of adhering to user-centered design principles in chatbot development, ensuring intuitive interfaces and clearly elucidated functionalities. Additionally, cultivating positive attitudes towards chatbots and instilling confidence in one's ability to learn effectively using them further enhances acceptance. Creating engaging and culturally relevant chatbot experiences can foster a positive attitude, while framing chatbot interactions as opportunities for independent learning can bolster self-efficacy.

However, the study also identified areas for improvement. PI and US exhibit a moderate influence on acceptance. This suggests that learners who are more receptive to trying new technologies are more likely to accept chatbots as a language learning tool. Similarly, learners who find chatbots easy to use and navigate are more likely to integrate them into their learning routine. In essence, learners who are more innovative and adaptable, along with those who perceive chatbots as user friendly, are more likely to embrace chatbots as a language learning aid. This alignment highlights the need for chatbots that are not only pedagogically effective but also inclusive, user friendly, and accessible to diverse learners in order to ensure equal opportunities for language acquisition.

While the study found overall positive reception, both PBC and BI scores were comparatively lower. These scores suggest that students may have had mixed feelings about their level of control over their learning experience using the chatbot and may not have expressed a strong intention to use it frequently. Future research could explore these factors in more detail, investigating specific aspects of chatbots that may be hindering learners' willingness to utilize them consistently. This could involve delving deeper into learner perceptions of speech recognition accuracy, limitations in chatbot response creativity, or concerns over data privacy.

In summary, while the findings suggest potential benefits in terms of ease of use, user attitudes, and learner confidence, the data also highlight the need for further development to enhance perceived usefulness, address concerns about usability, and encourage more consistent engagement with the chatbot as a learning tool.

4.2 Students' perspectives on the benefits and challenges of utilizing AI-chatbots in Korean language learning

In the survey, students were asked to share their experiences with the benefits and challenges of using the Sejong AI chatbot for Korean speaking practice. Their responses are presented in the following paragraphs, highlighting the key benefits and challenges. It is important to note that these findings are specific to the Sejong AI chatbot and may not be generalizable to all Korean AI chatbots.

The benefits of using AI chatbots

Students identified three primary benefits of using the Sejong AI chatbot in Korean language learning: enhanced flexibility, reduced language-related anxiety, and an engaging learning experience.

First, learners emphasized the significant flexibility afforded by chatbot utilization. Chatbots offer 24/7 accessibility, allowing learners to practice Korean at their convenience, regardless of time or location. This feature is particularly valuable for those studying Korean in areas with limited native speaker interactions. This finding aligns with Lee (2022) and Park and Lee (2021) who emphasize the accessibility and self-directed learning opportunities chatbots offer. Additionally, students particularly valued the ability to repeat exercises as often as needed, potentially promoting stronger vocabulary retention and grammar mastery. This report contrasts with studies like Fryer et al. (2017), where repetitive interactions with chatbots might decrease engagement.

Second, students noted the benefit of chatbots in mitigating language-related anxiety. Learners can interact with chatbots without the fear of negative judgment or embarrassment. In other words, learners do not have to worry about making mistakes in Korean or feeling embarrassed, which can alleviate anxiety levels as chatbots create a non-judgmental and low-pressure learning environment. Furthermore, learners can control the pace of their interactions and progress at their own comfortable speed. This finding aligns with Fryer et al. (2017), Liu et al. (2022), and Kim and Su (2024), who highlight the importance of non-judgmental learning environments. Additionally, students appreciated the real-time feedback mechanism for error correction, potentially fostering a sense of progress and boosting confidence compared to studies where chatbots lacked such features (Lee, 2022).

This feedback mechanism not only enhances the learning process but also augments students' confidence, thus reducing anxiety associated with making mistakes.

Last, students found that using chatbots was engaging and enjoyable. Learners noted that chatbots enhance the learning experience by integrating interactive elements like quizzes, games, and conversations, which adds dynamism and engagement to the process. Learners appreciated that chatbots provide a variety of activities and exercises in Korean, preventing monotony and thereby sustaining their own engagement and motivation. The use of interactive elements like quizzes and games aligns with Park and Lee (2021). However, unlike their study, this research suggests a wider range of activities might be beneficial. Students also found the ability to practice real-life scenarios engaging, enabling them to apply their Korean language skills in practical contexts. This active participation in real-world situations adds an enjoyable dimension to learning, as it closely resembles actual conversations they may encounter in Korean. This suggests that chatbots can complement traditional methods that might lack such context.

These findings have important implications for the use of AI chatbots in enhancing Korean speaking skills among learners. Specifically, AI chatbots offer flexible and accessible language learning, accommodating diverse learning styles and schedules. Moreover, they provide a supportive environment that reduces anxiety and promotes learner confidence. They also incorporate interactive and real-life scenarios, making the learning experience more engaging and enjoyable, and potentially leading to better retention and mastery of speaking skills. Overall, the combination of flexibility, reduced anxiety, and increased engagement creates a powerful learning experience that can significantly enhance Korean speaking skills.

The challenges of using of AI chatbots

This section explores the challenges students encountered while using the Sejong AI chatbot for Korean language learning. They reported encountering two primary challenges when using chatbots for educational purposes in language learning: frustration arising from misunderstood speech and a perceived lack of creativity in the conversational scripts.

Students reported the most frequent challenge as the chatbot's difficulty understanding spoken Korean, especially for learners with strong accents or non-native pronunciations. For instance, L2 learners with strong accents or non-native pronunciations may encounter difficulties, because chatbots are often trained on a standardized form of a language, making it challenging for them to comprehend diverse accents, regional pronunciations, or variations in speaking styles. Consequently, learners with non-standard Korean accents or pronunciations may find it challenging to interact effectively with chatbots. This frustration arose when students had to repeat themselves multiple times for the chatbot to understand their responses.

Beyond pronunciation issues, students also experienced frustration when using complex sentence structures, idiomatic expressions, or slang that chatbots may not be equipped to handle, leading to subtle nuances in the Korean language that can result in misunderstandings. This finding is consistent with Lee (2022), who found limitations in chatbot conversations beyond scripted scenarios despite advancements in sound recognition technology. Sejong AI's inability to handle unrestricted, spontaneous interactions remains a significant hurdle to its seamless incorporation into L2 pedagogy.

In addition, students criticized the absence of nuanced variety and creativity in the AI-generated Korean scripts. These elements are considered essential in everyday human conversations but are often lacking due to the inherent rigidity of chatbot responses. Chatbots that lack creativity may struggle to engage in authentic-sounding dialogues, resulting in interactions that feel artificial and less conducive to meaningful language practice for L2 learners seeking genuine communication experiences. During a 2-week practice period with the AI Korean chatbot focused on a specific topic, students encountered difficulties in expanding their vocabulary and grasping nuanced language aspects because the chatbot consistently provided repetitive responses. This limitation can hinder the depth and breadth of Korean language acquisition. Students reported that the repetitive and scripted responses quickly became monotonous and tedious, potentially leading to disengagement and reduced motivation to continue using the chatbot for learning or interaction.

Park and Lee (2021) highlighted similar technological challenges in their study, demonstrating that chatbots, while valuable tools for language learning, still face significant hurdles in achieving human-level conversational abilities and delivering adaptable knowledge that could replace human educators. Furthermore, Fryer et al. (2017) found that tasks involving human partners were predictive of future course interest, whereas interest levels diminished under chatbot partner conditions. These findings suggest that the lack of nuanced variety and creativity in chatbot responses can adversely impact long-term interest and overall enthusiasm for learning when compared to human interactions. In contrast, Liu et al. (2022) revealed that students who engaged in conversations with chatbots developed a profound sense of social connection, maintaining a consistent level of situational interest in the content. Taken together, these supporting studies suggest that while chatbots can foster engagement through social interaction, their current limitations in creativity and variety remain a significant challenge.

Overall, AI chatbots have significant potential for enhancing Korean language learning by offering flexibility, reducing anxiety, and fostering engagement through diverse activities and real-life scenario practice. However, current limitations in speech recognition accuracy can limit effective interactions. Moreover, students may find chatbot responses repetitive due to a lack of nuanced variety and creativity. To address these challenges, developers should prioritize expanding training datasets to include a wider range of accents and dialects to improve speech recognition, enhancing contextual understanding and response generation to enable more dynamic and adaptive chatbot response. Also, they should consider providing personalized feedback to offer tailored corrections and suggestions and refining natural language generation capabilities for more natural and engaging dialogue that reflects the complexities of human conversation.

These advancements would not only mitigate speech recognition issues but also create more contextually relevant and engaging interactions for Korean language learners, ultimately enhancing their learning outcomes.

5. Practical suggestions for integrating AI chatbots in Korean language education

The findings of this study offer valuable insights for Korean language educators seeking to incorporate AI chatbots into their teaching practices. By strategically integrating chatbots and focusing on specific user-centered design principles, teachers can create a more engaging and effective learning environment for L2 learners.

First, educators should focus on cultivating PEU by platforming chatbots with intuitive interfaces and clear instructions. This focus can be achieved by providing tutorials and practice opportunities that allow students to build confidence and familiarity with the chatbot's functionalities and features. In doing so, teachers can mitigate initial anxiety or uncertainty that students may experience when interacting with new technology.

Second, educators should leverage chatbots to promote SE by framing interactions as opportunities for independent learning and skill development. This can be accomplished by assigning chatbot-based exercises that target specific learning objectives, enabling students to practice at their own pace and receive immediate feedback. By empowering students to take ownership of their learning journeys, educators can foster a sense of agency and motivation that is critical for language acquisition.

Third, educators should highlight the practical applications of chatbot-learned skills by integrating scenarios that address real-life communication needs. For instance, chatbot interactions could involve practicing greetings, ordering food at a restaurant, or asking for directions. By showcasing the relevance and utility of chatbot-learned skills, educators can demonstrate the value of chatbot-assisted language learning and cultivate a positive attitude towards this innovative approach.

Finally, educators should strive to create engaging and interactive chatbot experiences that are culturally relevant and promote a sense of enjoyment. By doing so, educators can harness the unique capabilities of chatbots to create a more dynamic and immersive learning environment that motivates students to learn and practice Korean language skills.

These recommendations provide tangible ways in which Korean language educators can harness the potential of AI chatbots to create a more engaging, effective, and student-centered learning environment, ultimately supporting language acquisition journey of their students.

6. Conclusions

This study investigates the acceptance of AI chatbots in Korean language learning by utilizing the TAM2 framework to evaluate students' perceptions. The findings reveal a generally positive acceptance of chatbots, with high scores in PEU, PU, AT, and SE. These results suggest that learners are more likely to adopt chatbots designed with user-friendliness, practical benefits, and a focus on fostering positive attitudes and confidence in learning.

Additionally, the moderate level of PI and US scores indicate that some students are more receptive to this type of learning tool than others and that the specific chatbot used in this study has the potential to enhance Korean language learning.

However, the study also highlights areas for improvement. The relatively low scores for PBC and BI suggest that some barriers hinder consistent chatbot use. Future research could explore these aspects in more detail, examining factors such as speech recognition accuracy, chatbot response creativity, and data privacy concerns.

Student feedback highlighted both the benefits and challenges of AI chatbots in language learning. On the one hand, chatbots offer flexibility, reduce anxiety, and enhance engagement. On the other hand, they also present challenges such as frustration due to misunderstood speech and perceived limitations in conversational creativity. To address these challenges, it is essential to develop chatbots with improved speech recognition to minimize misunderstandings, personalized feedback to address individual learning needs, and enhanced natural language generation capabilities to increase conversational creativity.

Altogether, the results of this study show that combining chatbot-based learning with human interaction can provide a comprehensive and engaging language learning experience that leverages the strengths of both approaches to support students' language acquisition journeys.

7. Limitations and future research directions

This study has two main limitations that present valuable opportunities for future research. First, the present study focused on a single chatbot, which may limit the generalizability of other chatbots used for Korean language learning. Future research could explore a wider range of chatbots to establish a more comprehensive understanding of their effectiveness across different platforms and functionalities. Second, this study investigated student perceptions of chatbot use over a 2-week period, leaving the long-term efficacy of chatbot-assisted language learning unexplored. Future research design could incorporate extended learning periods to assess the impact of chatbots on language acquisition and retention over time.

Building upon the insights gleaned from this study, I plan to expand upon the findings with future research directions: (1) conducting a comparative analysis to assess the efficacy of three prominent AI chatbots (Sejong AI tutor, Langotalk, and Eggbun) in fostering Korean speaking skills. This analysis will involve both L2 learners and Korean language instructors, providing insight into user experiences across different demographics, and (2) investigating the impact of chatbot-assisted language learning on long-term speaking fluency and retention. This project will explore how consistent chatbot use influences learners' ability to maintain and develop their Korean speaking proficiency over extended periods.

By overcoming these limitations and exploring new directions, AI chatbot research can unlock deeper dives into its potential, foster innovative teaching methods, and further strengthen the AI-language learning connection. This, in turn, will create a more immersive and enriching learning experience for language learners worldwide.

Acknowledgments

This research was supported by the 2024 Korean Studies Grant Program of the Academy of Korean Studies (AKS-2024R-014).

Note

1 https://app.ksif.or.kr/eng/study/aiTeacher.do

References

Al-Emran, M., Mezhuyev, V., & Kamaludin, A. (2018). Technology acceptance model in M-learning context: A systematic review. *Computers & Education, 125*, 389–412.

Alfadda, H. A., & Mahdi, H. S. (2021). Measuring students' use of zoom application in language course based on the technology acceptance model (TAM). *Journal of Psycholinguistic Research, 50*(4), 883–900.

Baylor, A. L. (2011). The design of motivational agents and avatars. *Educational Technology Research and Development, 59*(2), 291–300.

Belda-Medina, J., & Calvo-Ferrer, J. R. (2022). Using chatbots as AI conversational partners in language learning. *Applied Sciences, 12*(17), 8427.

Chocarro, R., Cortinas, M., & Marcos-Matás, G. (2023). Teachers' attitudes towards chatbots in education: A technology acceptance model approach considering the effect of social language, bot proactiveness, and users' characteristics. *Educational Studies, 49*(2), 295–313.

Davis, F. D. (1985). *A technology acceptance model for empirically testing new end-user information systems: Theory and results* [Doctoral dissertation, Massachusetts Institute of Technology]. https://dspace.mit.edu/handle/1721.1/15192

Fryer, L. K., Ainley, M., Thompson, A., Gibson, A., & Sherlock, Z. (2017). Stimulating and sustaining interest in a language course: An experimental comparison of chatbot and human task partners. *Computers in Human Behavior, 75*, 461–468.

Hobert, S., & Meyer von Wolff, R. (2019). Say hello to your new automated tutor – A structured literature review on pedagogical conversational agents. In *14th International Conference on Wirtschaftsinformatik* (pp. 301–314).

Hsieh, J. S. C., Huang, Y. M., & Wu, W. C. V. (2017). Technological acceptance of LINE in flipped EFL oral training. *Computers in Human Behavior, 70*, 178–190.

Hsu, H. T., & Lin, C. C. (2022). Extending the technology acceptance model of college learners' mobile-assisted language learning by incorporating psychological constructs. *British Journal of Educational Technology, 53*(2), 286–306.

Huang, W., Hew, K. F., & Fryer, L. K. (2022). Chatbots for language learning – Are they really useful? A systematic review of chatbot-supported language learning. *Journal of Computer Assisted Learning, 38*(1), 237–257.

Hwang, G. J., & Chang, C. Y. (2023). A review of opportunities and challenges of chatbots in education. *Interactive Learning Environments, 31*(7), 4099–4112.

Jeon, J. (2024). Exploring AI chatbot affordances in the EFL classroom: Young learners' experiences and perspectives. *Computer Assisted Language Learning, 37*(1–2), 1–26.

Kerry, A., Ellis, R., & Bull, S. (2008). Conversational agents in e-learning. In *International Conference on Innovative Techniques and Applications of Artificial Intelligence* (pp. 169–182). Springer London.

Kim, A., & Su, Y. (2024). How implementing an AI chatbot impacts Korean as a foreign language learners' willingness to communicate in Korean. *System, 122*, 103256.

Kim, N. Y. (2018). Chatbots and Korean EFL students' English vocabulary learning. *Journal of Digital Convergence, 16*(2), 1–7.

Kuhail, M. A., Alturki, N., Alramlawi, S., & Alhejori, K. (2023). Interacting with educational chatbots: A systematic review. *Education and Information Technologies, 28*(1), 973–1018.

Kuleto, V., Ilić, M., Dumangiu, M., Ranković, M., Martins, O. M., Păun, D., & Mihoreanu, L. (2021). Exploring opportunities and challenges of artificial intelligence and machine learning in higher education institutions. *Sustainability, 13*(18), 10424.

Lee, S. (2022). A study on the development of Korean language learning and scoring tools applying artificial intelligence. *Grammar Education, 44*, 29–54.

Lee, Y. F., Hwang, G. J., & Chen, P. Y. (2022). Impacts of an AI-based chatbot on college students' after-class review, academic performance, self-efficacy, learning attitude, and motivation. *Educational Technology Research and Development, 70*(5), 1843–1865.

Liu, C. C., Liao, M. G., Chang, C. H., & Lin, H. M. (2022). An analysis of children's interaction with an AI chatbot and its impact on their interest in reading. *Computers & Education, 189*, 104576.

Luan, W. S., & Teo, T. (2009). Investigating the technology acceptance among student teachers in Malaysia: An application of the technology acceptance model (TAM). *Asia-Pacific Education Researcher, 18*(2), 261–272.

Nghi, T. T., Phuc, T. H., & Thang, N. T. (2019). Applying AI chatbot for teaching a foreign language: An empirical research. *International Journal of Scientific and Technology Research, 8*(12), 897–902.

Nikou, S. A., & Economides, A. A. (2017). Mobile-based assessment: Investigating the factors that influence behavioral intention to use. *Computers & Education, 109*, 56–73.

Okonkwo, C. W., & Ade-Ibijola, A. (2021). Chatbots applications in education: A systematic review. *Computers & Education: Artificial Intelligence, 2*, 100033.

Park, J., & Lee, H. (2021). AI chatbot builders utilization plan to develop AI chatbots for Korean language education. *Teaching Korean as a Foreign Language, 63*, 51–91.

Pindeh, N., & Suki, N. M. (2016). User acceptance on mobile apps as an effective medium to learn Kadazandusun language. *Procedia Economics and Finance, 37*, 372–378.

R Core Team. (2017). *R: A language and environment for statistical computing*. R Foundation for Statistical Computing. www.R-project.org

Suh, J. (2021). A study on the design method of Korean speaking practice chatbot for beginners based on scenarios. *The Society of Korean Culture and Convergence, 43*(9), 53–76.

Suh, J. (2023). A study on the conformity of chatbot builder as a Korean speech practice tool. *The Society of Korean Culture and Convergence, 45*(1), 61–70.

Thomas, H. (2020). Critical literature review on chatbots in education. *International Journal of Technical Research and Science Discovery, 4*(6), 786–788.

Venkatesh, V., & Davis, F. D. (2000). A theoretical extension of the technology acceptance model: Four longitudinal field studies. *Management Science, 46*(2), 186–204.

Wang, Y. F., Petrina, S., & Feng, F. (2017). VILLAGE – Virtual immersive language learning and gaming environment: Immersion and presence. *British Journal of Educational Technology, 48*(2), 431–450.

Winkler, R., & Söllner, M. (2018). Unleashing the potential of chatbots in education: A state-of-the-art analysis. In *Academy of Management Proceedings* (Vol. 2018, No. 1, p. 15903). Academy of Management.

Yin, J., Goh, T. T., Yang, B., & Xiaobin, Y. (2021). Conversation technology with micro-learning: The impact of chatbot-based learning on students' learning motivation and performance. *Journal of Educational Computing Research, 59*(1), 154–177.

Yoo, J. Y., & Yoo, H. S. (2021). The effects of smart-learning in Korean language education through chatbots: A focus on learner perception. *Multimedia-Assisted Language Learning, 24*(2), 82–105.

Zhang, S., Shan, C., Lee, J. S. Y., Che, S., & Kim, J. H. (2023). Effect of chatbot-assisted language learning: A meta-analysis. *Education and Information Technologies, 28*(11), 15223–15243.

3 Large language models for Korean grammar and spelling corrections
Comparative evaluation of Bard, Bing, ChatGPT, CLOVA X, and Perplexity AI

Narae Jung

1. Introduction

This chapter aims to critically evaluate the effectiveness of six large language models (LLMs) – Bard, Bing, ChatGPT (including GPT-3.5 and GPT-4), CLOVA X, and Perplexity AI – in the specific context of correcting Korean grammar and spelling errors. LLMs are a subset of generative artificial intelligence (GAI), specialized in producing text-based content such as prose, poetry, and programming code, within the broader capacity of GAI to create diverse digital content including language, images, video, and music (Byrd et al., 2023). LLMs have been the subject of active research, advancing the domain of natural language processing (NLP) and have surpassed cutting-edge outcomes in diverse natural language tasks such as question answering, summarization, and text generation (Pallagani et al., 2022).

In the realm of LLMs, OpenAI's ChatGPT has not only gained widespread popularity since its release in November 2022 (Leiter et al., 2023) but also emerged as a significant term synonymous with LLMs, especially in the context of text generation (Oh, 2023). This study considers ChatGPT one of the LLMs or a representative of LLMs. ChatGPT, which stands for "generative pre-trained transformer," is defined as a LLM that allows people to interact with a computer in a more natural and conversational way (Sabzalieva & Valentini, 2023). It specializes in understanding and generating natural language, facilitating more human-like and interactive conversations with computers. Its application in foreign language education is notable, providing services like writing assistance, language translation, and digital tutoring (Skrabut, 2023). Furthermore, ChatGPT has proven valuable in writing, offering grammar, vocabulary, and sentence composition feedback (Ferlazzo, 2023).

Despite these positive attributes, there are concerns regarding ChatGPT's potential negative impacts, particularly in academic contexts. Notably, Noam Chomsky has critiqued it as a form of "high-tech plagiarism" and a means to bypass traditional learning processes, highlighting the challenges it poses to academic integrity (Open Culture, 2023). However, in this era of continual technological advancement, it is not feasible to simply tell students not to use LLMs. Therefore, it is important to find ways to use them effectively rather than avoiding their use. Writing in a foreign language can be challenging and demanding, but with the help of LLMs for correction, writing skills can be significantly improved.

DOI: 10.4324/9781032725307-5

Yet, while ChatGPT's utility in English-language contexts is well established, its ability in handling non-English texts, particularly Korean, is less robust. ChatGPT has been primarily trained on English texts and thus has encountered comparatively less data in Korean, leading to limitations in its processing capabilities for this language (Noh & Hong, 2023). Although ChatGPT's capabilities are expected to improve in the future, its current proficiency in Korean is about intermediate, with many errors in interpreting idiomatic expressions (Baek, 2023). This linguistic gap underscores the importance of conducting a comparative analysis of various LLMs to determine the most effective model for correcting Korean text. Such an analysis, central to this study, aims to shed light on the potential of LLMs as language learning tools, particularly for languages other than English.

2. Literature review

To provide a comprehensive understanding of the current landscape in LLMs research, this section delves into two critical areas: comparative studies on various LLMs and their application in language education.

2.1 Comparative research on LLMs

While ChatGPT has been the subject of extensive examination in recent scholarship, studies exploring alternative LLMs have been relatively scarce. Notably, some studies have juxtaposed ChatGPT's capabilities with those of conventional translators, chatbots, Bard and Bing. For instance, Jiao et al. (2023) scrutinized ChatGPT's efficacy in multilingual translation, setting it against established commercial products like Google Translate and DeepL Translate. The findings indicate that while ChatGPT competes effectively in translating high-resource European languages, it is considerably less successful with low-resource or linguistically distant languages (Jiao et al., 2023).

In a similar vein, Shin et al. (2023) assessed Cleverbot, Kuki, and ChatGPT to explore the potential of chatbots as tools for content-based English instruction. They discovered that, based on education experts' feedback, ChatGPT surpassed Cleverbot and Kuki in information provision and language proficiency. Despite lower ratings in social skills and moral discernment, ChatGPT was deemed highly effective for English learning and teaching.

Beyond the realm of linguistic pedagogy, LLMs have been subjected to comparative analyses within the medical domain. Lim et al. (2023) compared the capabilities of three leading LLMs – Google's AI BARD, Bing's AI, and OpenAI's ChatGPT-4 – in providing advice for patients with hand lacerations. Their analysis revealed that ChatGPT-4 outperformed BARD and Bing AI in delivering reliable, evidence-based clinical advice, highlighting the challenges LLMs face in achieving the depth and specificity necessary for personalized decision-making.

Rahsepar et al. (2023) analyzed how accurately and consistently ChatGPT-3.5 and Google Bard answered non-expert questions related to lung cancer prevention, screening, and terminology commonly used in radiology reports. Their findings indicated that ChatGPT-3.5 was more accurate than the other platforms tested. However, none, including ChatGPT, Google Bard, or the Bing and Google search engines, provided completely correct and consistent responses to all queries.

Although such comparative evaluations exist, the focus of research frequently remains ChatGPT or involves discussions about several models collectively. Terms such as "ChatGPT et al." (Teubner et al., 2023) and "ChatGPT and its Friends" (Loukdes, 2023) treat a multitude of LLMs as a single categorical entity. Furthermore, Egli (2023) cited ChatGPT, Bard, Claude, Jasper, and Writesonic as examples of LLMs launched in 2022, acknowledging them as chatbot technologies but abstaining from a comparative analysis.

2.2 LLMs in language education

There has been a marked increase in research focusing on GAI and LLM, particularly centered around ChatGPT. This surge in interest spans a range of topics, with a notable focus on foreign language education, including languages from English to Korean.

In the realm of English language education, several studies have illuminated the versatile applications of ChatGPT. Park (2023) explored the integration of ChatGPT as an English learning platform in flipped classrooms and online courses, as well as its potential in student assessment. Cha (2023) found it beneficial in elementary English education for text generation, feedback provision, and picture book recommendations. Lee and Shin (2023) observed that ChatGPT can boost interest, confidence, and writing proficiency in middle school English free-writing classes. In the context of university-level education, Lee (2023) reported a preference among students for using ChatGPT in English poetry writing due to its ability to produce high-quality, sophisticated texts swiftly compared to the traditional method of using a dictionary. Furthermore, Shin (2023) investigated its application in writing instruction with pre-service teachers, emphasizing its support in idea generation and text revision, with a caution against overdependence.

Shifting the focus to language studies beyond English, several researchers have investigated the efficacy of ChatGPT across different linguistic disciplines. Jin (2023) highlighted the potential of ChatGPT in the field of Chinese grammar research, where it proves beneficial for a range of tasks from vocabulary and sentence analysis to thesis structuring and translation work. Jung (2023) posited that AI tools like ChatGPT can act as an advantageous supplementary aid for students majoring in Spanish as a second foreign language, particularly in improving classroom learning through increased interaction at intermediate levels and beyond. In a related vein, Koo and Hong (2023) delved into the advantages of ChatGPT for German language learners, noting significant improvements in grammar and vocabulary when beginners used the AI to correct their texts. The study also found that editing texts generated by ChatGPT can deepen learners' understanding of new expressions and sentence structures, indicating the tool's effectiveness in enhancing writing skills at the novice level.

Building upon ChatGPT's successful applications in diverse language domains, research has expanded to include its role in facilitating Korean language acquisition.

Han (2023) conducted an extensive study on teaching Korean speaking through talk-to-ChatGPT. This conversational generative AI, equipped with real-time interactive voice response capabilities, proved especially beneficial for speaking practice via role-playing exercises, emphasizing its value as a learner-centered tool.

In a complementary study, H. Kim (2023) examined ChatGPT's impact on advanced Korean learners, particularly in writing and speaking tasks. Despite some limitations, the AI chatbot was found to be effective for speaking practice, offering personalized learning experiences, alleviating speaking anxiety, and promoting autonomous learning among students.

Further, M. Kim (2023) devised and assessed a ChatGPT-integrated method for teaching Korean writing, aimed at improving the composition skills of foreign learners. Through a progression of writing tasks, from drafting emails to composing essays, students prepared initial drafts which they refined with ChatGPT's assistance, followed by their teacher's final feedback. This approach was successful in correcting linguistic errors and refining writing techniques, with its positive effects on learners' writing proficiency and their favorable perception confirmed by pre- and post-surveys and assessments.

The literature review has provided a thorough exploration of the current state and advancements in LLMs research, emphasizing comparative studies between various LLMs and their implementation in language education. While significant strides have been made in utilizing LLMs for multilingual translation, language learning, and specialized domains like medical advice, this critical review revealed that challenges remain in achieving linguistic accuracy and contextual relevance, particularly in languages with less data and specific educational settings. This review underscores the evolving nature of LLMs and their potential to revolutionize language learning and application across disciplines. Building on these insights, the subsequent phase of this study aims to extend the understanding of LLMs' abilities by specifically evaluating their effectiveness in identifying and correcting grammatical and spelling errors in Korean texts. This targeted investigation will contribute to refining the application of LLMs in language education, particularly focusing on Korean, thereby addressing a gap in current research, and offering a nuanced perspective on the practical utility and limitations of LLMs in enhancing language skills and learning outcomes.

3. Methods

The methodology of this study is structured to evaluate the ability of various LLMs in correcting Korean text, specifically focusing on grammatical and spelling errors. This section details the selection of representative LLMs, as well as the preparation and utilization of test materials, to ensure a systematic and unbiased assessment.

3.1 Selection of LLMs for comparative analysis

The emergence of LLMs has profoundly influenced various aspects of natural language processing, including language learning and text correction. However, the capability of these models to handle specific linguistic challenges, particularly in Korean, a language with complex grammatical structures and distinct phonetics, remains underexplored. Therefore, this research focuses on assessing the ability of various LLMs in identifying and rectifying grammatical and spelling inaccuracies in Korean texts.

The study focuses on a comparative analysis of six prominent LLMs, chosen based on their relevance and abilities in language processing. The models under evaluation are Bard, Bing, ChatGPT (including its GPT-3.5 and GPT-4 iterations), CLOVA X, and Perplexity AI. This selection encompasses a diverse spectrum of LLMs, ensuring a comprehensive examination of the current state of language processing abilities in this field. Table 3.1 provides a detailed overview of the LLMs evaluated in this study. It serves as an essential reference, outlining the developer, cost, and website for each LLM.

The following descriptions outline the main features of each of the LLMs selected for this study.

- Bard, developed by Google, can be accessed through Bard's official website for free. It represents Google's foray into advanced language models, leveraging their extensive search engine data.
- Bing, a product of Microsoft, is also free to use. Its details can be found on Bing's chat page. Bing's integration with Microsoft's search technology potentially offers unique insights into language processing.
- ChatGPT-3.5 is created by OpenAI. This version of ChatGPT is available at no cost. Users can interact with ChatGPT-3.5 via OpenAI's chat interface. As an earlier iteration of OpenAI's model, it provides a basis for comparison with its successor.
- ChatGPT-4, also developed by OpenAI, is a more advanced version and comes with a subscription cost of USD 20 per month. Accessible through the same platform as ChatGPT-3.5, it represents the cutting-edge of OpenAI's language model offerings.
- CLOVA X is developed by Naver, a South Korean online platform, and is also freely accessible. It can be accessed through its dedicated webpage. As a product of a non-Western company, it adds valuable diversity to the range of models analyzed.

Table 3.1 Overview of LLMs compared in the study

	Company	Cost	Website
Bard	Google	Free	https://gemini.google.com
Bing	Microsoft	Free	www.bing.com/chat
ChatGPT-3.5	Open AI	Free	https://chat.openai.com
ChatGPT-4	Open AI	US$20 per month	https://chat.openai.com
CLOVA X	Naver	Free	https://clova-x.naver.com
Perplexity AI	Perplexity AI	Free	www.perplexity.ai

- Perplexity AI, developed by Perplexity AI, is free for use. Information and access to this model are available at Perplexity AI's website. It is an emerging contender in the LLM space, noted for its specific approach to information retrieval and language understanding.

The criteria for selecting these LLMs included factors such as ease of access, cost-free (except for ChatGPT-4), widespread availability, and conversational features. Models like Llama (https://ai.meta.com/llama) were not considered due to their current requirement for download. Similarly, Claude (www.claude.ai) was excluded from this analysis due to its limited availability, being accessible only in the US and UK at the time of this study. It is, however, worth noting that the availability of such models might change in the future. Given the rapid advancements in the field of LLMs, numerous LLMs currently under development are not covered in this study. The constantly evolving landscape of language models means that this study, while aiming to provide a comprehensive analysis, cannot encompass all existing or rapidly emerging LLMs.

3.2 Design and selection of test materials

This study utilized reading passages from the *Seoul National University Korean 2A* textbook as test material. This source was chosen due to its authentic representation of beginner-level Korean language usage, making it highly relevant for real-world language learning scenarios. The reading passages in the textbook serve as examples for subsequent writing tasks, providing students with a diverse range of writing styles to emulate, including advertisements, emails, and blog entries. This variety provides a broad spectrum of linguistic contexts for evaluation, crucial for testing the adaptability of LLMs to various forms of written Korean, encompassing both formal and informal tones and structures.

The passages used in this study, sourced from the textbook, typically comprised 6 to 13 sentences. This range inherently provided a balance between text complexity and manageability for analysis, facilitating a focused yet comprehensive examination of each LLM's correction capabilities. Consequently, these passages offered a consistent basis for comparing the performance of the various models under review, ensuring that the evaluation process remained standardized across all tests.

To assess the LLMs' proficiency in correcting Korean grammar and spelling, 100 errors were purposefully introduced into nine selected Korean passages. These errors were evenly divided between grammatical and spelling mistakes, simulating common errors made by foreign learners of Korean. The details of these errors and the passages in which they were embedded can be found in the appendix.

In the case of spelling errors, common mistakes were incorporated, primarily involving similar spellings or identical pronunciations. For example, '찰고' and '찻고' are pronounced '찰꼬 [chatgo]' but only '찰고' is correctly spelled, while '찻고' is incorrect. Another example is '잃다', meaning 'to lose' and '잊다', meaning 'to forget'. Although both are correctly spelled, they have different meanings and are easily confused due to their similar spellings and slightly related meanings, presenting a challenge in spelling accuracy.

For grammatical errors, the focus was on commonly confused particles such as place particles '에' versus '에서', and subject particles '이/가' versus object particles '을/를'. These particles, which do not have direct equivalents in languages like English and Chinese, frequently pose difficulties for learners of Korean as a foreign language. Additionally, errors were introduced in tense usage, varying from present to past or future tense. A typical example of such confusion is seen in the verbs '좋아하다', meaning 'to like' and '좋다', meaning 'to be good'. While '좋아하다' is a verb requiring a direct object, '좋다' is an adjective but can sometimes be used in contexts similar to 'to like', leading to common mistakes among learners.

The nine Korean texts containing the 100 deliberate errors were presented to six LLMs for correction. Initially, the instruction given to the models was simply to "correct grammar and spelling". However, when the models attempted to rephrase or improve the sentences beyond error correction, the prompt was modified to "correct grammar and spelling, keeping the original sentences" to maintain the focus on error correction alone. This study observed that the LLMs' performance varied depending on the prompts used. To ensure a more objective comparison, prompts like "proofread" or "check grammar" were deliberately avoided. These terms might have shifted the focus away from the specific task of grammar and spelling correction. Consequently, the standardized prompt "correct grammar and spelling, keeping the original sentences" was uniformly used for all texts and all LLMs.

4. Results

4.1 Overall results

Six LLMs were evaluated on their ability to correct errors in Korean texts during a November 2023 study; it is important to acknowledge the dynamic nature of LLM technology, emphasizing that the results of this study may change as these models undergo further development. The evaluation provided valuable insights into the effectiveness of each model in correcting Korean grammar and spelling errors. The performance of the models was assessed based on their accuracy in addressing the errors within the diverse set of Korean text samples. Table 3.2 presents a comprehensive summary of these findings, detailing the performance of each LLM in both

Table 3.2 Comparative performance of LLMs in Korean text correction

Rank	LLMs	Spelling correction	Grammar correction	Total correction
1	ChatGPT-4	47/50	45/50	92%
2	CLOVA X	49/50	42/50	91%
3	Bard	45/50	41/50	86%
4	ChatGPT-3.5	41/50	44/50	85%
5	Bing	44/50	38/50	82%
6	Perplexity AI	37/50	35/50	72%

spelling and grammar correction and including their overall correction rates. These following results offer a clear view of the capabilities and limitations of each model in handling the complexities of the Korean language.

- ChatGPT-4 demonstrated superior performance in this evaluation. It achieved an impressive spelling correction rate of 94% (47/50) and a grammar correction rate of 90% (45/50), resulting in an overall correction rate of 92%. This high performance emphasizes ChatGPT-4's advanced proficiency in processing the complexities of the Korean language.
- CLOVA X followed closely, exhibiting exceptional strength in spelling correction with a perfect score of 98% (49/50). Its grammar correction rate was 84% (42/50), leading to an overall correction rate of 91%. CLOVA X's results highlight its robust accuracy, particularly in spelling correction.
- Bard showed balanced capabilities with a spelling correction rate of 90% (45/50) and a grammar correction rate of 82% (41/50), culminating in an overall correction rate of 86%. This indicates a solid performance in both spelling and grammar aspects.
- ChatGPT-3.5, the precursor to ChatGPT-4, displayed commendable effectiveness with a spelling correction rate of 82% (41/50) and a grammar correction rate of 88% (44/50), resulting in an overall correction rate of 85%. This underscores the iterative improvements in ChatGPT models.
- Bing ranked fifth with a spelling correction rate of 88% (44/50) and a grammar correction rate of 76% (38/50), achieving an overall correction rate of 82%. Its performance, while proficient, was slightly behind the other models in this study.
- Perplexity AI, with a spelling correction rate of 74% (37/50) and a grammar correction rate of 70% (35/50), had an overall correction rate of 72%. Although respectable, this indicates potential areas for enhancement compared to the other LLMs evaluated.

The study's findings illustrate a varied range of proficiency among LLMs in handling corrections in Korean text. Notably, models such as ChatGPT-4 and CLOVA X demonstrate superior capabilities in understanding and accurately amending Korean language errors. This heightened proficiency can be attributed to ChatGPT-4's advanced algorithmic framework and CLOVA X's extensive exposure to Korean language datasets, a result of its development by a Korean company. These factors collectively contribute to their exceptional performance in Korean language correction tasks.

4.2 Detailed results

A closer look at the Korean spelling correction cases of LLMs reveals that only ChatGPT-4 and CLOVA X correctly corrected the spelling error in '되요' to '돼요' in the sentence "우리 집으로 6시까지 오면 돼요(*되요)". This is a common spelling error, even among Koreans, as '되다' in its base form changes to '돼요' when combined with '아/어요', although '되' and '돼' sound the same. This example was presented to examine the spelling correction capabilities of LLMs. In this case of spelling error, Bing, Bard, and Perplexity AI left '되요' unchanged. ChatGPT-3.5, however, changed it to '됩니다', which is grammatically correct but not consistent with the informal polite ending of the rest of the sentences.

In terms of grammar, for the sentence "한국어를 잘 못해서 아픈(*아프는) 것을 설명할 수 없었습니다" since '아프다' is an adjective, it should be used as '(으)ㄴ 것' not '는 것'. ChatGPT-4, CLOVA X, and Bard correctly corrected it to '아픈 것', while Bing and Perplexity AI left it as '*아프는 것'. ChatGPT-3.5 changed it to '아프다고', which is grammatically correct in isolation but not a correct correction in the overall meaning.

Although all LLMs exhibited a correction capability exceeding 70%, they did not uniformly produce the same correction outcomes, thus posing challenges for precise analysis. Upon examining the unexpected responses from each LLM specifically, it was observed that ChatGPT-4's corrections occasionally deviated from the intended results. For instance, the correction of the spelling error '*배콰점' to '백화점' was anticipated to be straightforward. However, ChatGPT-4 unexpectedly altered it to '배움터'. While '배움터' is correct in itself, it does not correspond with '문화센터' in the sentence "백화점 문화센터에서 한국 요리를 배우고 있습니다", thus rendering it an incorrect modification. This is akin to the findings of Koo and Hong (2023), which indicate that while ChatGPT can perform basic and superficial corrections in German sentences, it lacks depth in corrections considering textuality. The same appears to be true for Korean; ChatGPT-4 seems to struggle with making detailed corrections that consider the overall meaning of sentences and the coherence between words. This illustrates that it is important to consider the overall context and meaning of sentences when evaluating corrections.

CLOVA X initially did not correct the sentence "저는 일본에서 온 마리코라고(*이라고) 합니다.", leading to the assumption that it missed the rule of using '라고' after a vowel-ending name like 'Mariko'. However, seeing Perplexity AI also leaving it unchanged suggested that the name might have been perceived as '마리코이'. When asked again with "Her name is Mariko. Can you correct again?", it correctly revised it to "저는 일본에서 온 마리코라고 합니다." Perplexity AI also correctly revised it upon being asked again with the name 'Mariko' clearly distinguished with quotation marks. This underscores the importance of precise and specific prompts, aligning with Jin's (2023) assertion that the effectiveness of ChatGPT is contingent upon the specificity of the prompt, and detailed prompts are crucial for obtaining specific results.

In the case of Bard, explanations were provided for its corrections, although at times, these reasons were inaccurate. For instance, with the correct sentence "시험을 봐야 해요?", Bard revised it to "시험을 봐야 하나요?" and explained that since "시험을 봐야 해요?" is a question directed at someone else, it could be rephrased to "시험을 봐야 하나요?" for questioning purposes. However, this explanation is incorrect because both expressions are equally valid for asking questions. This example demonstrates that not all information provided by LLMs is reliable, even when it seems correct. It aligns with the 'hallucination' phenomenon, identified by

Kang (2023), which refers to the tendency of LLMs to generate plausible but false or non-existent information, posing potential problems in language education This emphasizes the necessity for caution with LLMs that, despite providing seemingly accurate explanations, can fabricate information without any factual basis.

ChatGPT-3.5 often unnecessarily changed correct expressions to different expressions. For example, the error-free sentence "방이 많지 않아서 신청한 학생이 모두 이용할 수 있는 것은 아닙니다." was changed to "방이 제한적이기 때문에 신청한 학생 모두에게 이용이 보장되지는 않습니다.". This could lead students to mistakenly think the original sentence was incorrect and needed correction. Moreover, using difficult words like '제한' and '보장' makes the sentence harder for beginners to understand, indicating that LLMs may not be easy for beginners to use for correction purposes. It was mentioned in Shin (2023) that some participants expressed disappointment in how English sentence structures became simpler and the vocabulary easier after being revised by ChatGPT. Contrarily, in this study, it is concerning to observe that sentences became more complex, posing significant challenges for beginner learners in utilizing LLMs for Korean language correction.

In Bing's case, there were instances where it inaccurately modified correct elements. For example, in the Korean sentence "우리 나라 말로 이야기를 하면(*하면서) 즐겁습니다.", Bing incorrectly altered the accurate phrase '즐겁습니다' to '*즐거웁니다' incorrectly. This issue is compounded by the fact that LLMs like Bing often provide responses with a tone of certainty, with little to no indication of potential error. This characteristic can lead learners, particularly beginners, to accept these responses as accurate without questioning or verifying them. As Kohnke et al. (2023) highlighted, this can be a problem for young students who may not have the ability to "fact-check" the information provided by LLMs.

Perplexity AI had instances where it entirely omitted the incorrect parts. For instance, in the sentence, "직접 가서 사는 것보다 더 싸서(*사서) 좋은 것 같습니다.", it did not correct the error but simply omitted it, writing "직접 가서 사는 것보다 더 좋은 것 같습니다". In the case of "좋은(*조은) 날씨와 맛있는(*마싰는) 음식, 그리고 친절한 사람들이 있는 터키를 만나(*만나서) 보세요.", it deleted the entire sentence and added information about Türkiye instead. On November 10, the incorrect sentence was removed and unnecessary additional information was provided, leading to all three being counted as incorrect. Perplexity AI scored the lowest among the LLMs. However, on November 29, when asked again with the same prompt, it correctly revised it to "좋은 날씨와 훌륭한 음식, 그리고 친절한 사람들이 있는 터키를 만나보세요." As such, different outcomes can arise from the same prompt, and especially since LLMs are evolving day by day, it is important to acknowledge that the results of this experiment can change.

5. Conclusion and suggestions

The development of learners' writing skills is critically enhanced by personalized and customized feedback. Traditional methods of providing feedback on writing tasks are often time-consuming, posing challenges for teachers in offering timely and essential responses for student improvement. The emergence of LLMs has introduced a paradigm shift, facilitating prompt initial feedback to students and thus expediting their learning process. This immediate feedback mechanism, as emphasized by Hong (2023), reinforces the role of LLMs as personal language tutors by providing writing suggestions, correction recommendations, and detailed vocabulary explanations with relevant examples. This study aimed to evaluate the efficacy of LLMs in providing feedback on Korean writing and to determine which LLMs are better suited for Korean text correction in a field predominantly centered on English.

Conducted in November 2023, this study revealed that all six LLMs are capable of correcting grammatical and spelling errors in Korean texts. However, the ranking of the correction rate (ChatGPT-4 at 92%, CLOVA X at 91%, Bard at 86%, ChatGPT-3.5 at 85%, Bing at 82%, and Perplexity AI at 72%) might not be very important, considering the small data set of the test materials and the ongoing improvements in LLMs' capabilities. Therefore, if the same experiment is conducted later with more data, the results may change. It is more significant to consider the broader implications of these LLMs in educational contexts, particularly in enhancing Korean writing skills, rather than comparing them directly.

One key finding of this study is the need for cautious reliance on LLMs. Instances where LLMs inaccurately modified correct elements or struggled with contextually detailed corrections highlight the importance of not relying solely on these tools. While LLMs can generate more detailed feedback on students' writing than human instructors (Dai et al., 2023), this study found that their explanations can occasionally be inaccurate. This suggests that LLMs can be valuable for Korean text correction, but they should be used with an understanding of their current limitations.

Another important aspect is the role of specific and clear prompts in eliciting accurate responses from LLMs. The study observed that detailed prompts led to more accurate corrections but also revealed the possibility of obtaining different answers from the same prompt over time. This variability, as echoed by Choi and Park (2023), illustrates the dynamic nature of LLM technology and the need for users to be aware of these inconsistencies.

Furthermore, the study suggests that LLMs might be more beneficial for advanced learners than beginners. The models often provided complex words and expressions, posing challenges for Korean beginners. This aligns with Cha's (2023) observation that the English texts generated by ChatGPT may include words not suitable for the learner's level, requiring additional verification. The same applies to Korean, where corrections made with words more difficult than the learner's level can be challenging for Korean beginners using LLMs for writing correction.

These findings lead to the recommendation of a combined approach in language learning, integrating both AI tools and traditional teaching methods. As advocated by Jeon and Lee (2023), a synergistic collaboration between teachers and AI can foster a more effective and comprehensive learning experience. This approach maximizes the strengths of both human instruction and artificial intelligence, ensuring a balanced and holistic educational process.

In conclusion, as LLMs continue to evolve, their thoughtful integration into language education is imperative. They offer significant advantages, but their effective utilization requires a careful balance of their benefits and limitations. The future of language education is poised to be enriched by technology, but it requires a thoughtful approach that harmoniously combines the unique contributions of both AI and human educators.

References

Baek, M. (2023). A study on the assessment of Korean language proficiency of ChatGPT: Focusing on the reading section of TOPIK and idioms. *Language Facts and Perspectives, 59*, 279–308.

Byrd, A., Flores, L., Green, D., Hassel, H., Johnson, S., Kirschenbaum, M., Lockett, A., Losh, E., & Mills, A. (2023). MLA-CCCC joint task force on writing and AI working paper: Overview of the issues, statement of principles, and recommendations. In *Modern Language Association of America and Conference on College Composition and Communication*. https://aiandwriting.hcommons.org/working-paper-1/

Cha, S. (2023). Exploring the utilization of ChatGPT in elementary English education. *Multimedia-Assisted Language Learning, 26*(3), 130–150. https://doi.org/10.15702/mall.2023.26.3.130

Choi, S., & Park, J. (2023). Exploring the utilization of ChatGPT for composition assessment in the era of artificial intelligence. *Journal of Cheong Ram Korean Language Education, 95*, 65–109.

Dai, W., Lin, J., Jin, F., Li, T., Tsai, Y., Gasevic, D., & Chen, G. (2023). *Can large language models provide feedback to students? A case study on ChatGPT*. https://doi.org/10.35542/osf.io/hcgzj

Egli, A. (2023). ChatGPT, GPT-4, and other large language models – the next revolution for clinical microbiology? *Clinical Infectious Diseases*. https://doi.org/10.1093/cid/ciad407

Ferlazzo, L. (2023). 19 ways to use ChatGPT in your classroom. *Education Week*. www.edweek.org/teaching-learning/opinion-19-ways-to-use-chatgpt-in-your-classroom/2023/01

Han, S. (2023). A study on Korean speaking using interactive generative AI ChatGPT: Focused on role-playing, using talk-to-ChatGPT, to the utilization of AIPRM-for-ChatGPT. *Journal of Learner-Centered Curriculum and Instruction, 23*(18), 651–674.

Hong, W. (2023). The impact of ChatGPT on foreign language teaching and learning: Opportunities in education and research. *Journal of Educational Technology and Innovation*, 37–45. www.researchgate.net/publication/369369955

Jeon, J., & Lee, S. (2023). Large language models in education: A focus on the complementary relationship between human teachers and ChatGPT. *Education and Information Technologies*. https://doi.org/10.1007/s10639-023-11834-1

Jiao, W., Wang, W., Huang, J., Wang, X., & Tu, Z. (2023). *Is ChatGPT a good translator? A preliminary study*. https://wxjiao.github.io/downloads/tech_chatgpt_arxiv.pdf

Jin, J. (2023). How to utilize the 'generative AI language model service: ChatGPT' in Chinese grammar research? *China and Chinese Studies, 50*, 165–196.

Jung, W. (2023). The applicability of ChatGPT in Spanish language education. *Revista Asiatica de Estudios Iberoamericanos, 34*(2), 67–98.

Kang, D.-H. (2023). The advent of ChatGPT and the response of Korean language education. *Korean Language and Literature, 82*(82), 469–496.

Kim, H. (2023). Exploring the potential application of a conversational AI Chatbot in Korean language education: An interaction analysis between advanced learners and ChatGPT. *The Study of Korean Language and Literature, 76*, 261–292.

Kim, M. (2023). A study on teaching and learning methods for Korean writing using ChatGPT. *The Journal of Korean Literary Creative Writing, 22*(2), 55–86.

Kohnke, L., Moorhouse, B. L., & Zou, D. (2023). ChatGPT for language teaching and learning. *RELC Journal*, 1–14. https://journals.sagepub.com/home/rel

Koo, Y., & Hong, M. (2023). A study on the composition practice of beginner German learners using ChatGPT. *German Language and Literature, 100,* 47–69.

Lee, C., & Shin, N. (2023). Enhancing middle school English free writing with ChatGPT: A lesson plan development and usability study. *Journal of Knowledge Information Technology and Systems (JKITS), 18*(3), 685–696. https://doi.org/10.34163/jkits.2023.18.3.017

Lee, Y. (2023). Utilizing ChatGPT in writing poem in English. *The Jungang Journal of English Language and Literature, 65*(2), 23–46. http://dx.doi.org/10.18853/jjell.2023.65.2.002

Leiter, C., Zhang, R., Chen, Y., Belouadi, J., Larionov, D., Fresen, V., & Eger, S. (2023). ChatGPT: A meta-analysis after 2.5 months. https://doi.org/10.48550/arXiv.2302.13795

Lim, B., Seth, I., Bulloch, G., Xie, Y., Hunter-Smith, D. J., & Rozen, W. M. (2023). Evaluating the efficacy of major language models in providing guidance for hand trauma nerve laceration patients: A case study on Google's AI BARD, Bing AI, and ChatGPT. *Plastic and Aesthetic Research, 10,* 43. https://doi.org/10.20517/2347-9264.2023.70

Loukdes, M. K. (2023). *What are ChatGPT and its friends? Opportunities, costs, and risks for large language models* (1st ed.). O'Reilly Media, Inc.

Noh, D., & Hong, M. (2023). Strategies for solving the AI plagiarism problem and educational applications of ChatGPT. *The Journal of Korean Language and Literature Education, 82,* 71–102.

Oh, K. (2023). The impact of generative artificial intelligence on Korean education and response strategies – ChatGPT: A tool or threat for Korean education? *The Journal of Korean Language and Literature Education, 82,* 143–189.

Open Culture. (2023, February). *Noam Chomsky on ChatGPT: It's "basically high-tech plagiarism" and "a way of avoiding learning."* www.openculture.com/2023/02/noam-chomsky-on-chatgpt-its-basically-high-tech-plagiarism-and-a-way-of-avoiding-learning.html

Pallagani, V., Muppasani, B., Murugesan, K., Rossi, F., Horesh, L., Srivastava, B., Fabiano, F., & Loreggia, A. (2022). *Plansformer: Generating symbolic plans using transformers.* https://doi.org/10.48550/arXiv.2212.08681

Park, H.-Y. (2023). Application of ChatGPT for an English learning platform. *Journal of English Teaching through Movies and Media, 24*(3), 30–48. https://doi.org/10.16875/stem.2023.24.3.30

Rahsepar, A. A., Tavakoli, N., Kim, G. H. J., Hassani, C., Abtin, F., & Bedayat, A. (2023). How AI responds to common lung cancer questions: ChatGPT vs Google bard. *Radiology, 307*(5). https://doi.org/10.1148/radiol.230922

Sabzalieva, E., & Valentini, A. (2023). *ChatGPT and artificial intelligence in higher education: Quick start guide.* UNESCO (United Nations Educational, Scientific and Cultural Organization). https://etico.iiep.unesco.org/en/chatgpt-and-artificial-intelligence-higher-education-quick-start-guide

Shin, D. (2023). Utilizing ChatGPT in guided writing activities. *Journal of the Korea English Education Society, 22*(2), 197–217. http://dx.doi.org/10.18649/jkees.2023.22.2.197

Shin, D., Jung, H., & Lee, Y. (2023). Exploring the potential of using ChatGPT as a content-based English learning and teaching tool. *Journal of the Korea English Education Society, 22*(1), 171–192.

Skrabut, S. (2023). 80 ways to use ChatGPT in the classroom: Using AI to enhance teaching and learning. *ProQuest Ebook Central.* http://ebookcentral.proquest.com/lib/ntusg/detail.action?docID=7193594

Teubner, T., Flath, C. M., Weinhardt, C., van der Aalst, W., & Hinz, O. (2023). Welcome to the era of ChatGPT et al.: The prospects of large language models. *Business & Information Systems Engineering, 65*(2), 95–101. https://doi.org/10.1007/s12599-023-00795-x

Appendix

This appendix includes nine Korean texts, each accompanied by their English translation. These texts incorporate a total of 100 intentionally inserted errors to facilitate the study of Korean grammar and spelling correction of LLMs. In each instance, the correct grammar and spelling are underlined for easy identification. Any intentional error is enclosed within parentheses and marked with an asterisk (*) next to the correct form that immediately follows. For example, in the case of '전화(*전하) 주세요', '전화' is the correct usage and is underlined, while the incorrect '(*전하)' is placed in parentheses with an asterisk. This format is intended to provide a clear comparison between common errors and their correct grammatical or spelling counterparts.

Text 1 스페인어 할 수 있으세요?

안녕하세요? 저는 서울대학교 2학년 박민영이라고 합니다. 저는 여행을 아주 좋아하고 *다른*(*다룬) 나라의 언어나 문화에 관심 *이*(*을) *많습니다*(*만습니다). 이번 가을 *에*(*에서) 중남미를 여행 *하려고*(*하러) 스페인어를 공부하고 있습니다. 스페인어 공부는 *재미*(*채미)있지만 발음이 조금 *어렵습니다*(*어려웠습니다). 그래서 매주 두 시간 정도 스페인어 연습을 *도와줄 수 있는*(*도와드릴) 분을 *찾고*(*찾고) 있습니다. 저는 한국어를 *가르쳐*(*가르켜) 드리겠습니다. *전화*(*전하) 주세요! (010-0880-5488)

Can you speak Spanish?

Hello, my name is Minyoung Park, a sophomore at Seoul National University. I really love traveling and am very interested in the languages and cultures of other countries. I'm studying Spanish as I plan to travel to Central and South America this fall. Spanish study is fun, but the pronunciation is a bit challenging. Therefore, I'm looking for someone who can help me practice Spanish for about two hours each week. In exchange, I will teach Korean. Please call me! (010-0880-5488)

Text 2 마리코의 블로그

안녕하세요. 저는 일본에서 온 마리코 *라고*(*이라고) 합니다. *제*(*재) 취미는 요리와 한국 드라마 *를*(*가) 보는 것입니다. 매주 *금요일*(*굼요일)에 우리 집에서 한국 드라마를 *좋아하는*(*좋은) 친구들과 모임을 합니다. 저는 *친구*(*칭구)들에게 맛있는 음식을 만들어 줍니다. 제가 좋아하는 요리도 하고 친구들과 재미있는 시간을 보내서 참 좋습니다. 요즘 저는 드라마 *에서*(*에) 본 한국 음식을 만들어 보고 싶어서 *백화점*(*배콰점) 문화 센터에서 한국 요리를 *배우고*(*배워고) 있습니다. 별로 잘하지는 못하지만 제가 만든 한국 음식 *사진*(*사전)을 블로그에 올리고 있습니다. 제 블로그에 자주 *놀러*(*놀으러) 오세요.

Mariko's blog

Hello. My name is Mariko, and I'm from Japan. My hobbies are cooking and watching Korean dramas. Every Friday, I gather with friends who love Korean dramas at my house. I make delicious food for my friends. It's great to cook my favorite dishes and have fun with my friends. Recently, I've been wanting to try making Korean food that I've seen in dramas, so I am learning Korean cooking at a department store culture center. I'm not very good at it yet, but I'm posting photos of the Korean food I make on my blog. Please visit my blog often.

Text 3 한국에서 여행해 본 곳

저는 *작년*(*장년) 봄에 한국에 왔습니다. 그동안 한국에서 많은 곳에 가 봤는데 특히 부산에 간 것이 가장 *기억*(*기역)에 남습니다. 저는 부산에서 영화제에 갔습니다. 부산에서는 매년 가을에 일주일 동안 영화제를 하는데 세계 여러 나라 *에서*(*에) 감독과 배우들이 많이 옵니다. 거기서 다른 나라 영화도 많이 보고 유명한 배우*들도*(*를도) 만날 수 있어서 참 *좋았습니다*(*좋아했습니다). 그리고 부산은 바다와 가까워서 생선 요리도 맛있고 구경할 것도 많습니다. 저는 부산에서 생선회*를*(*가) 처음 먹어 봤는데 정말 맛있었습니다. 시간이 있으면 부산에 *또*(*도) 가고 싶습니다.

Places I've traveled to in Korea

I came to Korea last spring. During my time there, I visited many places, but my trip to Busan was the most memorable. I attended a film festival in Busan. Every year in the fall, Busan hosts a week-long film festival attended by directors and actors from many countries around the world. It was great to watch films from other countries and meet famous actors. Busan is also close to the sea, so the seafood dishes are delicious and there's a lot to see. I tried sashimi for the first time in Busan and it was really tasty. If I have the time, I would like to visit Busan again.

Text 4 한국에서 쇼핑해 봤어요?

저는 쇼핑하는 것*을*(*이) 좋아합니다. 시간이 있으면 백화점이나 시장에 *가서*(*가고) 구경을 합니다. *특히*(*트키) 시장은 우리 *고향*(*고양)에 없는 여러 가지 물건을 구경할 수 있어서 재미있습니다. *그리고*(*그렇지만) 한국 사람들과 이야기하면서 한국말 연습도 할 수 있어서 좋습니다. 하지만 요즘은 공부할 것이 많아서 쇼핑할 시간이 별로 없습니다. 그래서 필요한 것 *이*(*을) 있으면 인터넷으로 삽니다. 인터넷으로 사면 시간도 *절약*(*절략)할 수 있고 직접 가서 사는 것보다 더 *싸서*(*사서) 좋은 것 같습니다. 어제 인터넷에서 티셔츠와 운동화를 주문했는데 오늘 *오후*(*우호)에 받았습니다. 티셔츠는 사이즈도 잘 맞고 디자인도 마음에 *들었지만*(*들지만) 운동화는 좀 작아서 불편했습니다. 그래서 큰 사이즈로 바꾸려고 *이메일*(*이멜)을 보냈습니다. 빨리 새 운동화가 왔으면 좋겠습니다.

Have you done shopping in Korea?

I enjoy shopping. Whenever I have time, I visit department stores or markets to browse. Especially, markets are fun as they offer a variety of items that are not available in my hometown. Also, it's nice to practice speaking Korean while chatting with Korean people. However, these days I have a lot of studying to do, so I don't have much time for shopping. Therefore, when I need something, I buy it online. Shopping online saves time and often costs less than buying in person. Yesterday, I ordered a t-shirt and sneakers online, and I received them this afternoon. The t-shirt fit well and I liked the design, but the sneakers were a bit small and uncomfortable. So, I sent an email to exchange them for a larger size. I hope the new sneakers arrive soon.

Text 5 동서양이 만나는 곳, 터키

터키는 아시아와 유럽 사이에 있어서 동양과 서양의 *역사*(*역싸)와 문화를 모두 느*낄*(*느킬) 수 있는 곳 *입니다*(*임니다). 터키에는 오래된 건축물과 *아름다운*(*아름답은) 자연 등 다양한 구경거리가 있습니다. 한 번의 여행으로 여러가지 경험을 하고 싶은 분*에게*(*에게서) 터키를 추천합니다. *좋은*(*조은) 날씨와 *맛있는*(*마싰는) 음식, 그리고 친절한 사람들이 있는 터키를 *만나*(*만나서) 보세요.

The place where East meets West, Turkey

Turkey, located between Asia and Europe, is a place where one can experience the history and culture of both the East and the West. Turkey is home to a variety of attractions, including ancient buildings and beautiful natural landscapes. I recommend Turkey to those who wish to have diverse experiences in a single trip. Enjoy the good weather, delicious food, and friendly people of Turkey.

Text 6 한국어교육센터 홈페이지 Q&A

Q: 언어교육원에서 한국어를 배우고 *싶은데*(*싶는데) 처음이라서 잘 몰라요. *어떻게*(*어떠케) 등록해야 해요?

A: 언어교육원 홈페이지에서 등록하시면 *됩니다*(*됍니다). 전화나 우편으로는 접수하지 *않습니다*(*안습니다).

Q: 언어교육원에 *등록하면*(*등록하니까) 기숙사를 이용할 수 있어요?

A: 네, 할 수 있습니다. *기숙사*(*키숙사) 이용 신청은 언어교육원 홈페이지에서 하시면 됩니다. 하지만 방이 많지 않아서 신청한 학생이 모두 이용할 수 있는 것은 아닙니다.

Q: 등록하려고 *하는데*(*한데) 시험을 봐야 해요?

A: 네, 처음 등록하는 학생은 배치 시험을 봐야 *합니다*(*했습니다). 하지만 한국어를 전혀 모르는 학생은 시험을 *보지*(*하지) 않고 바로 1급 수업을 *들으시면*(*듣으시면) 됩니다.

Korean language education center website Q&A

Q: I want to learn Korean at the Language Education Institute, but it's my first time and I'm not sure how to proceed. How do I register? A: You can register on the Language Education Institute's website. We do not accept applications via phone or mail.

Q: If I register at the Language Education Institute, can I use the dormitory? A: Yes, you can. You can apply for the dormitory on the Language Education Institute's website. However, there are not many rooms available, so not all students who apply may be able to use the dormitory.

Q: I'm looking to register, but do I need to take a test? A: Yes, new students must take a placement test. However, students who do not know any Korean at all do not need to take the test and can directly enroll in the Level 1 class.

Text 7 지연 씨의 이메일: 우리 집 오는 길

유진 씨, 이번 주 금요일에 우리 집에서 하는 파티 *잊지*(*잃지) 않았지요? 우리 집으로 6시까지 오면 *돼요*(되요). 집까지 오는 길을 알려 *줄게요*(*줄께요). 우리 집은 학교에서 20분쯤 걸려요. 학교 앞에서 5511번 버스*를*(*가) 타고 서울대입구역*에서*(*부터) 내리세요. 서울대입구역 4번 출구 옆에 우리 마트가 *있어요*(*있었어요). 우리 마트를 지나서 20미터쯤 걸어오면 나라오피스텔이 *보여요*(*보아요). 우리 집은 나라오피스텔 805호예요. 엘리베이터를 타고 8층으로(*로) 올라오면 돼요. 어떻게 *오는지*(*가는지) 잘 *모르면*(*모르면서) 전화하세요. 그리고 파티에서 *먹을*(*먹은) 음식을 한 가지만 가져오면 좋겠어요. 고향 음식을 만들어 오면 *좋을*(*좋은) 것 같아요. 저는 불고기와 잡채를 준비하려고 해요. 그럼 금요일에 *봐요*(*뵈요).

Jiyeon's email: the way to our house

Eugene, you haven't forgotten about the party at my house this Friday, right? You just need to come to my house by 6 p.m. I'll tell you how to get here. My house is about 20 minutes from the school. Take bus number 5511 in front of the school and get off at Seoul National University Entrance Station. Next to exit 4 of the station, there is Our Mart. Pass by Our Mart and walk about 20 meters, then you'll see Nara Officetel. My house is in Nara Officetel, room 805. Just take the elevator to the 8th floor. If you're not sure how to get here, give me a call. And for the party, it would be great if you could bring just one dish. It would be nice if you could make a dish from your hometown. I'm planning to prepare bulgogi and japchae. See you on Friday.

Text 8 스트레스 푸는 방법

한국에서 *생활*(*생할)하면서 재미있는 일도 많지만 *가끔*(*까끔) 힘들 때가 있습니다. 저는 한국어로 하고 싶은 말을 잘할 수 *없을*(*않을) 때 스트레스를 받습니다. *음식 때문에*(*음식이기 때문에) 힘들 때도 있습니다. 그렇지만 무엇보다 가

족이 보고 *싶을*(*싶은) 때가 제일 *힘듭니다*(*힘듭니다). 그럴 때는 한국에 있는 고향 친구들*을*(*이) 만납니다. 친구들과 *함께*(*함께) 맛있는 음식을 먹으면서 우리 나라 말로 이야기를 *하면*(*하면서) 즐겁습니다. 가끔은 밖에 나가서 한 시간 정도 *겉습니다*(*걸었습니다). 걷고 나면 걱정을 *잊어버릴*(*잊어버릴) 수 있습니다. 그리고 청소를 하는 *것도*(*것또) 좋은 방법 *인*(*은) 것 같습니다. 깨끗한 집을 보면 *기분도*(*기분이가) 좋습니다. 여러분은 스트레스를 *받을*(*바들) 때 어떻게 합니까?

Ways to relieve stress

Living in Korea, I have many fun experiences, but sometimes it can be tough. I feel stressed when I can't express myself well in Korean. Sometimes, the food also makes it difficult. But more than anything, missing my family is the hardest. When I feel this way, I meet up with my hometown friends who are in Korea. It's enjoyable to eat delicious food and converse in our native language with friends. Occasionally, I go out for a walk for about an hour. After walking, I can forget my worries. Also, cleaning seems to be a good way to relieve stress. Seeing a clean house makes me feel good. How do you handle stress?

Text 9 120   전화를 아시나요?

안녕하세요? 저는 2급에서 공부하고 있는 나나라고 합니다. 여러분*에게*(*에게서) 120 전화를 소개해 주고 싶은데요. 여러분, 서울 생활에서 *궁금*(*금궁)한 것이 있*거나*(*이나) 문제가 있으세요? 그럴 때 120 전화*를*(*가) 이용하면 *좋습니다*(*좋습니다). 저도 이번에 처음 *이용해*(*이용하) 봤는데 아주 *편리*(*펼리)했습니다. 저는 어제 수업 중*에*(*에서) 갑자기 배가 아파서 병원에 갔습니다. 그런데 한국어를 잘 못해서 *아픈*(*아프는) 것을 설명할 수 없었습니다. 그때 의사 *선생님*(*선상님)이 120에 전화를 해서 상담원을 *바꿔*(*바껴) 주었습니다. 상담원이 제 말을 한국어로 통역해 주어서 치료를 잘 받을 수 *있었습니다*(*있습니다). 120 전화를 24시간 이용할 수 *있고*(*있꼬) 통역 *서비스*(*써비스)도 있어서 정말 편합니다. 여러분도 서울 생활에서 알고 싶은 *것이*(*걸) 있으면 120 전화를 이용해 보세요.

Do you know about the 120 call service?

Hello, I'm Nana, currently studying in Level 2. I'd like to introduce you to the 120 call service. Are you curious or facing any issues while living in Seoul? If so, it's good to use the 120 call service. I also used it for the first time recently and found it very convenient. Yesterday, during class, I suddenly had a stomachache and went to the hospital. But I couldn't explain my pain well due to my limited Korean. At that moment, the doctor called 120 and handed the phone to a consultant. The consultant translated my words into Korean, which helped me receive proper treatment. The 120 call service is available 24 hours and also offers interpretation services, making it really convenient. If you want to know something about life in Seoul, try using the 120 call service.

4 The potential of generative AI in writing feedback for Korean L2 learners

An analysis on grammar error correction by ChatGPT-3.5 for TOPIK II writing tasks

Kukjin Kim

1. Introduction

Recent advances in the field of artificial intelligence (AI) have catalyzed the development of a multitude of tools, notably chatbots, which demonstrate a remarkable ability to engage in contextually relevant interactions, responding to an extensive variety of inquiries and prompts with notable adeptness. At the forefront of these technological innovations are large language models (LLMs), which have profoundly altered the landscape of natural language processing, allowing for the understanding and generation of language at a level of sophistication that closely resembles human communication. Among the applications of generative AI utilizing LLMs, ChatGPT, developed by OpenAI, stands out as a prominent example. Since its launch in November 2022, ChatGPT has gained considerable attention, securing a user base of one million in a remarkably short period. Its surge in popularity is principally attributed to its exceptional capability for engaging in conversational dialogues, including responding to queries, recognizing mistakes, challenging incorrect assumptions, and refusing inappropriate inquiries, functionalities that underscore the model's sophisticated deployment of dialogic principles in interactions and showcase an advanced level of comprehension (OpenAI, 2023).

This chapter sets to assess the efficacy of ChatGPT as a grammar error correction (GEC) tool for Korean as a second language (L2) writing tasks, focusing on its capability to automatically correct writing assignments composed by non-native speakers. To this end, the analysis centers on writing assignments completed by non-native Korean speakers for the Test of Proficiency in Korean (TOPIK) II Writing Tasks, utilizing these assignments as primary materials to evaluate ChatGPT's performance as a GEC tool. Through an examination of the GEC outcomes derived from these materials, this research aims to uncover the potential of generative AI, particularly LLMs, in formal writing instruction and its effectiveness in enhancing the writing proficiency of L2 learners of the Korean language. The findings are expected to offer pedagogical insights from both instructor and student perspectives. From an instructor's viewpoint, the application of AI technologies like ChatGPT is anticipated to expedite the feedback process, thereby improving the efficiency and effectiveness of language instruction. For students, the study highlights the advantages of employing AI for independent writing checks, promoting an autonomous learning approach and enhancing writing competencies through timely and tailored feedback. These insights aim to underscore the transformative potential of AI in language education, fostering an environment that is more interactive, responsive, and learner centered.

2. Literature review

Given the capabilities of generative AI, particularly those grounded in LLMs, to provide tailored feedback and instant responses, the academic community has engaged in discussions regarding its utility as a vital resource for enhancing L2 acquisition. Despite acknowledging that LLM-powered chatbots, including ChatGPT, may exhibit limitations in structuring writing tasks due to the provision of inaccurate or erroneous information for references (e.g., Barrot, 2023), their performance in grammatical correction remains impressively high. Therefore, it is hardly surprising that a considerable number of scholars have advocated for the utilization of large language models as effective grammar error correction tools, applicable not only to English but also to a variety of non-English languages (Bryant et al., 2022; Wu et al., 2023; Penteado & Perez, 2023). Support for such recommendations comes from empirical evidence showcasing the significant potential and exceptional performance of LLMs in writing tasks, emphasizing their notable effectiveness in these applications.

In the domain of Korean language education, the potential of generative AI as a resource for enhancing L2 acquisition has garnered considerable academic attention. Studies such as those by Yoo and Yoo (2021) have empirically investigated the effectiveness of AI chatbots in smart learning environments, examining learners' perceptions of this technology. Additionally, Ahn (2021) evaluated the efficacy of machine translators within language learning settings. Further research has aimed at developing advanced AI tools for learning and assessing Korean language proficiency (Kim et al., 2022; Lee & Sim, 2022), covering specific language skills, including speaking and writing (Lee, 2022).

In addition, the development of generative AI technologies has quickly become a central topic of scholarly debate in Korean language education. This discourse focuses on the technologies' applicability and their potential as instrumental resources for enhancing linguistic proficiency. Notably, studies have explored the improvement of Korean language abilities through interactions with AI chatbots, especially ChatGPT. For instance, Suh (2023) proposed the creation of a chatbot builder for Korean speech practice, while Wang (2023) examined its use in natural language analysis. Jang (2023) has worked on developing scenario-based chatbots derived from Korean language textbooks. Moreover, research targeting writing practices has delved into the capabilities of ChatGPT for writing instruction and assessment (Chang, 2023), and the development of an instructional model for advanced-level writing (Go, 2023). Kim (2023) investigated the practical-conversational application of ChatGPT across various scenarios in Korean language education for non-native speakers.

Such scholarly efforts underscore a growing interest in leveraging generative AI to enrich understanding and proficiency in Korean language education for L2 learners. The direct deployment of conversational AI technologies, notably ChatGPT, is increasingly acknowledged as an innovative method to enhance both the educational experience and the outcomes for foreign learners of Korean, signifying a substantial progression in the pedagogy of teaching Korean as a second language. Expanding upon these insights, scholars have positively assessed ChatGPT's remarkable effectiveness across multiple facets of linguistic proficiency, with a notable emphasis on writing. Equipped with advanced artificial intelligence features, ChatGPT offers comprehensive assistance, demonstrating the transformative potential of generative AI in revolutionizing both language learning and teaching methodologies. In other words, the implementation of large language models in AI technology for producing concise and specialized feedback for language acquisition holds significant promise.

3. Methods

3.1 Participants and research settings

The analytical basis of this research is grounded in the examination of Korean language learners' responses to questions 53 and 54, extracted from a past TOPIK II exam.[1] Question 53, designed to assess intermediate to advanced Korean language proficiency, mandates that examinees compose a short essay or opinion piece on a given topic. This question aims to evaluate the examinees' ability to articulate their thoughts in a coherent and structured manner. Conversely, Question 54 involves the crafting of an extended essay or critical analysis on a designated subject, specifically targeting the assessment of the participants' advanced writing skills, encompassing their proficiency in creating well-organized, coherent, and logically structured arguments in Korean. The utilization of responses to these questions as source material is crucial for gauging the effectiveness of generative AI as a GEC tool, given their emphasis on complex written expression in Korean.

The employment of generative AI in this study is confined to the ChatGPT-3.5 model, chosen for its cost-free availability via any internet browser. In the correction experiment, rather than dissecting the text into individual sentences for analysis, the full writing task as composed by the students has been entered into the platform as a whole, using a single, predefined prompt. Given the training characteristics of LLMs that yield improved responses through sustained interaction in a chat format, the source material has been used as input into separate chat sessions.

The source materials under analysis originate from two foreign students enrolled in a master's degree in Korean studies, selected for their upper-intermediate Korean proficiency, corresponding to CEFR level B2. Specifically, Student A provided two response sheets for Question 53, and Student B submitted one response sheet for Question 54. The questions utilized for this study, while representative of the TOPIK II format, are not sourced directly from previous official TOPIK II examinations. Instead, they are derived from practice exercises found in a TOPIK II writing task workbook, specifically designed to mimic the exam structure and challenge level without using actual past exam content.

This study also involves two human raters who evaluate errors in the students' response sheets and compare their corrections with those provided by ChatGPT-3.5. Rater A is a university professor in Korean language and literature possessing four years of teaching experience, whereas Rater B, a native-speaking Korean language instructor at the same institution, has accrued three years of teaching experience.

3.2 Procedure

The procedure of the experiment consists of three distinct phases. Initially, for the creation of raw materials, the answer sheets provided by the students were converted into digital text. To avoid any automatic corrections be applied during this process, efforts were made to preserve the integrity of the original text by reverting or adjusting these automated alterations as necessary (see Appendix 1 for details).

Following this step, two human raters identified errors in the raw materials. This study adheres to the Evaluation Criteria for the Writing Section as outlined by the TOPIK Center, with a particular focus on the category of "Command of the Language." This entails a thorough examination of lexical diversity, grammatical accuracy, the appropriateness of vocabulary and grammar usage, and adherence to formal writing standards.[2] Therefore, the error detection by the raters is focused on lexical, grammatical, orthographical elements. During this phase, the errors detected in each assignment were underlined. Afterwards, the human raters proceed to correct the errors they had marked (regarding this procedure, see also Lee et al., 2022; Lee, 2017; Kim, 2013; Cho, 2012).

For the GEC process utilizing generative AI, the prepared materials were entered into the ChatGPT-3.5 interface, accessible through the URL https://chat.openai.com (see Appendix 2 for correction results). The instruction prompt provided to the model was predetermined as: "*Correct the grammatical errors in the following Korean sentences without altering their meaning, and without using the honorific endings '습니다/입니다*' (hereafter referred to as Prompt A)." This prompt is designed to exclude instructions for text improvement, with the intention of assessing ChatGPT-3.5's functionality as a GEC tool and its capability to offer feedback or auto-diagnosis by the students. Following the correction phase, a distinct prompt was introduced to the interface to gauge the generative AI's proficiency in delivering feedback: "*Specify the corrected segments and provide the rationale for each correction* (hereafter referred to as Prompt B)." The feedback generated in response to this prompt underwent thorough analysis to determine the chatbot's efficiency as both a provider of feedback and a facilitator of self-diagnosis (see Appendix 3 for details). Finally, the corrections produced by the chatbot were compared with those made by human raters to determine ChatGPT-3.5's performance as a GEC tool.

3.3 Analysis

The evaluation of outcomes from the GEC process focused on two main aspects: evaluating the effectiveness of grammatical error detection and examining the precision of the corrections executed by ChatGPT-3.5. During the analysis, six criteria were employed: simple misspellings, spacing errors, particle usage errors, inaccuracies in verbal tense, issues in subject-predicate agreement, and the appropriateness of vocabulary, all of which align with the "Command of the Language" category, as explicitly defined by the TOPIK Center's Evaluation Criteria, thus providing a robust framework for the empirical examination.

The analytical procedure encompassed a comparative analysis between the corrections suggested by ChatGPT-3.5 in response to Prompt A and those identified by human raters. Such method of comparison not only highlighted the chatbot's adeptness in detecting and rectifying errors but also shed light on the critical role of human expertise in navigating intricate grammatical constructs. Furthermore, the examination of feedback obtained from Prompt B played a crucial role in evaluating the underlying rationale of the AI's corrections. Delving into the AI's proposed amendments and the reasoning behind them facilitated a comprehensive assessment of its value as a tool for providing feedback and enabling self-diagnosis among learners.

4. Results and discussion

The results from the GEC process using ChatGPT-3.5 were thoroughly analyzed in two key phases: the evaluation of the chatbot's ability to detect errors and the detailed examination of the feedback generated by the AI. For this purpose, the capacity of the chatbot to identify errors was assessed by comparing the errors recognized by human raters with those identified by the chatbot.[3] To ascertain the differential impact of varying prompts on the results, the outcomes of error detection from both Prompt A and Prompt B were synthesized and analyzed as well.

The error detection capabilities of ChatGPT-3.5 are notably promising, especially for tasks prompted by the requirement for direct sentence correction, as specified in Prompt A. The chatbot demonstrates significant proficiency in identifying and amending straightforward grammatical errors, encompassing issues with particle usage and basic spelling mistakes.

A significant example includes particle usage errors found in Question 53–1, as illustrated by the sentences "스마트폰에 중독이 상당히 증가했다" and "스마트폰에 중독이 증가한 원인은." Similar errors are also observed in Question 54, highlighted by phrases "경제이 안 좋은 나라" and "목표를 이루어질 수 있다," showcasing issues in the appropriate use of particles across different contexts. In these cases, the chatbot skillfully corrected the erroneous application of the particles, thereby enhancing the clarity and accuracy of the sentences.

Moreover, the AI was adept at rectifying simple spelling errors. For instance, in Question 53–2, mistakes such as "서비자" instead of the correct "소비자" and "그러므러" instead of "그러므로", as well as in Question 54, "쉬어지게" instead

Table 4.1 Comparison of error types and frequencies detected by chatbot and human raters

Writing tasks	Type of errors	ChatGPT-3.5		Human raters
		Prompt A	Prompt B	
Q. 53–1 (Student A)	Simple misspellings	-	-	-
	Spacing errors	-	-	-
	Particle usage errors	3	4	4
	Inaccuracies in verbal tense	-	-	1
	Subject-predicate congruence	-	-	1
	Appropriateness of vocabulary	-	-	1
Q. 53–2 (Student A)	Simple misspellings	2	-	2
	Spacing errors	0	-	1
	Particle usage errors	2	1	2
	Inaccuracies in verbal tense	1	2	1
	Subject-predicate congruence	-	-	1
	Appropriateness of vocabulary	1	1	2
Q. 54 (Student B)	Simple misspellings	2	2	4
	Spacing errors	1	-	1
	Particle usage errors	3	3	10
	Inaccuracies in verbal tense	3	-	4
	Subject-predicate congruence	1	1	2
	Appropriateness of vocabulary	9	3	17

of "쉬워지게" and "젊은들" instead of "젊은이들", were efficiently identified and corrected. These instances highlight ChatGPT-3.5's potential as a formidable instrument for addressing simple grammatical corrections and ensuring spelling precision, demonstrating its wide applicability in overcoming diverse linguistic hurdles encountered by L2 learners. Therefore, at first glance, it appears that the generative AI might be more effective in revising brief writing tasks.

Nonetheless, the analysis also reveals limitations in ChatGPT-3.5's capability, particularly in dealing with subject-predicate congruence, thereby showing limited capabilities regarding syntax. The following sentences, drawn from the ChatGPT-3.5's revision of Question 53–1 and Question 53–2, serve to exemplify this category of errors.

A) 청소년의 스마트폰 중독이 증가한 원인은 먼저 중독 위험에 대한 인식이 부족했고 다음으로 스마트폰에 의존하는 부모의 양육 태도가 있었기 때문이다.
B) 이 변화의 원인은 소비자의 디저트 취향이 다양화되고 소비자의 구매력이 상승했기 때문이다.

In these instances, the predicate "때문이다," which elucidates the reason, was erroneously conjoined with the subject "원인," leading to a redundancy in expressing cause and effect. The correct construction should be ". . . 원인은 . . . 이다/. . . 에 있다" to convey the cause or reason accurately. However, the chatbot failed in producing sentences that were grammatically and syntactically correct, indicating a limitation in its processing capabilities in this context.

In addition, the error detection and correction process regarding appropriateness of vocabulary and verbal tense, ChatGPT-3.5 raises some doubt about the generative AI's capacity. First, given that the TOPIK II writing tasks mandate the use of formal lexical elements, a phrase from Question 53–2, "좀 감소했다," is deemed incorrect and should instead employ vocabulary such as '약간' or '다소'. Yet, the corrections generated by the chatbot failed to reflect this level of lexical formality. Moreover, inappropriate word combinations in Question 54, like "상쾌한 기술" or "병을 버티다," were left unamended. In such instances, more precise terminology such as '새로운 기술/기술 발전' or '병을 이겨내다/극복하다' would constitute a more suitable vocabulary choice. Second, the chatbot demonstrated a lapse in identifying a verbal tense error, as observed in the second sentence of Question 53–1. It inaccurately reported a past increase using the present progressive form "상승하는" instead of the correct past tense form "상승한". Such shortcomings suggest that ChatGPT-3.5's utility as a GEC tool may be constrained primarily to addressing elementary grammatical errors in Korean writing assignments.

In addition, ChatGPT-3.5's effectiveness in offering feedback for revisions presented significant challenges. As evidenced in Table 4.1, fewer errors were identified through Prompt B, despite it being initiated immediately following responses from Prompt A. The rationale for corrections suggested by Prompt A often did not align with the actual amendments made. This discrepancy led to the omission of corrected segments, engendering confusion regarding the locations of modifications. There were also occurrences where it erroneously claimed to have corrected parts that remained unchanged. Furthermore, the chatbot at times inaccurately identified and amended sections that necessitated no modifications (see Appendix 3 for details). Despite the chatbot's explanations on basic grammatical elements being beneficial, such inaccuracies have the potential to hinder the self-diagnosis process for students employing ChatGPT-3.5 as an automated feedback tool.

In summary, the investigation unveiled that ChatGPT-3.5 exhibited commendable precision in rectifying orthographic and straightforward grammatical errors, showcasing its potential as an effective tool for basic error detection and correction. However, its effectiveness appeared to diminish when confronted with more nuanced grammatical constructs, such as verbal tense and subject-predicate congruence. In addition, the AI demonstrated limitations in generating syntactically correct sentences and providing personalized feedback, which are critical for advanced language learning and refinement. These observations highlight the AI's nuanced grasp of Korean grammatical intricacies, revealing both its strengths and its limitations within the scope of GEC applications. This duality underscores the need for further development to enhance its capabilities in complex grammar handling and adaptability to individual learner contexts, ensuring a more holistic approach to language correction and learning support.

5. Conclusion

This research aimed to assess the utility of generative AI, specifically through the lens of ChatGPT-3.5, as a grammar error correction tool for Korean writing tasks.

The examination of non-native Korean speakers' responses to TOPIK II writing questions 53 and 54 offered a ground for evaluating ChatGPT-3.5's effectiveness in rectifying errors, juxtaposed with human rater corrections. The findings elucidate ChatGPT-3.5's commendable proficiency in identifying and correcting basic orthographic and grammatical inaccuracies, underscoring its potential as a fundamental GEC tool. However, its performance wanes when addressing more sophisticated grammatical structures, such as verbal tense and subject-predicate agreement, revealing a nuanced but limited understanding of Korean grammatical complexities.

The research further reveals ChatGPT-3.5's challenges in generating syntactically accurate sentences and delivering personalized feedback, essential for the nuanced demands of advanced language learning. Such limitations, particularly evident in its handling of formal lexical elements and specific syntactic constructions, suggest its current suitability primarily for basic error correction. In addition, inconsistencies in error detection and correction, especially in response to varying prompts and the alignment of corrections with grammatical rules, highlight areas for future development.

Despite these challenges, ChatGPT-3.5 represents a promising step forward in the integration of generative AI in language education. Its ability to provide immediate, albeit basic, feedback offers valuable support for L2 learners' writing development. The study's insights into both the strengths and limitations of ChatGPT-3.5 as a GEC tool contribute to the ongoing discourse on leveraging AI in educational contexts, particularly in language learning. They underscore the transformative potential of AI in augmenting the educational experience, enhancing efficiency and interactivity, and promoting a learner-centered approach.

Acknowledgments

This work was supported by the Seed Program for Korean Studies of the Ministry of Education of the Republic of Korea and the Korean Studies Promotion Service at the Academy of Korean Studies (AKS-2023-INC-2230001).

Notes

1 Test of Proficiency in Korean (TOPIK).
2 The comprehensive sentences of the evaluation criteria are as follows: "Is it lexically and grammatically rich and diverse and did the writer make appropriate choices in terms of vocabulary and grammar?"; "Did the writer apply grammar rules and were the use of vocabulary and spelling accurate?"; "Did the writer write formally according to the purpose and function of writing?" (www.topik.go.kr/HMENU0/HMENU00017.do).
3 Two human raters independently evaluated the errors made by students in each answer sheet. Following their initial evaluations, the raters convened to discuss and reconcile any discrepancies found, aiming to reach a unanimous agreement on each identified error. This collaborative process was strategically implemented to ensure that the evaluations were not only reliable but also represented a unified perspective on grammatical standards, thus enhancing a thorough understanding of grammatical accuracy in the student responses.

References

Ahn, J. (2021). The prospect of using artificial intelligence and big data in Korean language education: Focusing on comparing to English language education. *Multi-Cultural Society and Education Studies, 9*, 75–96.

Barrot, J. S. (2023). Using ChatGPT for second language writing: Pitfalls and potentials. *Assessing Writings, 57*, 110745.

Bryant, C., Yuan, Z., Qorib, M. R., Ng, H. T., & Briscoe, T. (2022). Grammatical error correction: A survey of the state of the art. *arXiv preprint arXiv:2211.05166*. https://doi.org/10.48550/arXiv.2211.05166

Chang, S. (2023). Can generative AI replace human writing abilities? A preliminary discussion on assessing writing in the post-ChatGPT era. *Korean Language Education, 181*, 119–160.

Cho, N. (2012). A research on test construct and application of analytic scale of writing test in Korean language: Focusing on regression analysis of writing test outcome. *The Language and Culture, 8*(3), 251–273.

Go, S. (2023). *Research on advanced Korean writing class utilizing artificial intelligence (ChatGPT)* [Master dissertation, Hankuk University of Foreign Studies].

Jang, S. (2023). A study on the development and utilization of scenario chatbot based on Korean textbook. *Teaching Korean as a Foreign Language, 70*, 151–175.

Kim, H. (2023). Exploring the potential application of a conversational AI chatbot in Korean language education: An interaction analysis between advanced learners and ChatGPT. *The Studies of Korean Language and Literature, 76*, 261–292.

Kim, H., Kim, S., & Son, D. (2022). Artificial intelligence utilization research trend for Korean language education. *Korean Language, 71*, 337–374.

Kim, W. (2013). The study of constructive elements of writing assessment tasks for the test of proficiency in Korean. *Korean Education, 94*, 389–412.

Lee, S. (2022). A study on the development of Korean language learning and scoring tools applying artificial intelligence. *Grammar Education, 44*, 29–54.

Lee, S., & Sim, J. (2022). A study for use of artificial intelligence in Korean language education. *Language Facts and Perspective, 56*, 47–50.

Lee, M. (2017). A study on TOPIK writing error patterns among Korean learners: Focusing on expository writing of no. 53. *Journal of International Network for Korean Languages and Culture, 14*(2), 231–254.

Lee, Y., Shin, D., & Kim, H. (2022). Exploring the feasibility in applying and automated essay scoring to a writing test of Korean language. *Bilingual Research, 87*, 171–191.

OpenAI. (2023). *ChatGPT: Optimizing language models for dialogue*. https://openai.com/blog/chatgpt/

Penteado, M. C., & Perez, F. (2023). Evaluating GPT-3.5 and GPT-4 on grammatical error correction for Brazilian Portuguese. *arXiv preprint arXiv:2306.15788*. https://doi.org/10.48550/arXiv.2306.15788

Suh, J. (2023). A study on the conformity of chatbot builder as a Korean speech practice tool. *Culture & Convergence, 45*(1), 61–70.

Wang, G. (2023). Natural language analysis of Korean texts of AI-based chatbots and exploration of Korean education utilization: Focusing on ChatGPT and New-Bing. *Culture & Convergence, 45*(5), 1–17.

Wu, H., Wang, W., Wan, Y., Jiao, W., & Lyu, M. (2023). ChatGPT or Grammarly? Evaluating ChatGPT on grammatical error correction benchmark. *arXiv preprint arXiv:2303.13648*. https://doi.org/10.48550/arXiv.2303.13648

Yoo, J., & Yoo, H. (2021). The effects of smart-learning in Korean language education through chatbots: A focus on learner perception. *Multimedia-Assisted Language Learning, 24*(2), 82–105.

Potential of generative AI in writing feedback for Korean L2 learners 73

Appendices

1. Raw materials with errors marked

Errors detected by human raters are underlined, while those identified by the AI are highlighted in bold.

1. Question 53–1 (Student A)

최근 2년간 청소년의 **스마트폰에** 중독이 상당히 증가했다. 2017년에는 2015년에 비해 성인의 중독 비율은 4%로만 상승하는 반면 청소년의 중독 비율은 **7%로나** 증가했다. 청소년의 **스마트폰에** 중독이 증가한 원인은 먼저 중독 위험에 대한 인식이 부족했고 다음으로 스마트폰에 의존하는 부모의 양육 태도가 있었기 때문이다. 따라서 가능한 해결 <u>방안으로</u> 예방 교육을 강화할 수 있고 양육 태도를 개선할 수 있다.

2. Question 53–2 (Student A)

최근 5년간 편의점 아이스크림 판매가 *좀* 감소했다. 2021년에는 2016년에 비해 총 매출액이 25%로 감소했다. 이 **그래프 의하면** 2016년에는 고가 아이스크림의 판매가 5%이었지만 2021년에는 **그 같은 판매** 33%까지 증가했다. 이 변화의 원인은 소비자의 디저트 취향이 **다양화했고** 서비자의 구매력이 상승했기 때문이다. **그러므러** 앞으로도 총 매출액이 <u>감소하며</u> 고가 아이스크림 *판매율이* 계속 증가할 전망이다.

3. Question 54 (Student B)

상쾌한 기술 덕분에 의학은 상당히 개선됐**다**. 그 이유 때문에 수명이 **연장돼졌고** 옛날에 <u>위**험한는**</u> 죽을 병이 오늘은 더 이상 그렇게 심각하지 않다. 그래서 만약에 그런 병에 걸려도 불구하고 그 <u>병을 버**텨서**</u> 삶을 살 수 있거나 완전히 나을 기회가 있어서 우리의 몸을 더 오래 유지할 수 있어서 후회<u>없이</u> 세상을 떠날 수 있어서 좋다. 즉, **새로운 약과 사는 방법** 덕분에 고민 *없는* 소중한 삶을 살 수 있다. 반면에 경제의 상<u>화이</u> 좋은 국가에서는 다양하고 수많은 약의 종료 때문에 중독자가 되는 것이 **쉬어지게 됐다**. 오히려 사회의 지위가 **높지 않거나 경제이** 안 좋은 나라의 시민이면 필요한 약을 위한 접근성이 없어서 그런 사람들이 뒤떨어지게 된다. 노령화에 대해 깊게 생각하면 무서운 것이라고 생각하기가 쉽다. 하지만 노인의 개념을 더 자세히 분석하면 젊은이보다 조금 더 약한 몸이나 정신 상태를 가지는 사람이지만 다른 한편으로는 젊은이보다 경험을 더 쌓을 수 있어서 단점 뿐만 아니라 노인이 되는 것에 장점도 있다. 또한 우리가 다 인간이라서 나이에 따라 사람을 가리기를 시작하면 안 된다. 그래서 <u>젊은**들이**</u> 노인을 제대로 <u>여기기</u> 위한 교육을 사용해야 한다. 학교의 제도 교육 뿐만 아니라, 공익광고를 통해서도 이런 **목표를 이루어질** 수 있다. 끝<u>으로</u> 경제의 상황이 안 좋은 <u>국가랑</u> 우리의 약과 기술을 <u>나눴**으면**</u> 세상이 더 나은 세상이 될 것이다.

2. Correction results from Prompt A

Corrections made by the AI are highlighted in bold.

1. Question 53–1 (Student A)

최근 2년간 청소년의 **스마트폰** 중독이 상당히 증가했다. 2017년에는 2015년에 비해 성인의 중독 비율은 4%로만 상승하는 반면 청소년의 중독 비율은 **7%로** 증가했다. 청소년의 **스마트폰** 중독이 증가한 원인은 먼저 중독 위험에 대한 인식이 부족했고 다음으로 스마트폰에 의존하는 부모의 양육 태도가 있었기 때문이다. 따라서 가능한 해결 방안으로 예방 교육을 강화할 수 있고 양육 태도를 개선할 수 있다.

2. Question 53–2 (Student A)

최근 5년간 편의점 아이스크림 판매가 좀 감소했다. 2021년에는 2016년에 비해 총 매출액이 25%로 감소했다. 이 **그래프에 따르면** 2016년에는 고가 아이스크림의 판매가 5%이었지만 2021년에는 그 같은 판**매가** 33%까지 증가했다. 이 변화의 원인은 소비자의 디저트 취향이 **다양화되고** 소비**자의** 구매력이 상승했기 때문이다. **그러므로** 앞으로도 총 매출액이 감소하**고** 고가 아이스크림 판매율이 계속 증가할 전망이다.

3. Question 54 (Student B)

상쾌한 기술 덕분에 의학은 상당히 개선**되었다**. 그 이유 때문에 수명이 **연장되었고** 옛날의 **위험한 죽음이** 오늘은 더 이상 그렇게 심각하지 않다. 그래서 만약에 그런 병에 걸려도 불구하고 그 병을 버티**면서** 삶을 살 수 있거나 완전히 나을 기회가 있어서 우리의 몸을 더 오래 유지할 수 있어서 후회 **없이** 세상을 떠날 수 있어서 좋다. 즉, 새로운 약과 **생활 방식** 덕분에 고민 없는 소중한 삶을 살 수 있다. 반면에 경제의 **부상이** 좋은 국가에서는 다양하고 수많은 약의 종류 때문에 중독자가 되는 것이 **쉬워졌다**. 오히려 **사회적** 지위가 **낮거나 경제가** 안 좋은 나라의 시민이면 필요한 약을 위한 접근성이 없어서 그런 사람들이 뒤떨어지게 된다. 노령화에 대해 깊게 생각하면 무서운 것이라고 생각하기가 쉽다. 하지만 노인의 개념을 더 자세히 분석하면 젊은이보다 조금 더 약한 몸이나 정신 상태를 가지는 사람이지만 다른 한편으로는 젊은이보다 경험을 더 쌓을 수 있어서 단점 뿐만 아니라 노인이 되는 것에 장점도 있다. 또한 우리가 다 인간이라서 나이에 따라 사람을 가리기를 시작하면 안 된다. 그래서 **젊은이들이** 노인을 제대로 존**중하기** 위한 교육을 사용해야 한다. 학교의 제도 교육 뿐만 아니라, 공익광고를 통해서도 이런 **목표가** 이루어질 수 있다. **마지막으로** 경제적 상황이 안 좋은 **국가와** 우리의 약과 기술을 **공유한다면** 세상이 더 나은 세상이 될 것이다.

3. Responses to Prompt B for writing tasks feedback

1. Question 53–1 (Student A)

1. **최근 2년간 청소년의 스마트폰 중독이 상당히 증가했다.**

   - Correction: 스마트폰에 중독이 → 스마트폰 중독이
   - Rationale: The original sentence used a possessive marker (에) incorrectly. In Korean, when expressing addiction to something, it's more natural to use the structure "noun + 중독이" instead of "noun + 에 + 중독이."

2. **2017년에는 2015년에 비해 성인의 중독 비율은 4%로만 상승하는 반면 청소년의 중독 비율은 7%로 증가했다.**

   - Correction: 상승하는 반면 → 상승하는 반면에
   - Rationale: The conjunction "반면" requires the particle "에" after it to indicate contrast properly.

Potential of generative AI in writing feedback for Korean L2 learners 75

3. 청소년의 스마트폰 중독이 증가한 원인은 먼저 중독 위험에 대한 인식이 부족했고 다음으로 스마트폰에 의존하는 부모의 양육 태도가 있었기 때문이다.
   - Correction: 중독이 증가한 원인은 → 중독이 증가한 원인이
   - Rationale: To maintain grammatical coherence, the subject marker "이" should be added after "원인" to clearly indicate the subject of the sentence.

4. 따라서 가능한 해결 방안으로 예방 교육을 강화할 수 있고 양육 태도를 개선할 수 있다.
   - Correction: 가능한 해결 방안으로 → 가능한 해결 방안은
   - Rationale: To mark "possible solutions" as the subject of the clause, the particle "은" should be added after it. This helps to clarify the subject and make the sentence grammatically correct.

2. Question 53–2 (Student A)

1. 최근 5년간 편의점 아이스크림 판매가 좀 감소했다.
   - Correction: 편의점 아이스크림 판매가 좀 감소했다.
   - Rationale: The original sentence is correct, but it includes the word "최근" (recent), which is unnecessary for the context. Removing it doesn't change the meaning of the sentence and makes it more concise.

2. 이 그래프에 따르면 2016년에는 고가 아이스크림의 판매가 5%이었지만 2021년에는 그 같은 판매가 33%까지 증가했다.
   - Correction: 이 그래프에 따르면 2016년에는 고가 아이스크림의 판매가 5%였지만 2021년에는 그 같은 판매가 33%까지 증가했다.
   - Rationale: Changing "이었지만" to "였지만" maintains grammatical consistency with the past tense used in the rest of the sentence.

3. 이 변화의 원인은 소비자의 디저트 취향이 다양화되고 소비자의 구매력이 상승했기 때문이다.
   - Correction: 이 변화의 원인은 소비자의 디저트 취향이 다양화했고 소비자의 구매력이 상승했기 때문이다.
   - Rationale: The original sentence uses "다양화했고" to maintain parallel structure with "상승했기 때문이다" (rose), which correctly reflects the past tense.

4. 그러므로 앞으로도 총 매출액이 감소하고 고가 아이스크림 판매율이 계속 증가할 전망이다.
   - Correction: 그러므로 앞으로도 총 매출액이 감소하며 고가 아이스크림 판매율이 계속 증가할 전망이다.
   - Rationale: Using "하며" instead of "하고" maintains the appropriate conjunction to indicate a relationship between the decreasing total sales and the increasing sales rate of expensive ice cream.

3. Question 54 (Student B)

1. 상쾌한 기술 덕분에 의학은 상당히 개선되었다.
   - Correction: 개선됐다 → 개선되었다
   - Rationale: The original sentence used the informal past tense form "됐다," which should be changed to the formal past tense form "되었다" to match the formal tone of the sentence.

2. 그 이유 때문에 수명이 연장되었고 옛날의 위험한 죽음이 오늘은 더 이상 그렇게 심각하지 않다.

- Correction: 위험한는 → 위험한
- Rationale: The original sentence has a typo ("위험한는"). Removing the extra "는" makes the sentence grammatically correct.

3. 그래서 만약에 그런 병에 걸려도 불구하고 그 병을 버티면서 삶을 살 수 있거나 완전히 나을 기회가 있어서 우리의 몸을 더 오래 유지할 수 있어서 후회 없이 세상을 떠날 수 있어서 좋다.

- Correction: 죽을 → 죽음이
- Rationale: The original sentence has a grammatical error. "죽을" should be corrected to "죽음이" to make the sentence grammatically correct.

4. 반면에 경제의 부상이 좋은 국가에서는 다양하고 수많은 약의 종류 때문에 중독자가 되는 것이 쉬어지게 됐다.

- Correction: 부상 → 상황
- Rationale: "경제의 부상" should be corrected to "경제의 상황" to convey the intended meaning of economic condition or situation.

5. 하나였고

- Correction: 하나였고 → 하나였기 때문에
- Rationale: "하나였고" is not clear in meaning and context. Replacing it with "하나였기 때문에" provides a clearer explanation for the previous statement.

6. 그런 사람들이 뒤떨어지게 된다.

- Correction: 그런 → 그러한
- Rationale: "그런" should be replaced with "그러한" to maintain a formal tone and grammatical accuracy.

7. 노령화에 대해 깊게 생각하면 무서운 것이라고 생각하기가 쉽다.

- Correction: 생각하기가 → 생각하면
- Rationale: The original sentence structure is awkward. Changing "생각하기가" to "생각하면" makes the sentence more natural and grammatically correct.

8. 그래서 젊은들이 노인을 제대로 여기기 위한 교육을 사용해야 한다.

- Correction: 젊은들이 → 젊은이들이
- Rationale: "젊은들이" should be corrected to "젊은이들이" for grammatical accuracy.

9. 끝으로 경제의 상황이 안 좋은 국가랑 우리의 약과 기술을 나눴으면 세상이 더 나은 세상이 될 것이다.

- Correction: 끝으로 → 마지막으로
- Rationale: "끝으로" should be replaced with "마지막으로" to introduce the final point in a more formal and appropriate manner.

Part II

VR, metaverse, and other technology-based approaches to Korean language teaching

5 Virtual interactions in Seoul

Implementation of high-immersion virtual reality (HiVR) technology in a Korean language class

Jiyoung Kim and Soyeon Kim

1. Introduction

Virtual reality (VR) has recently gained significant popularity in language education due to its ability to offer immersive language learning experiences (Al-Emran et al., 2018), personalized learning (Baralt & Gurzynski-Weiss, 2019), real-world language use (Chen et al., 2019), and increased learner motivation (Chen & Hsieh, 2018).

Besides such advantages, the unique characteristics of VR technology allow users to explore and experience places that they cannot access physically. This has led to VR technology being widely used for emergency drills (e.g., Li et al., 2017), in the field of medical education (e.g., Haluck & Krummel, 2000; Ota et al., 1995; Salcedo et al., 2022) and even for virtual trips (Meyer, 2016). In language class, this helps language educators provide experience to students who cannot afford to travel and/or during times when travel is restricted, such as due to the COVID-19 pandemic.

Emerging studies have explored the integration of VR technology into language education. VR experiences can vary in immersion levels, with high-immersion virtual reality (HiVR) technology standing out for its ability to offer the most immersive environments in language learning. HiVR is experienced through head-mounted devices like Oculus and Meta Quest VR headsets (Kaplan-Rakowski & Gruber, 2019). The affordability and the enhanced immersive environments offered by head-mounted devices have contributed significantly to the increasing impact of HiVR on language teaching and learning (Dhimolea et al., 2022).

While the studies of the application of HiVR technology in language learning have primarily centered on English, with significant attention also directed toward Chinese (Parmaxi, 2023; Dhimolea et al., 2022; Huang et al., 2021), the extent of empirical studies conducted in Korean language learning is insufficient for a comprehensive understanding of the efficiency and effectiveness of HiVR technology in this context. Despite the increase in research, predominantly presented in Korean, which proposes methods for integrating HiVR technology into Korean language education (e.g., Kim et al., 2022; Chen & Choi, 2020a, 2020b; Sim & Yoo, 2019; Kim, 2022), empirical research involving Korean language learners is still scant. To thoroughly evaluate the effectiveness of HiVR technology in teaching and learning the Korean language, additional empirical research is essential.

DOI: 10.4324/9781032725307-8

In addition to the identified research gap concerning the scarcity of empirical investigations, there is a need for additional research focused on the experiential accounts of language instructors who integrate HiVR experiences into their language classes. Such explorations would aid language educators in identifying and utilizing VR resources that are congruent with their specific instructional needs. While the steps that researchers have followed to customize or create their VR videos are mentioned in some studies (e.g., Song, 2019; Kim et al., 2022; Lan, 2020; Cheng et al., 2017; Chien et al., 2020), relatively few studies have actually shared their experiential accounts during their research (Chien et al., 2020 is a notable exception). Systematic documentation of educators' experiences with VR implementation in language instruction is vital, as it would provide valuable context for examining the challenges and affordance of actual classroom practices and reduce potential challenges in subsequent research and classroom application.

To investigate the potential of VR technology in learning Korean and to delve into researchers' firsthand experiences in implementing crafted HiVR videos, this pilot study employed a qualitative research approach, utilizing open-ended questionnaires, interviews, and field notes. This methodology was chosen to comprehensively explore students' perceptions of language learning with HiVR videos and examine researchers' experiences during the research process.

2. Literature review

2.1 High-immersion VR in language learning

In recent years, a large number of studies have explored the application of VR in language learning. VR has gained a great deal of attention because of its advantages of offering a realistic simulated language learning environment (Chen et al., 2022). As language learning is regarded as a social process (Vygotsky, 1978), VR has been a valuable tool for language educators to provide learners with opportunities to interact with each other in meaningful contexts (Lan, 2020).

As technologies are increasingly advancing, VR has become more accessible and more affordable than before, and even the use of high-immersion VR (HiVR) has increased since 2015 (Dhimolea et al., 2022). Low-immersion VR (LiVR) and high immersion VR (HiVR) represent distinct approaches to delivering virtual experiences. LiVR, often referred to as "desktop VR," allows students to engage with virtual content through a flat screen using a mouse or keyboard. In contrast, HiVR is experienced through head-mounted devices like Oculus and Meta Quest VR headsets (Kaplan-Rakowski & Gruber, 2019). With HiVR, students can immerse themselves in a 360° environment by simply turning their heads in any direction and using a controller to navigate between scenes, answer questions, or access additional information. The affordability and enhanced immersive environments provided by head-mounted devices have contributed to the growing impact of HiVR on language teaching and learning (Dhimolea et al., 2022).

Among studies on language learning using HiVR technology published between 2015 and 2023, empirical studies involving Korean language learners are few. The largest portion of these studies have concentrated on teaching and learning English, either as a target or native language (e.g., Acar & Cavas, 2020; Lee, 2019; Monteiro & Ribeiro, 2020; Soto et al., 2020), followed by Chinese (e.g., Xie et al., 2019). Additionally, there have been multiple studies focused on Spanish, German, Portuguese, Japanese, and French, with at least three or more publications for each (Parmaxi, 2023; Dhimolea et al., 2022; Huang et al., 2021).

However, it is noteworthy that only two studies during this period (Song, 2019; Kim et al., 2022) have collected their data from Korean language learners. Song's study (2019) conducted qualitative research with Korean language learners at a North American university to examine how VR enhanced intercultural competence. The other study (Kim et al., 2022) was presented in Korean and employed a quantitative approach, surveying 53 Asian foreign students in South Korea to evaluate the efficacy of VR-based Korean language education.

Although there is a notable array of Korean-language publications proposing various strategies for incorporation of HiVR technology into Korean language education based on textbook analysis, and/or numerous pedagogical considerations (e.g., Kim et al., 2022; Jung & Seo, 2022; Chen & Choi, 2020a, 2020b; Sim & Yoo, 2019; Kim, 2022), the field is marked by a noticeable deficit of empirical data derived directly from Korean language learners themselves. Closing this gap in the literature necessitates further research to comprehensively gauge the effectiveness of HiVR technology in Korean language classrooms.

2.2 *Implementation of HiVR in language learning*

Language educators contemplating the incorporation of HiVR into their instruction have a spectrum of content options that vary by the level of effort required for design and development. Although the delineation between these types is not always sharp and might intersect in practice, categorizing them is beneficial for contrasting our pilot VR with other VR content and providing a rationale for discussing the challenges involved in creating VR videos for language courses.

Within the extant literature, a triad of VR content types has been observed in terms of their development complexity. The first category comprises readily available VR resources. Language educators can integrate off-the-shelf VR resources into their classes via various applications from app stores and existing VR videos accessible to the public like YouTube 360° videos. Instances of applications employed include Mondly VR (Christoforou et al., 2019; Kaplan-Rakowski & Wojdynski, 2018), House of Languages (Alfadil, 2020), and ImmerseMe (Soto et al., 2020). Although these applications and existing videos are convenient, they offer limited flexibility for adapting content to meet specific educational outcomes.

The second category involves modifying existing resources or customizing content by utilizing the options available within the platform or application. Cheng and his colleagues (2017) adapted pre-existing language-learning games on *Crystallize* and ported them to VR. Moreover, certain platforms and applications allow educators to craft content, as seen with *Second Life*, which has been featured in research (Lo & Lan, 2021; Chen, 2016). *Second Life* offers an online multimedia platform where users can craft avatars, generate content, and interact in virtual worlds. This category enables language educators to personalize content to a greater degree compared to the first category.

The third and involved category is the creation of custom-developed VR content tailored to meet specific learning goals. Various studies (e.g., Khatoony, 2019; Pack et al., 2020; Song, 2019; Chien et al., 2020) have demonstrated the production of VR videos designed explicitly to meet their specific instructional objectives for their targeted learners. This approach demands the most significant investment in time and creative input from educators but also offers unparalleled flexibility and creative control.

When selecting VR content for language learning, it is important to understand the difficulties and challenges of different VR content types. Addressing shortcomings can be an improvement basis for those who want to integrate VR videos into their instructions. While some issues such as dizziness, technical difficulties, and students' frustration over programs that are inappropriate for their actual language levels are commonly noticed across studies (e.g., Chien et al., 2020; Cheng et al., 2017; Chen, 2016; Huang et al., 2023), different types of VR content will pose challenges specific to the kind of VR content employed. In addition, those considering the most labor-intensive option – custom development – must take into account additional steps, such as design, development, and testing for usability. While previous studies on tailor-made VR content detail procedures to design and develop content (e.g., Song, 2019; Kim et al., 2022; Lan, 2020; Cheng et al., 2017; Chien et al., 2020), discussions on the inherent challenges are scant. Consequently, this study aims to elucidate the challenges encountered in the development of VR content, offering critical insights for its refinement and serving as a guide for future educators who aspire to innovate by creating and integrating their own VR content within their teaching practice.

2.3 Evaluation of effectiveness of HiVR in language learning

Evaluation plays a crucial role in determining the effectiveness of VR experiences and collecting valuable user feedback. The impact of VR on language learning has yielded mixed results. Positive learning outcomes have been observed in areas such as vocabulary improvement (e.g., Alfadil, 2020; Legault et al., 2019; Tai et al., 2022), oral communication skills (e.g., Yang et al., 2020), individual speaking and listening skills (e.g., Lee, 2019), and intercultural competence (e.g., Song, 2019). However, some studies have reported negative or insignificant outcomes (e.g., Ebert et al., 2016; Hartfill et al., 2020; Cheng et al., 2017).

Despite the mixed results in measurable language acquisition, participants in most studies have reported positive affective responses to learning experiences with VR. Students actively engaged in VR experiences, displaying notable interest and motivation (Alfadil, 2020; Pack et al., 2020; Kaplan-Rakowski & Wojdynski, 2018; Lee, 2019). Additionally, certain studies have found that VR reduces students' anxiety associated with speaking (Soto et al., 2020).

Despite the burgeoning interest in VR and its prospects as an ever-evolving educational platform, current HiVR research is characterized by a discernible lack of definitive evidence regarding its pedagogical efficacy (Dhimolea et al., 2022). As such, with the continuous advancement of technology, it remains imperative to conduct further research for a deeper comprehension of HiVR's impact and capabilities. In pursuit of this objective, our empirical study was guided by the following research questions:

1) In what ways did HiVR videos enhance learners' understanding of Korean culture?
2) To what extent were the HiVR videos effective in facilitating Korean language acquisition?
3) What were the specific challenges or difficulties encountered by researchers when integrating tailor-made HiVR videos into the language classroom?

3. Methodology

To address the aforementioned research questions, this study employed qualitative research methods. We leveraged open-ended questionnaires, interviews, and document analysis to investigate students' perceptions of the HiVR videos related to Korean language learning and cultural exposure. Additionally, we documented the challenges and difficulties experienced by the research team throughout this study. Given the pivotal role the HiVR videos designed and developed by our research team played as both an educational tool and a research instrument, we offer a detailed description of the procedure we employed to both produce the VR videos and subsequently implement them within the classroom setting.

3.1 Custom-developed HiVR videos

The development of the VR videos adhered to a structured process overseen by the Center for Academic Innovation at the University of Michigan. The initial phase centered on articulating the learning goals, objectives, and activities envisioned for the project. Our objective was to simulate an interactive engagement where students could converse with native Korean speakers, thereby gaining insight into everyday Korean life. With a specific focus on learners at the high novice to low intermediate level, we crafted two interactive scenarios grounded in chapters from the *Integrated Korean Beginning 2* and *Integrated Korean Intermediate 1* textbooks, pertaining to "At a Restaurant" and "Clothing and Fashion," respectively.

In the first scenario, learners were transported to an outdoor park scene, a typical setting for food delivery in Korea, where they were prompted to order food – reflecting a departure from the conventional textbook interaction of placing an order at a restaurant. The second scenario positioned the learner within one of Seoul's renowned shopping malls, directing them to initiate a conversation with a clothing sales assistant and later, engage with Korean traditional handcrafts at a souvenir shop.

Following the definition of learning objectives, we meticulously drafted scripts and storyboards for each scenario, outlining the actors' dialogue and plotting the scene sequences essential for fulfilling the learning objectives. An "experience web" was also designed to map out potential learner pathways and scene correlations. For instance, the shopping mall scenario begins with the learner consulting a directory to navigate to the clothing store, with each choice leading to distinct scenes and interactions.

With the scripts and storyboards in place, a film crew was commissioned in Seoul to capture the scenes using a 360° camera. The integration of interactive features was facilitated through Uptale, an immersive learning platform, enabling the enrichment of 360° videos with interactive buttons and questions. The inclusion of multiple-choice queries and voice recognition capabilities through Uptale transformed these videos into dynamic, interactive language learning experiences. Samples of both VR videos can be found in the appendix.

In the classroom, the students experienced both VR videos through Oculus Quest 2 headsets. With help from the technology service team at our university, the students were able to access the Uptale application on their headsets and interact with the videos via the two hand-held controllers that accompany the Oculus Quest 2 headset. To accommodate the spatial requirements of the headsets and guarantee the safety of the users, the VR sessions were conducted in a spacious computer lab.

3.2 Participants

In this pilot study taking place at a North American university, most participants were recruited from second-year Korean courses in the fall of 2021, as the videos were designed for students nearing the completion of their first year of Korean and/or beginning their second year. Before introducing the videos to our target group (44 students), we recruited 11 volunteer students from upper-level Korean classes and sought feedback from them to make final revisions to our VR content. To ensure the acquisition of rich data, we extended the introduction of the videos to two additional groups: four students who participated in the first-year intensive Korean course during the summer of 2022 and ten students from the first-year accelerated Korean course in the fall of 2022.

3.3 Data collection

To gather qualitative data efficiently from a substantial number of participants within a limited time frame, we employed two primary data collection methods. Participants who completed at least one of the videos were requested to respond to open-ended questions via a dedicated Google form during a 50-minute class period. This method facilitated the collection of insights from a large cohort of students. Additionally, we conducted interviews with a subset of willing participants (five students) to further explore their experiences and perceptions of the videos. Individual interviews were conducted with two research assistants. We conducted group interviews with four students from the first-year intensive Korean course and ten students from the first-year accelerated Korean course. These interviews occurred during their respective class periods. These diverse data collection approaches allowed us to gain comprehensive insights into the impact of the videos on their language learning.

Additionally, this study entailed the collection of various documents and materials generated throughout the research process to examine the challenges and difficulties encountered. This dataset encompasses field notes annotated with observations made during the implementation of VR in classroom settings, as well as insights gleaned from student interviews and reflective discussions within the research team.

3.4 Data analysis

For data analysis, we employed the constant comparative method of data analysis as proposed by Glaser and Strauss (2017). Our process began with identifying segments in the data that pertained to our research questions. This involved an initial stage of "open coding," where we remained receptive to all possibilities in the early phases of our analysis, annotating notes alongside segments of data (Merriam, 2009). Subsequently, we proceeded with "axial coding" (Corbin & Strauss, 2008) or "analytical coding" (Merriam, 2009), which entailed the systematic grouping of open codes into cohesive and related categories.

4. Findings

In this study, we pose three research questions, and these are each addressed in order over the following three subsections. Section 4.1 responds to our first research question about Korean cultural understanding, Section 4.2 responds to our second question about the facilitation of Korean language learning, and Section 4.3 addresses our third question about the practical challenges faced by researchers in implementing HiVR in the classroom.

4.1 Achieving cultural understanding

We found that VR was a valuable tool for introducing and experiencing various cultural aspects, typically taught verbally by instructors in traditional language classes. In particular, the immersive environments and visuals of VR provided students with a genuine sense of being in Seoul. Several participants described the experiences as "very real" and felt as though they existed "in an actual space." The following excerpts, taken from responses to open-ended questions, are representative of the ways students expressed such feelings.

> S1:[1] I was able to move around as if I was present in Korea.
> S2: Ordering food is interesting because it imitates real-life order!
> S3: You feel like you are actually in the middle of the park.

This aspect of VR made students excited and helped keep them engaged with the VR experiences.

The VR videos also helped students increase their curiosity and sensitivity to cultural differences. In the first video, filmed by the Han River, several participants discussed various differences in delivery services between Korea and the US. Some of the examples are:

> S3: Delivery services . . . are significantly more efficient in South Korea, . . . open container laws are relaxed in South Korea so you theoretically could have fried chicken with beer in a park which you cannot do in most parts of the US.
> S4: When they deliver the food, it is normally by motorcycle.

In the second video, set in a large shopping mall in Korea, eight participants shared their observations about different shopping experiences compared to the US. They made observations such as the following:

> S5: In America, store employees welcome you in and offer, but most people kindly decline and never really make use of the employees' knowledge. . . . . In Korea, it seems as though store employees are helpful and more involved in the shopping experience.

Additionally, some participants enjoyed exploring the mall's unique features and various clothing styles and as S6 noted, "learning about cultural items" they had not encountered before.

Both VR videos also helped students understand cultural differences in non-verbal communication. Nine students mentioned the "politeness" of people in Korea. Among those, two students commented:

> S7: People tend to bow after every greeting or exchange.
> S8: They use honorific language when speaking to those they do not know.

During interviews, one student also made the following observation:

> S9: We heard people's conversations in Korean, but we had not seen the body language of people. So, it helps to know.

This student thought it was helpful to see the different body language used in Korean culture, something that they had not had the chance to observe in more authentic contexts during their regular classroom work.

Contrary to the majority of participants' experiences, several students did not notice significant differences in the videos. This was often the case for some Korean heritage students and those who had previously visited Korea, although a few heritage students also found it "new and amazing" to revisit familiar places via VR headsets. Additionally, some students had exposure to Korean culture through media like K-dramas and movies, making them already familiar with certain aspects of Korean culture.

In summary, VR videos offer significant potential for conveying cultural aspects and fostering an understanding of cultural differences in non-verbal communication particularly for those with limited exposure to Korean culture.

4.2 Meeting linguistic and affective objectives

The VR videos aimed to enhance students' linguistic skills and reduce speaking anxiety, but their effectiveness in meeting these goals remains inconclusive. The participants' responses were mixed, encompassing both negative and positive feedback. Most negative opinions about the effectiveness of VR in improving their communication skills were primarily related to technical difficulties, which are discussed in detail in the following section.

In practicing Korean, more than half of the participants had positive responses regarding the "interaction" features of the VR videos. In the videos, students were required to answer questions to proceed to the next scene. Consequently, they had to comprehend the conversations to provide correct answers. The following are two representative responses from students who appreciated this interactive element:

S9: I appreciated my interaction with the delivery person.
S10: The aspect of speaking into the VR headset was the most interesting part, I did not expect the experience to be interactive.

While many students found it helpful for enhancing their listening comprehension, eight students expressed frustrations, referring to it as a "guessing game" or an "overwhelming" task due to their inadequate language ability. As a result, some students requested "pop-up translations" or "Korean subtitles" within the videos to aid their understanding of the conversations.

In addition, one of the interaction features, the recording function for verbal answers caused some frustration. This speaking component was incorporated with the expectation that students could practice Korean in the VR videos with reduced foreign language anxiety and eventually have confidence speaking in real situations. While recording voices within the videos, the voice recognition function performed poorly due to the limited Korean data in the software, causing students to lose confidence, which contradicted our goal to improve their affective response to holding a conversation in Korean. The following are some representative examples of students expressing this frustration:

S11: I kept getting stuck on the microphone response questions.
S12: The recording part was a bit frustrating when it did not understand me.
S13: I thought I was saying the right thing but maybe my wording was off.

Additionally, the videos were sometimes perceived as computer games rather than learning tools. We included responses for incorrect answers in the interactive tasks with the expectation that students would still learn useful expressions even when choosing wrong answers. However, many students opted to press the button to listen to the conversations again in the task to find the correct answer, and it was thus relatively rare for them to actually encounter the different responses for incorrect answers. During interviews, five participants mentioned that they felt compelled to "find correct answers" to complete the tasks and achieve high scores, a framework similar to that presented by many video games.

Due to difficulties in designing content tailored to individual student levels, the absence of proper AI voice recognition support, and the tendency amongst some students to approach VR through a video game-style, "point-scoring" framework, it is challenging to assert that our interactive VR videos successfully achieved the linguistic and affective goals of this pilot study.

4.3 Challenges and difficulties of utilizing tailored VR for language learning

In addition to the voice recognition issues briefly mentioned previously, we encountered a range of challenges and difficulties in the development and deployment of VR videos, including issues with setup, technical glitches, hardware limitations, and motion sickness concerns. As non-specialists in VR video development, it took us some time to become proficient in using the Uptale platform. Operating on a limited budget, we enlisted the services of an amateur filming team along with actors and actresses. Obtaining permissions for filming locations presented another hurdle, leading us to adapt by shooting on the streets or changing locations – for instance, moving from a cultural item shop to an outdoor street scene or from the Han River to a park.

After the completion of the VR videos, we undertook a series of preparatory steps before using these videos in class. For instance, we needed to request the management team to create accounts for our students in advance, as the Uptale application mandates the use of an account (active for only 14 days) for login to access the videos. At times, some students did not receive their accounts in time, which required us to occasionally loan our own accounts to them. Additionally, we had to reserve a larger room than our regular classroom (which had a maximum capacity of 18 students) because the VR headsets require ample space without obstacles to ensure user safety. We also worked with a technology specialist who was in charge of the management, storage, and maintenance of the VR headsets. The specialist provided technical support in the classroom as well. Even in cases like ours where such assistance is available, we realized that it would be difficult for us to offer VR experiences regularly in the future due to these procedural requirements.

Despite our preparatory efforts, students also struggled with technical issues during the class sessions in which we used the VR headsets. Even accessing the videos on the headsets was time consuming for students, as it involved several steps to log in to the application. Additionally, the VR headsets, the application, and Meta accounts (Oculus headsets use Meta accounts) occasionally required updates or renewal, resulting in delays lasting hours in some cases. Furthermore, several students faced issues, some of which stemmed from the application. Specifically, several became stuck in one scene, some students were unexpectedly ejected from the videos, necessitating a restart of the application, and others were unable to progress, resulting in an inability to complete the videos at all. Another challenge was the unfamiliarity with navigating the new technology. For some students, it was their first experience with VR headsets. Despite their excitement about the new technology, a few students struggled with setting up the headsets and locating buttons on the controllers or within the videos.

Another issue pertained to the headsets themselves. Several students reported difficulties in wearing headsets comfortably, finding it challenging to adjust them properly for optimal viewing. Additionally, five students had to choose between taking off their glasses to use headsets or viewing the videos on computer monitors due to difficulties using the headsets with glasses. Two students, along with one researcher, experienced motion sickness while exploring the scenes. Furthermore, a few students found the headsets to be heavy for prolonged use. As a solution to mitigate these issues, we concluded that the VR experiences should be kept relatively short in duration.

The final challenge pertains to the design, development, and potential reuse of VR content. While custom-made VR materials offer a tantalizing promise of higher efficacy due to their ability to align closely with specific language learning goals and the needs of particular student groups, the time required to craft these resources is non-trivial. Such an endeavor can pose significant difficulties for language teachers who are already coping with demanding teaching schedules, an observation supported by Lan (2020). Furthermore, editing and repurposing 360° immersive videos for different objectives presents its own set of complexities. Often, it necessitates additional filming, including travel to relevant locations and engagement of actors, raising concerns regarding the cost efficiency and practicality of utilizing custom VR content in educational settings. These considerations bring into question the overall feasibility of implementing VR videos in the classroom with respect to both time and financial resources.

5. Discussion

In this pilot study, it was found that the VR videos were beneficial for introducing and experiencing Korean culture. In particular, immersive environments and visuals increased students' sense of presence, leading to their excitement and active engagement with the VR videos. This positive perception toward VR was similarly found in other studies (Alfadil, 2020; Pack et al., 2020; Kaplan-Rakowski & Wojdynski, 2018; Lee, 2019; Cheng et al., 2017; Huang et al., 2023).

In addition, the VR videos helped students increase their curiosity for and sensibility to cultural differences. They were valuable in teaching cultural differences in both verbal and non-verbal communication. These findings align with discussions in the studies confirming that VR had a significant impact on cultural learning (Cheng et al., 2017; Song, 2019). Song (2019) used the term "intercultural competence," which she describes as "1) enjoyment, curiosity, and sensitivity toward another culture; 2) deeper cultural knowledge and awareness; and 3) increased sociopragmatics (the ability to use the language appropriately to a particular context or situation)." These aspects of intercultural competence can be enhanced by VR.

On the other hand, we remained inconclusive about the impact of VR technology on improving language proficiency and reducing foreign language anxiety in our current study. While the majority of students found the videos beneficial for improving their listening skills, some also expressed their frustration because of the challenging language levels presented. When it comes to speaking skills, the interactive features of the videos garnered mostly positive feedback from participants. However, the lack of proper voice recognition support led to a loss of confidence in their speaking abilities. Also, the interactive tasks, which included responses for incorrect answers, were not fully utilized by students who tended to view the use of the headsets through a video game-style framework where the goal was to complete tasks and gain a high score by seeking only correct answers.

In other studies, the impact of VR on language learning remains inconclusive, with some studies showing a significant positive impact of VR (e.g., Garcia et al., 2019; Yang et al., 2020), while others described negative effects (e.g., Ebert et al., 2016; Hartfill et al., 2020; Christoforou et al., 2019). Cheng and his colleagues (2017) also observed no obvious evidence that language learning improved. After reviewing 32 articles on high-immersion VR for language learning, Dhimolea and his colleagues (2022) found that multiple exposures to VR are necessary for effective learning. However, our pilot study was designed as a one-time event, so it may be premature to conclude that the impact of VR on language learning is either positive or negative.

To increase the frequency of the use of VR in language learning and measure its efficiency and effectiveness, the challenges and difficulties associated with the current videos and headsets need to be addressed. In addition to improving AI voice recognition support, we discussed setup issues, technical glitches, hardware limitations, motion sickness, and difficulty in the development and reuse of VR videos. The Uptale platform that we used to develop the videos may not be suitable for the Korean language until it improves its Korean voice recognition support. We found that voice recognition functions available on the market for practicing Korean conversations that works very well. For example, TEUIDA is a software application that offers interactive Korean lessons with a voice recognition. This suggests the possibility of incorporating a better voice recognition function even at this time.

Regarding other issues, such as setup issues, technical glitches, headset issues, and even editing and reusing 360° videos, we believe that these can be overcome with advancing technology. To avoid the technical issues that we encountered and reduce the cost of headsets and their maintenance, a possible, short-term solution may be to use VR sets composed of a cardboard frame around a smartphone (Qiu et al., 2021). This setup enables users to experience VR content using a simple, affordable, and lightweight device. It has only been in recent years that VR has seen significant use in language education and thus the use of VR as an educational tool is still in the primary stages of development (Qiu et al., 2021), and little software has been created to make fuller use of the mature application systems that are just now coming on the market. Considering the popularity of VR technology and the increase in studies on high-immersion VR in recent years (Dhimolea et al., 2022), technical issues and even the shortcomings of headsets are expected to be solved in the foreseeable future. Chang and Wang (2019) anticipate that the current preference for computer-generated VR spaces will diminish as computer vision and image-based capturing and rendering advance, addressing the current issues with editing and recycling 360° videos. This anticipated technological progression promises to resolve many of the challenges and difficulties uncovered in the course of our research.

6. Implications for language educators

This pilot study makes a significant contribution to a burgeoning area of educational technology by offering empirical evidence of the impact of VR technology on language learning, particularly within the realm of Korean language education where little research has been done. There is a distinct need for a deeper understanding of the strengths and limitations of VR technology for Korean language pedagogy. To conduct a rigorous evaluation of VR videos and their implementation, language educators should consider integrating VR exposure more regularly within their curricula, as sporadic use has been associated with negligible or negative outcomes (Dhimolea et al., 2022). A structured approach, such as incorporating VR into existing curriculums or designing specific courses centered around VR-assisted language learning, could provide a more consistent measurement of its efficacy beyond the initial novelty.

Furthermore, the integration of learning theories is paramount in underpinning the design and deployment of VR applications. In the development phase of the VR content used in our study, explicit learning theories were not applied. Retrospectively, we recognize this as a missed opportunity for enhancing the educational alignment and efficacy of VR in language learning contexts. Educators developing VR content could benefit from employing established conceptual frameworks that have been demonstrated to be effective, such as those conceptual frameworks recommended by Salcedo et al. (2022).

Last, it is imperative for language educators to embrace innovation and adapt to the rapid advancements in educational technologies. With the pace of technological change and the evolving profiles of student populations, educators must be proactive in acquiring new knowledge and skills pertinent to tech-based teaching methods, including VR. For those educators for whom the design and development of custom VR content may prove challenging, leveraging existing resources is a recommended stepping stone. For instance, institutions like CLIC Rice University provide accessible 360° VR videos for learning Korean and Korean culture, offered on their YouTube channel – these can serve as valuable educational tools even in the absence of VR headsets or other specialized hardware.

By incorporating these approaches, language educators can more effectively harness the potential of VR technology, enrich the learning experience, and ultimately enhance student engagement and language proficiency.

7. Conclusion

This pilot study enhances the field of foreign language education by integrating HiVR technology with a focus on Korean language learning. Through empirical analysis, we have demonstrated a discernible positive impact on the cultural learning aspect of Korean language education, while the more direct effects of VR on Korean language proficiency and speaking anxiety remain inconclusive. This study has been a step towards a deeper understanding of the pedagogical impacts of VR and it indicates the need for continued investigation to further delineate the factors that influence the effects that VR can have on Korean language education.

Moreover, this research has navigated through and outlined a series of challenges, particularly in the design, development, and implementation of custom VR content. Addressing these challenges informs best practices and contributes to the knowledge base of VR in educational settings. Additionally, as VR technology evolves and the specific shortcomings identified in this research are mitigated, it is crucial that future studies build on these findings to explore the shifting efficacy of VR in language instruction.

We would also like to highlight the essential role of language educators in pioneering the use of innovative technologies. The positive reception from students signifies more than just appreciation. It underscores the profound potential impact that such initiatives have on learners' engagement and enthusiasm for emerging educational tools. These encounters serve not only as validation of our work but also as an impetus to continue pushing the boundaries of language education.

Acknowledgments

This work was made possible by funding from the Center for Academic Innovation at the University of Michigan. Our sincere appreciation goes to the center's team for their indispensable support during the entirety of the project. We are also grateful to Philomena Meechan, instructional learning lead at the Language Resource Center, for her insightful contributions during team meetings and her constructive feedback on our work. Further thanks are extended to John (Jan) Stewart, lead academic technology strategist at Literature, Science, and the Arts Technology Services, for his invaluable technical assistance.

Note

1 The numbering is arbitrary and is used to distinguish between different voices. Students' answers were collected anonymously.

References

Acar, A., & Cavas, B. (2020). The effect of virtual reality enhanced learning environment on the 7th-grade students' reading and writing skills in English. *Malaysian Online Journal of Educational Sciences*, 8(4), 22–33.

Al-Emran, M., Mezhuyev, V., & Kamaludin, A. (2018). Virtual reality as a new trend in language learning research: A meta-analysis study. *EURASIA Journal of Mathematics, Science and Technology Education, 14*(3), 1047–1058.

Alfadil, M. (2020). Effectiveness of virtual reality game in foreign language vocabulary acquisition. *Computers & Education, 153*, 103893.

Baralt, M., & Gurzynski-Weiss, L. (2019). The use of virtual reality in second language research: A review. *Language Learning & Technology, 23*(2), 1–23.

Chang, Y., & Wang, G.-P. (2019). A review on image-based rendering. *Virtual Reality & Intelligent Hardware, 1*(1), 39–54.

Chen, B., Wang, Y., & Wang, L. (2022). The effects of virtual reality-assisted language learning: A meta-analysis. *Sustainability, 14*(6), 3147.

Chen, C. M., & Hsieh, J. S. (2018). Effects of virtual reality learning environment on students' learning outcomes: Evidence from a meta-analysis. *Educational Research Review, 24*, 1–14.

Chen, C. M., Lin, Y. C., & Liu, Y. C. (2019). An exploration of using virtual reality to support language learning: A case study of college students learning Mandarin. *Educational Technology Research and Development, 67*(1), 71–89.

Chen, J. C. (2016). The crossroads of English language learners, task-based instruction, and 3D multi-user virtual learning in second life. *Computers & Education, 102*, 152–171.

Chen, X., & Choi, E. (2020a). A study on an elementary-level Korean language program using immersive content: Focusing on the textbook of Korean language institutes affiliated with universities. *Journal of Education & Culture, 26*(2), 837–864.

Chen, X., & Choi, E. (2020b). A study on an intermediate-level Korean language program using immersive content: Focusing on the Korean textbooks of D University. *The Academy for Korean Language Education, 125*, 291–328.

Cheng, A., Yang, L., & Andersen, E. (2017, May). Teaching language and culture with a virtual reality game. In *Proceedings of the 2017 CHI Conference on Human Factors in Computing Systems* (pp. 541–549). Association for Computing Machinery.

Chien, S. Y., Hwang, G. J., & Jong, M. S. Y. (2020). Effects of peer assessment within the context of spherical video-based virtual reality on EFL students' English-speaking performance and learning perceptions. *Computers & Education, 146*, 103751.

Christoforou, M., Xerou, E., & Papadima-Sophocleous, S. (2019). Integrating a virtual reality application to simulate situated learning experiences in a foreign language course. In F. Meunier, J. Vyver, L. Bradley, & S. Thouësny (Eds.), *CALL and complexity – short papers from EUROCALL* (pp. 82–87). Research-publishing.net.

Corbin, J., & Strauss, A. (2008). Strategies for qualitative data analysis. In *Basics of qualitative research (3rd ed.): Techniques and procedures for developing grounded theory* (pp. 65–86). SAGE.

Dhimolea, T. K., Kaplan-Rakowski, R., & Lin, L. (2022). A systematic review of research on high-immersion virtual reality for language learning. *TechTrends, 66*(5), 810–824.

Ebert, D., Gupta, S., & Makedon, F. (2016, June). Ogma: A virtual reality language acquisition system. In *Proceedings of the 9th ACM International Conference on Pervasive Technologies Related to Assistive Environments* (pp. 1–5). Association for Computing Machinery.

Garcia, S., Laesker, D., Caprio, D., Kauer, R., Nguyen, J., & Andujar, M. (2019). An immersive virtual reality experience for learning Spanish. In P. Zaphiris & A. Ioannou (Eds.), *Learning and collaboration technologies. Ubiquitous and virtual environments for learning and collaboration*. HCII 2019. Lecture Notes in Computer Science, Vol. 11591. Springer.

Glaser, B., & Strauss, A. (2017). *Discovery of grounded theory: Strategies for qualitative research*. Routledge.

Haluck, R. S., & Krummel, T. M. (2000). Computers and virtual reality for surgical education in the 21st century. *Archives of Surgery, 135*(7), 786–792.

Hartfill, J., Gabel, J., Neves-Coelho, D., Vogel, D., Räthel, F., Tiede, S., & Steinicke, F. (2020). Word saber: An effective and fun VR vocabulary learning game. In B. Preim, A. Nürnberger, & C. Hansen (Eds.), *Proceedings of Mensch und Computer 2020* (pp. 145–154). Association for Computing Machinery.

Huang, H. W., Huang, K., Liu, H., & Dusza, D. G. (2023). 360-Degree virtual reality videos in EFL teaching: Student experiences. In K. Nakamatsu, S. Patnaik, R. Kountchev, R. Li, & A. Aharari (Eds.), *Advanced intelligent virtual reality technologies. Smart innovation, systems and technologies, proceedings of 6th international conference on artificial intelligence and virtual reality (AIVR 2022)* (pp. 131–143). Springer Singapore.

Huang, X., Zou, D., Cheng, G., & Xie, H. (2021). A systematic review of AR and VR enhanced language learning. *Sustainability*, *13*(9), 4639.

Jung, Y., & Seo, E. (2022). A study on design and operation of Korea immigration and integration program (KIIP) class using Metaverse: Focusing on level 4 "Korean language and Korean culture". *Journal of Multi-Cultural Contents Studies*, *41*, 311–331.

Kaplan-Rakowski, R., & Gruber, A. (2019). Low-immersion versus high-immersion virtual reality: Definitions, classification, and examples with a foreign language focus. In Pixel (Ed.), *Proceedings of Innovation in Language Learning International Conference 2019* (pp. 552–555). Filodiritto Editore.

Kaplan-Rakowski, R., & Wojdynski, T. (2018). Students' attitudes toward high-immersion virtual reality assisted language learning. In P. Taals, J. Jalkanen, L. Bradley, & S. Thouësny (Eds.), *Future-proof CALL: Language learning as exploration and encounters – short papers from EUROCALL 2018* (pp. 124–129). Research-publishing.net.

Khatoony, S. (2019, December). An innovative teaching with serious games through virtual reality assisted language learning. In *2019 International serious games symposium (ISGS)* (pp. 100–108). IEEE.

Kim, D., Kim, Y., & Yoo, H. (2022). Based on VR (virtual reality) technology for Asian foreign students' effectiveness of Korean language education. *Design Convergence Study*, *21*(2), 17–36.

Kim, J. (2022). Basic research for the development of beginner Korean education contents applying virtual reality (VR) technology. *The Journal of Next-Generation Convergence Technology Association*, *6*(7), 1313–1320.

Kim, S., Kwak, J., Shon, S., & Han, S. (2022). A study on compositive principles of online Korean language education contents focusing on the development case of Y University basic level online Korean language education contents. *Teaching Korean as a Foreign Language*, *64*, 1–40.

Lan, Y. J. (2020). Immersion into virtual reality for language learning. In K. D. Federmeier & H.-W. Huang (Eds.), *Psychology of learning and motivation* (Vol. 72, pp. 1–26). Academic Press.

Lee, A. (2019). Using virtual reality to test academic listening proficiency. *Korean Journal of English Language and Linguistics*, *19*(4), 688–712.

Legault, J., Zhao, J., Chi, Y. A., Chen, W., Klippel, A., & Li, P. (2019). Immersive virtual reality as an effective tool for second language vocabulary learning. *Languages*, *4*(1), 13.

Li, C., Liang, W., Quigley, C., Zhao, Y., & Yu, L. F. (2017). Earthquake safety training through virtual drills. *IEEE Transactions on Visualization and Computer Graphics*, *23*(4), 1275–1284.

Lo, P. Y., & Lan, Y. J. (2021). An investigation into virtual immersion Mandarin Chinese writing instruction with student with autism. In Y. Wen, Y. Wu, G. Qi, S. Guo, J. Spector, S. Chelliah, Kinshuk, & Y. Lan (Eds.), *Expanding global horizons through technology enhanced language learning* (pp. 73–111). Springer Singapore.

Merriam, S. B. (2009). *Qualitative research: A guide to design and implementation*. Jossey-Bass.

Meyer, L. (2016). Students explore the earth and beyond with virtual field trips. *THE Journal*, *43*(3), 22–25.

Monteiro, A. M. V., & Ribeiro, P. N. D. S. (2020). Virtual reality in English vocabulary teaching: An exploratory study on effect in the use of technology. *Trabalhos Em Linguística Aplicada, 59*(2), 1310–1338.

Ota, D., Loftin, B., Saito, T., Lea, R., & Keller, J. (1995). Virtual reality in surgical education. *Computers in Biology and Medicine, 25*(2), 127–137.

Pack, A., Barrett, A., Liang, H. N., & Monteiro, D. V. (2020). University EAP students' perceptions of using a prototype virtual reality learning environment to learn writing structure. *International Journal of Computer-Assisted Language Learning and Teaching, 10*(1), 27–46.

Parmaxi, A. (2023). Virtual reality in language learning: A systematic review and implications for research and practice. *Interactive Learning Environments, 31*(1), 172–184.

Qiu, X. Y., Chiu, C. K., Zhao, L. L., Sun, C. F., & Chen, S. J. (2021). Trends in VR/AR technology-supporting language learning from 2008 to 2019: A research perspective. *Interactive Learning Environments, 31*(4), 2090–2113.

Salcedo, D., Regan, J., Aebersold, M., Lee, D., Darr, A., Davis, K., & Berrocal, Y. (2022). Frequently used conceptual frameworks and design principles for extended reality in health professions education. *Medical Science Educator, 32*(6), 1587–1595.

Sim, E., & Yoo, H. (2019). A Study on strategies for Korean education for marriage migrant women using VR tools. *Korean Association for Learner-Centered Curriculum and Instruction, 19*(15), 497–515.

Song, J. (2019). Enhancing intercultural competence with 360-degree virtual reality videos. *The Korean Language in America, 23*(1), 85–98.

Soto, J. B., Ocampo, D. T., Colon, L. B., & Oropesa, A. V. (2020). Perceptions of ImmerseMe virtual reality platform to improve English communicative skills in Higher Education. *International Journal of Interactive Mobile Technologies, 14*(7), 4–19.

Tai, T. Y., Chen, H. H. J., & Todd, G. (2022). The impact of a virtual reality app on adolescent EFL learners' vocabulary learning. *Computer Assisted Language Learning, 35*(4), 892–917.

Vygotsky, L. S. (1978). *Mind in society: Development of higher psychological processes.* Harvard University Press.

Xie, Y., Chen, Y., & Ryder, L. H. (2019). Effects of using mobile-based virtual reality on Chinese L2 students' oral proficiency. *Computer Assisted Language Learning, 34*(3), 225–245.

Yang, F. C. O., Lo, F. Y. R., Hsieh, J. C., & Wu, W. C. V. (2020). Facilitating communicative ability of EFL learners via high-immersion virtual reality. *Journal of Educational Technology & Society, 23*(1), 30–49.

96 *Innovative Methods in Korean Language Teaching*

Appendix

VR images

1. Food delivery at the Han river

Figure 5.1 Initiation of the experience: The participant receives a call

Figure 5.2 Gathering information: The participant interacts with locals

Virtual interactions in Seoul 97

Figure 5.3 Food ordering: Participant places a delivery order

Figure 5.4 Conclusion: Participant receives the order

98 *Innovative Methods in Korean Language Teaching*

2. Shopping in Seoul

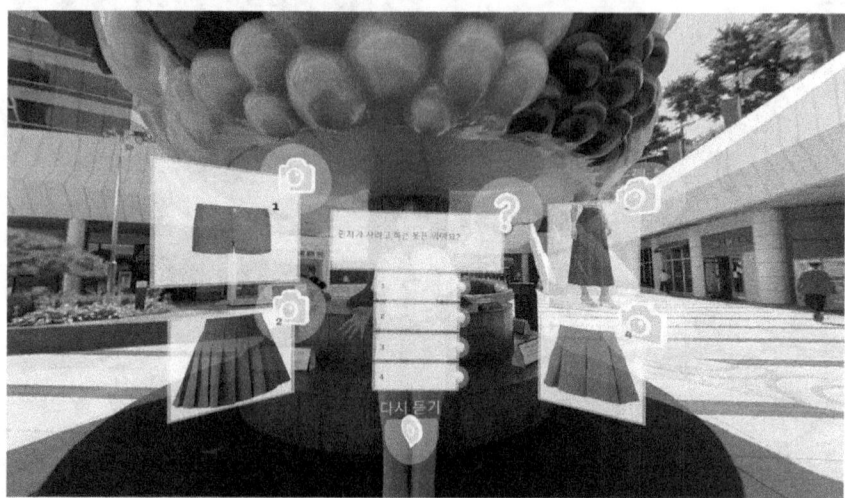

Figure 5.5 Entrance interaction with Minji at a mall in Seoul

Figure 5.6 Shopping assistance at a clothing store

Virtual interactions in Seoul 99

Figure 5.7 Learning cultural significance of Korean traditional souvenirs

Figure 5.8 Farewell with Minji outside the mall

6 Exploring the possibilities and limits of metaverse as a Korean teaching resource

The case of the Sejong Institute's metaverse proposal

Álvaro Trigo Maldonado

1. Introduction

The circumstances of the worldwide COVID-19 pandemic accelerated the adoption of remote work in numerous sectors, necessitating advancements in technology. Consequently, many individuals who transitioned to remote work during the pandemic continue to do so. This shift has also impacted education, with an increasing number of universities and institutions offering online education globally, eliminating the need for students to be physically present in the classroom.

However, many of these activities primarily rely on web 2.0 technology. Presently, emerging technologies are focusing on the development of metaverses. Coined from "meta," meaning virtual and transcendent, and "verse," referring to the world and universe, the term metaverse was first introduced in the novel *Snow Crash*, published in 1992 (Park & Kim, 2022, p. 3). Metaverses are real-time 3D virtual worlds where "users can collectively experience, interact, and collaborate with others, fostering a sense of individual presence" (Wu et al., 2023, p. 44). For instance, during the pandemic, Sungkyunkwan University held a virtual admission ceremony in 2021 for their students using VR technologies (Jeong & Seo, 2022), while other institutions utilized virtual environments to substitute on-site activities canceled due to the pandemic.

The fundamental characteristics of metaverses, as outlined by Ryu (2022), differ from traditional e-learning platforms. They require active engagement, sharing, and expansion of digital content, offering a space for unrestricted communication and real-time sharing across time and space. Moreover, metaverses interact with the real world, influencing and being influenced by it. Despite being virtual, users engage through avatars, impacting their real-world thoughts and lifestyles (Ryu, 2022).

Metaverses have been hailed for their potential in various sectors. In the tourism industry, cities like Incheon have integrated metaverse elements into their advertisement strategies, creating virtual replicas of the city accessible to users via platforms like Minecraft. Projects like "Incheoncraft" aim to enhance tourists' experiences by offering "unique interactions and historical insights" (Um et al., 2022). With technology companies increasingly investing in metaverses, the press views them as the third wave of the internet revolution, shaping its future.[1] Notably,

DOI: 10.4324/9781032725307-9

Facebook rebranded as Meta introduced augmented reality products, an investment that could be interpreted in the context of a future significant shift in mass communication via the internet.

In this context, it is worth exploring how these developments could impact second language teaching and acquisition, potentially advancing the concept of web-based e-learning. This paper aims to analyze the pedagogical characteristics and value of the Korean language education-oriented metaverse based on the ZEP (Zettaverse expansion platform), recently launched by the Sejong Institute Foundation to commemorate its tenth anniversary.

2. The use of metaverses in language learning

Despite metaverses still being in their infancy, there have already been several instances of attempts to utilize metaverses for language teaching. As early as 2015, Garrido-Iñigo and Rodríguez-Moreno (2015) published the outcomes of their experiment in teaching French to 108 tourism students using a virtual platform. The researchers developed a metaverse prototype based on OpenSim and utilized Imprudence (an open-source viewer based on Second Life code) as a viewer. For most of the students involved, it was their first experience with a metaverse. The program was structured across five islands, each offering various activities in French language set in different environments, such as an airport desk. It is worth noting that these activities were designed to complement previously studied content and were organized as part of a competitive contest.

Among the positive outcomes of this experiment, the researchers highlighted those related to the psychological implications of metaverse language learning. As early as 1977, Dulay and Burt proposed the concept of the "affective filter," encompassing variables influencing success in second language acquisition, mainly motivation, self-confidence, and anxiety. While the concept of affective filter theory was later further developed by prominent linguists such as Stephen Krashen (1981), among others, it has also been criticized for its limited consideration of broader social factors impacting learning (Bailey & Fahad, 2021), such as the relationship between identity and motivation or the influence of external factors, and it continues to underscore the significance of psychological and emotional factors in second language acquisition. However, how can metaverses impact our emotions when used for second language acquisition?

Metaverses possess characteristics that distinguish them from traditional classroom learning and are aligned with the affective filter theory. One such feature is gamification. Given that the primary users of metaverses are members of Generation Z, born after 1995, who have grown up with evolving PC and mobile technologies, they are familiar with videogaming. Game elements in education are believed to have positive effects on learner motivation, participation, and attitude (Park & Kim, 2022). Additionally, the possibility of using authentic materials rather than teaching-oriented ones, and the use of avatars as alternative identities, have the potential to enhance motivation and reduce anxiety in second language learners, respectively.

According to Garrido-Iñigo and Rodríguez-Moreno (2015), during their experiment, the use of avatars led to a "disguise" effect, providing a sense of liberation in both gestural and verbal interactions. In other words, the indirect interaction through virtual avatars may reduce anxiety when speaking a foreign language, creating a more relaxed learning environment. However, there appear to be a few disadvantages in using metaverses as learning environments. For instance, while the previously mentioned researchers found that student engagement in the activities increased as they felt part of the project, they also noted that the positive novelty soon wore off (Garrido-Iñigo & Rodríguez-Moreno, 2015), suggesting that short-term experiences may differ from long-term use of this resource. Perhaps the most significant issue raised in this study was related to technology; teachers needed to invest considerable time in designing activities, and the use of the metaverse requires a certain degree of IT skills.

More recently, there have been numerous similar empirical research experiments in Korea. As mentioned earlier, among other consequences, the COVID-19 pandemic prompted the online adaptation of several educational programs that were traditionally conducted offline. One such program was the government's Korea Immigration and Integration Program (KIIP), which offers four levels of Korean language training and an additional level on Korean culture and society. During the pandemic, the courses transitioned to remote video classes. Jeong and Seo's (2022) research examines the use of a ZEP open platform-based metaverse for teaching the last level. This methodological proposal involves activities across three phases, with the final phase adopting additional VR tools to introduce students to Korean cultural heritage in a 3D environment (Jeong & Seo, 2022). Among the limitations noted by researchers was the need for further integration of reading and listening materials, despite the usefulness of the platform for speaking and writing tasks (Jeong & Seo, 2022). However, it appears that technological issues once again hindered the development of the teaching program; teachers had to spend significant amounts of time creating activities, and access to technology (such as a stable internet connection, VR devices, and Android operating system limitations) became a barrier to the successful use of the metaverse as a tool for second language teaching.

Another relevant study for this research was carried out by Lee and Choi (2022), focusing on speaking classes for beginner-level Korean students. While the target group is too restricted to draw generalizable conclusions, this study was focused on the use of the ZEP platform, as in Jeong and Seo (2022). It is important to emphasize that ZEP is also the same platform used by the Sejong Institute in the case that will be analyzed in the following sections. Lee and Choi's (2022) study concentrated on speaking classes for beginner-level Korean students, selecting ten representative places for conversation practice: a park, coffee shop, subway, classroom, Han river park, city, library, restaurant, cinema, and a theme park. The classes "lasted 90 minutes and followed five stages: Introduction, presentation, practice, use, and conclusion" (Lee & Choi, 2022, p. 106). The study emphasized pedagogical proposals for daily conversation at a basic level. After receiving relevant explanations in the classroom, students could freely move to other locations, such as the coffee shop, where they assumed worker-customer roles and engaged in speaking exercises like ordering food and drinks. This starkly contrasts with online classes, where student interaction is limited. Therefore, one of the findings of this study is that online learners, especially, felt a strong sense of interaction in ZEP, perceived as a significant advantage compared to their online classes using Webex (Lee & Choi, 2022). While this sense of interaction might be lower compared to in-person classes, according to interviewed students, digital environments provided by the metaverse play a significant role in immersing students in assigned tasks. Nonetheless, the study speculates that while metaverses seem effective for conducting speaking classes, transferring entire regular classes to ZEP would be challenging due to the higher degree of freedom and less control over learners (Lee & Choi, 2022).

A similar study focused on basic Korean speaking was conducted at Ewha Womans University in 2021. This project offered speaking classes to 23 beginner students over a month using Gather.town instead of ZEP. There are differences between both platforms; for instance, researchers highlighted that in Gather.town, it is necessary to approach another user to listen to their voice or see their video, making interactions more realistic. Overall, the researcher emphasized aspects such as the high value of the metaverse for conversation practice, as it allows users to travel to virtual spaces, and the positive effects on speaking practice (Jang, 2021). The assignment execution was dynamic and closely resembled real-world situations, which in the case of speaking practice prompted students to go beyond class materials and ask their teacher how to solve certain situations that could arise in real life; for example, in a restaurant scenario, students asked which expressions they should use to call the owner (Jang, 2021). Thus, more immersive exercises can also lead students to imagine the expressions they would need in real situations and expand their vocabulary accordingly. However, technical issues, such as connectivity, and the initial difficulty in learning how to use Gather.town, were noted by some students (Jang, 2021).

Other studies have stressed the need to integrate various technologies, such as virtual reality, augmented reality, mirror worlds, lifelogging, and other elements, for more effective Korean language education in metaverses (Seok, 2023). This observation is significant because one of the drawbacks of metaverse technology appears to be its current heterogeneity, but it is also necessary to consider accessibility to the current technology, that is, whether most learners have specific devices such as VR headsets.

3. Methodology

In celebration of its tenth anniversary, the Sejong Institute Foundation, established by the Ministry of Culture, Sports and Tourism of Korea, launched a ZEP platform–based metaverse for Korean learners. The Sejong Institute, which started in 2007 with just 13 language centers in three countries, had 258 centers in the five continents as of April 2024 (Sejong Institute Foundation, 2024). This rapid expansion, which follows the past few years of growing overseas interest in the Korean language, has fostered the reputation of the institution as one of the main referents for Korean language education. The fact that such an institution has launched a metaverse is significant itself because it has the capacity to mobilize a large number of students and instructors, and consequently it opens the possibility of creating a community of Korean learners. In other words, it has the potential to engage students from around the world if the appropriate strategies are applied. According to the Sejong Institute's data, after launching the service there was a total of 4,643 visitors during the first day, and an average of 480 learners from 123 countries communicated in Korean each day (Sejong Institute, 2023a), which can be seen as proof of the international interest in the Korean language these days.

Since metaverse functions can vary according to the selected platform, it is convenient to first summarize the core characteristics of ZEP, the platform used by Sejong Institute for its educational proposal (see Table 6.1).

Besides the elements noted in Table 6.1, it is important to emphasize that ZEP can be accessed without separated program installations and allows smartphone access. Other key features are that, unlike other platforms like Gather.Town, ZEP provides Korean language support since it was co-developed with Naver. Additionally, it is also free to use regardless the number of users, while, for example, Gather. Town allows free use up to 25 simultaneous users (Lee & Choi, 2022).

As metaverses are recent technological developments, their potential application in education is still being researched. To analyze the Sejong's Institute metaverse, the theoretical framework proposed by Zhang et al. (2022) will be used

Table 6.1 Core characteristics of the platform ZEP

	Types of spaces	2D web-based spaces
Metaverse spatial environment	User space creation	Provides space creation via Space Maker
	Space templates	Forty basic templates (continuously updated), and users can purchase both free and paid templates from a store
	Access and invitation features	Allow access without membership and enables invitations through shared links
Teaching learning environment	Interaction between teachers and students	Supports: avatar, video chat, and voice functions
	Provision of teaching materials	Allows insertion of media: YouTube, web links, background music, and so on
	Sharing teaching materials	Provides screen sharing (multiple simultaneous screen sharing, zoom in and out of screens)
	File upload function	Allows the insertion of YouTube, image, files, and so on
	Separation of group class spaces	Setting designated areas with effects
	Provides collaboration tools	It is possible to use whiteboards

Source: (Adapted and translated from Gye et al., 2023)

as reference and applied to determine which learning-related characteristics are met by the case analyzed in this chapter. Among the different features mentioned, the chapter will focus on those defined as "features of metaverse in education" that are oriented to the specific purpose of language education.

According to Zhang et al. (2022), there are certain features that distinguish metaverse-based learning from in-person classroom learning or screen-based remote learning (normally referred to as online learning). These are the following: time and location for learners to participate in class, learner identity, the people learners interact with, learning scene, learning resource, learning activity, learning interaction, learning objective, and learning assessment (Zhang et al., 2022). Reflecting on these categories in relation to Sejong Institute's metaverse will shed light on the value of its pedagogical proposal and offer a complete case study on this initiative.

4. The case of the Sejong Institute's metaverse

4.1 Identity and time

Upon entering the Sejong Institute's metaverse, users are asked to select a nickname and customize a cartoonish avatar that will represent them. There is a certain degree of customization regarding the avatar's appearance (it is possible to choose among different facial types and hair colors) and clothing. The system offers the opportunity to type in Hangul and communicate in real time with other users who are online, but it also has microphone and webcam features. This is all related to **learner identity**. While in physical classrooms and videoconferences, learners attend classes displaying their real identities, in this case they display their virtual identities through their avatars. As has been mentioned, people can be recognized in a limited way compared to reality (Gye et al., 2021), and this gap between the avatar and the "real me" can lead learners to experience a higher degree of freedom and potentially lessen the anxiety of more active participation in the classroom. While this might be an advantage in language learning, there have been concerns, as anonymity also implies the possibility of committing cybercrimes more easily. IT limitations may also create a divide across learners. For example, one of the instructors of the Sejong Institute's metaverse stated that at first, teaching was challenging, as not every student was able to take part in the classes with their cameras. However, this led instructors to adapt classes to the metaverse environment and learn how to check students' interaction intuitively through their avatar movements and expressions instead of their faces (Sejong Institute, 2023c).

The next feature of Sejong's metaverse would be the **time and location for learners** to participate in classes. As can be seen in the mini map represented in Figure 6.1, this metaverse world is divided into two main areas: campus and cultural village.

The campus is a smaller area that comprises virtual classrooms, a library, and a materials room. The project combines different technologies to display media resources to students. For example, if the students enter the library, they can use

106 *Innovative Methods in Korean Language Teaching*

Figure 6.1 Metaverse map
(*Source:* zep.us/@ksif)

their avatar to interact with different e-books for Korean learning made by the Sejong Institute, which can also be read online. At the same time, in certain areas it is possible to interact with boards and open different cultural presentations and videos. The classes are conducted synchronically at certain times with Korean teachers in the virtual classroom. To explore its metaverse possibilities, the Sejong Institute has been offering free of charge classes through an application system. The classes take place twice a week for 90 minutes, with a maximum of 20 students per group. As can be inferred from the large interrogation mark in Figure 6.1, the metaverse is in constant expansion, and from time to time it rearranges existing areas or incorporate new ones.

4.2 Interaction and learning objectives

When it comes to **learners' interaction**, Zhang et al. (2022) define two main categories in their study: interaction with teachers' and peers' avatars and teachers' and peers' intelligent non-playable characters (NPCs) (Zhang et al., 2022). While the second category serves as a complement to fill up the metaverse with language learning–oriented tasks, what makes the environment feel alive is the interaction among humans. In this regard, it is challenging to keep the metaverse alive 24 hours a day, but the Sejong Institute has engaged a few voluntary teachers. This program is especially interesting for graduate students majoring in Korean teaching as a foreign language, as it provides them with opportunities to gain experience with students from all around the globe. For example, in an interview, one of the instructors reflects on how her experience in this metaverse has helped her to identify common errors made by Korean language students, learn about other cultures, and establish meaningful relationships while gaining experience in her field (Sejong Institute, 2023c).

While the campus is clearly oriented to language teaching, the much broader cultural village recreates different zones inspired by Seoul, such as the DDP Plaza in Dongdaemun. From a pedagogical perspective, the most interesting feature is perhaps the self-learning bots that can be found throughout the different areas. Students can interact with these bots to open speaking exercises assisted by artificial intelligence. Before opening one of these exercises, students can select a difficulty level. After that, a dialogue with a bot opens and users are given the choice to answer questions either by typing in Korean or by speaking through their microphones. In such a way, it is possible to maintain a conversation in Korean with these bots about a daily-life–related topic. However, it is important to emphasize that bots in their current state are just a complement to language education oriented towards specific exercises rather than a resource allowing independent learning without the supervision of instructors.

Other areas of the cultural village try to convey Korean culture in a more ludic manner. For example, in a folk village zone, it is possible to experience a variety of Korean traditional instruments and traditional games, such as *yutnori*, through multiplayer videogames (see Figures 6.2 and 6.3).

During the last years, the previously mentioned game-based learning (GBL), which refers to mainly digital games for learning, which are designed balancing the need to cover a subject with the desire to prioritize game play, has been in vogue. It is important to note that this differs from gamification, broadly defined as the use of certain game elements such as "incentive systems to motivate players to engage in a task they otherwise would not find attractive" (Plass et al., 2015, p. 259). Gamification has also started to play a big role in foreign language teaching as a

Figures 6.2 (left) and *6.3* (right). Embedded games portraying Korean traditional music and games

(*Source:* zep.us/@ksif)

108 *Innovative Methods in Korean Language Teaching*

tool that can boast students' motivation and competitiveness when used correctly. Certain apps, such as Kahoot, have started to be widely used as a support to traditional language learning. In this case, the inclusion of such multiplayer supportive games entirely in the Korean language has significance in terms of Vygotsky's formulation of collaborative learning as a learning potential through the interaction among peers sharing a learning environment (Vygotsky, 1978). It is important to emphasize that, as a learning tool, this metaverse has the potential to go beyond synchronic classes and chat with AI bots by providing a space for Korean language learners to practice among themselves while trying different games, which is also a key element in reinforcing language and culture immersion.

However, one of the main shortcomings of this metaverse is the sense of emptiness, that is, a lack of users, at certain times. As mentioned before, once the novelty of the proposal fades away, it is difficult to keep an engaged audience, and consequently the challenge consists in making this a lasting project. To do so, the Sejong Institute schedules monthly special events, promoted to gather students in the metaverse and also to convey Korean cultural elements. These activities take on the concept of gamification. Users can participate in group events such as quizzes and move their avatar towards the correct answer or type it. For example, for the lunar new year in 2024, there was an event about Korean winter snacks (see Figure 6.4).

Figure 6.4 Sejong's metaverse's special Seollal event instructions
(*Source:* zep.us/@ksif)

As can be seen in Figure 6.4, the Sejong Institute incentivizes participation in these events by providing a chance to earn Amazon gift cards. In the case of the event represented in Figure 6.4, students could follow a real-time cooking class in Korean, through which instructors ensured interaction using cultural quizzes. As can be seen in Figure 6.4, students are invited to cook the snacks themselves and submit their pictures for a chance of earning an Amazon gift card. It has been known for a long time (e.g., Dale, 1946) that actively simulating real experiences while learning supports retention of the material learned more than studying done through conventional textbooks, for example, and SLA research also shows how meaningful interactions positively impact the language acquisition process. Therefore, the experience of listening to a cooking class in Korean and imitating the steps shown could potentially become a valuable learning experience that will be remembered by students. This learning by doing aspect can be associated with what Zhang et al. (2022) defined as **learning objectives**. While in the traditional classroom, learning and screen-based remote learning are concentrated on the development of low-order cognitive skills (remembering, understanding, and applying), "metaverses enable learners to engage in various types of learning activities such as group work, creative learning or inquiry-based learning regardless of whether they are in classes or not" (Zhang et al., 2022, p. 10). Some of these learning activities seem to require a higher investment in activity development by instructors. Regarding this aspect, it must be kept in mind that the Sejong Institute metaverse allows smooth interaction between peers and a common place to practice their skills and also allows the instructors to design collaborative activities for students and immersive roleplay exercises where students can practice grammar patterns and vocabulary. Activities that use game elements so that learners find information on words or topics on their own are used. It must be noted that the more or less active use of such innovative gamification-related activities depends on the instructor, and it is difficult to quantify to what extent they play a role in the regular curriculum of metaverse-based courses.

4.3 Assessment

Finally, when it comes to **learning assessment**, Zhang et al. (2022) compare the limitations of learning results in conventional learning environments (largely collected through tests and other assignments) to the possibilities of collecting data through learning logging technologies. One of the main differences lies in the fact that such a collection of user-related data makes it possible to assess learners' performance progressively along time (Zhang et al., 2022). Regarding this, it is very significant that one of the Sejong Institute's metaverse instructors mentioned in her interview that she no longer felt a lack of communication in remote classes once she learned how to interpret student avatar movements (Sejong Institute, 2023b).

Metaverses' higher degree of movement freedom seems to make it more difficult to assess participation and students' progresses. However, this issue could be technologically solved if instructors received analytical data on learners' performance, as some teaching-oriented applications already do. For example, the app

Kahoot, which has become widely used for vocabulary acquisition tests, offers instructors reports on students' performance. ZEP already embeds paid functions, such as the Data Dashboard, that allow one to track number of visitors, object interaction, and other information, although it does not provide an education-oriented assessment tool yet.

5. Pedagogical implications

In its current state, the most positive aspects of the Sejong Institute's metaverse can be summarized as follows:

1. The possibility of creating a community that connects students from the Sejong Institute's centers around the world in their process of learning Korean.
2. The possibility of communicating in Korean and practicing with instructors, volunteers, peer learners, and AI bots.
3. Improved learner interaction, such as more realistic role-plays, compared to conventional online and offline learning spaces.

It is important to emphasize that most of the negative aspects experienced by users of metaverse are related to technology availability and adaptation. For example, in Kong and Kim (2022), users provided generally positive feedback on the use of the metaverse in the Korean language class but also noted negative aspects, such as "it was difficult to move around," "the laptop did not work well, which was frustrating," or "even a short usage could cause dizziness" (Kong & Kim, 2022, p. 3610). Other studies, such as Jang (2021), also highlighted the importance of having a fast internet connection to participate in this kind of class. While the ZEP metaverse may not be the most advanced option in terms of metaverses, its easy accessibility aligns with the Sejong Institute's goals of reaching a world-wide audience.

When it comes to adaptation time, most users can easily learn how to navigate the metaverse with a simple orientation session. Instructors may need to invest more time to prepare class materials, but it is also important to note that, similarly to conventional classes, those materials can be saved and become available for the future so that the initial time investment is justified in the long term.

While adapting the whole class to a ZEP-based metaverse may be challenging, the metaverse itself can be seen as an excellent complement, especially when it comes to tasks oriented towards oral and written production, because it offers dynamic and realistic ways to make the students feel immersed in the learning process.

6. Conclusions

Science fiction works have speculated for decades about a future in which a digital world would become a substitute for or a parallel experience of significant importance in people's lives. As people had restricted mobility during the COVID-19 pandemic, the situation triggered a significant interest in metaverse-related technologies and their potential in different areas.

Exploring the possibilities and limits of metaverse 111

It is important to emphasize that this interest, which reached its peak during the pandemic, also decreased drastically afterwards, when on-site activities started to be carried out again. This trend can be verified through Figure 6.5, which illustrates data collected by Google about the number of searches for the term "metaverse" in their search engine.

The downward trend shown in Figure 6.5 should not be interpreted as a failure of metaverses, because other statistics point out an increasing number of metaverse users and investment in related industries every year. For example, it is said that every month the metaverse attracts over 400 million active participants (Sagar, 2023). While many of these metaverses are game oriented, there are all sorts of projects involving them. Some initially conventional games such as Fortnite have also transitioned to a metaverse-like model in which users can enjoy concerts and socialize in different ways (Tassi, 2023). In such a context, it is to be expected that more research for its application to language learning will be carried out soon.

When it comes to the analyzed case based on ZEP, one of the main strengths of the Sejong Institute metaverse is that it has the potential to gather students from their institutes all around the world into a single virtual space, fostering a sense of community and allowing Korean language learners to practice among themselves and share their interest in Korean culture. At the same time, through the recruitment of instructors, the Sejong Institute can provide immersive classes for learners who cannot afford to attend physical centers or to study in Korea due to their geographical locations or economic circumstances. For example, recently there have been proposals for Korean learning metaverse-related projects that include mock interviews for Vietnamese Korean language major students who are hopping to get a job in a Korean company after their graduation (Yun & Dillan, 2023). These kinds of projects intend to capitalize on the increasing economic relations between the two countries and remove geographical barriers using digital environments.

Like other metaverses, the Sejong Institute's proposal offers the possibility for students to socialize through avatars, which may have a positive impact on learning anxiety. Learners may perceive their interaction increased, and the digital setup is helpful to carry out cooperative learning activities in groups, in contrast to conventional learning environments. The metaverse world also provides an interaction with instructors and AI bots. As mentioned by Jang (2021), this environment

Figure 6.5 Number of Google searches for the term "metaverse" over time collected from Google trends[2]

facilities a transition to a less teacher-led learning where instructors act as facilitators and lesson designers and students take a more active role in their learning processes.

Perhaps one of the weaknesses of the Sejong Institute metaverse, in the long term, is the base technology. In the metaverse industry, changes occur fast, and while ZEP is an intuitive, easy-to-use service to create virtual worlds, its 2D interface seems less immersive than hyperrealistic 3D or VR-related services (see Kim & Kim, Chapter 5). For example, unlike other platforms like Immerse or Mondly VR, ZEP does not integrate VR headset technology. This feature is not only related to visualization but also movement. For example, through platforms like Immerse, language students can experience activities such as cooking a burger, which requires them to coordinate all their senses and makes the task much more immersive than pen-based learning (Wu et al., 2023). While Immerse is available so far in only three languages, Mondly VR offers 30 languages, including Korean. Mondly VR offers language learners recreations of situational conversations; however, according to the mixed opinions provided by reviewers, it seems that Mondly VR has many aspects to improve for appropriate use in Korean language instruction. Moreover, although VR headsets may become affordable in the future, nowadays they are still expensive, and exploring platforms like ZEP, which are free, seems the best option to reach a larger audience. Another challenge for metaverses to become broadly used is the heterogeneous nature of these technologies. Since they are not integrated in a single digital environment and multiple metaverses are available to users, it will be challenging to create lasting projects for institutions without large networks. In that regard, it seems if the Sejong Institute continues investing in and promoting its metaverse, it could have potential to become a meaningful learning resource for learners around the world.

Notes

1 For a recent example, see: The metaverse: Shaping the future of the internet and business through AI integration. *Forbes*. Retrieved Last March 25, 2024, www.forbes.com/sites/forbestechcouncil/2023/09/18/the-metaverse-shaping-the-future-of-the-internet-and-business-through-ai-integration/?sh=1ae105dfeab7.
2 https://trends.google.com/trends/explore?date=all&q=metaverse&hl=es

References

Bailey, F., & Fahad, A. K. (2021). Krashen revisited: Case study of the role of input, motivation and identity in second language learning. *Arab World English Journal*, *12*(2), 540–550.
Dale, E. (1946). *Audiovisual methods in teaching*. The Dryden Press.
Dulay, H., & Burt, M. (1977). Remarks on creativity in language acquisition. In M. Burt, H. Dulay, & M. Finocchiaro (Eds.), *Viewpoints on English as a second language* (pp. 95–126). Regents Press.
Garrido-Iñigo, P., & Rodríguez-Moreno, F. (2015). The reality of virtual worlds: Pros and cons of their application to foreign language teaching. *Interactive Learning Environments*, *23*(4), 453–470. https://doi.org/10.1080/10494820.2013.788034

Gye, B., Han, N., Kim, E., Park, Y., & Jo, S. (2021). Educational applications of metaverse: Possibilities and limitations. *Journal of Educational Evaluation for Health Professions*, 18. https://doi.org/10.3352/jeehp.2021.18.32

Gye, B., Lee, D., Lee, E., Jo, A., Kim, E., & Kwon, M. (2023). *Design research on future education learning environments based on the metaverse*. Korea Education and Research Information Service.

Jang, J. (2021). A study on a Korean speaking class based on metaverse: Using Gather.town. *Journal of Korean Language Education, 32*(4), 279–301.

Jeong, Y., & Seo, E. (2022). A study on design and operation of Korea immigration and integration program (KIIP) class using metaverse: Focusing on level 4 "Korean language and Korean culture." *Multicultural Content Research, 41*, 312–331.

Kong, H., & Kim, Y. (2022). Satisfaction survey and demand analysis study on metaverse-using classes for learners majoring in Korean language education. *Humanities and Social Sciences, 13*(5), 3603–3617.

Krashen, S. (1981). *Second language acquisition and second language learning*. Pergamon Press.

Lee, B., & Choi, E. (2022). A study on beginner Korean speaking education using metaverse: Focusing on metaverse platform ZEP. *Culture and Convergence, 44*(10), 99–115. https://doi.org/10.33645/cnc.2022.10.44.10.99

Park, S., & Kim, S. (2022). Identifying world types to deliver gameful experiences for sustainable learning in the metaverse. *Sustainability, 14*(1361). https://doi.org/10.3390/su14031361

Plass, J. L., Homer, B. D., & Kinzer, C. K. (2015). Foundations of game-based learning. *Educational Psychologist, 40*(4), 258–283.

Ryu, S. (2022). An exploratory study on the possibility of metaverse-based Korean language subject design. *Korean Journal of General Education, 16*(2), 289–305. https://doi.org/10.46392/kjge.2022.16.2.289

Sagar, J. (2023, September 25). *52 Metaverse statistics that will shape our virtual world*. LearnG2. https://learn.g2.com/metaverse-statistics

Sejong Institute. (2023a, March 27). *Learn and speak Korean easily with 'Metaverse Sejong Hakdang!'* Retrieved March 25, 2024, from www.ksif.or.kr/cop/bbs/selectBoardArticle.do?nttId=9220000004880&bbsId=BBSMSTR_000000000071

Sejong Institute. (2023b, December 1). *Instructor Park Geun-young of metaverse King Sejong Institute, exploring the possibilities of metaverse Korean learning*. Retrieved March 25, 2024, from www.ksif.or.kr/cop/bbs/selectBoardArticle.do?nttId=9220000005794&bbsId=BBSMSTR_000000000141&pageIndex=1

Sejong Institute. (2023c). *Korean-speaking supporter Hong Hyun-jin, a friend of learners at Metaverse King Sejong Institute*. www.ksif.or.kr/cop/bbs/selectBoardArticle.do?nttId=9220000005795&bbsId=BBSMSTR_000

Sejong Institute. (2024). *We build Korea all over the world. The power that makes the world dream of Korea! It is in the King Sejong Institute*. Retrieved April 30, 2024, from www.ksif.or.kr/ste/ksf/hkd/lochkd.do?menuNo=31101100

Seok, J. (2023). Exploratory application research of special purpose Korean language education in the metaverse. *Journal of Language and Literature, 94*, 325–363. https://doi.org/10.15565/jll.2023.3.93.325

Tassi, P. (2023, December 10). 'Fortnite' has actually made the metaverse after everyone else quit. *Forbes*. www.forbes.com/sites/paultassi/2023/12/10/fortnite-has-actually-made-the-metaverse-after-everyone-else-quit/?sh=17fbc6ab45e8

Um, T., Kim, H., Kim, H., Lee, J., Koo, C., & Chung, N. (2022). Travel Incheon as a metaverse: Smart tourism cities development case in Korea. In *Information and Communication Technologies in Tourism 2022, Proceedings of the ENTER 2022 eTourism Conference* (pp. 226–231). Springer.

Vygotsky, L. (1978). *Mind in society: The development of higher psychological processes.* Harvard University Press.

Wu, J. G., Zhang, D., & Lee, S. M. (2023). Into the brave new metaverse: Envisaging future language teaching and learning. *IEEE Transactions on Learning Technologies.* https://doi.org/10.1109/TLT.2023.3259470

Yun, S., & Dillan, H. (2023). A basic study on the metaverse platform for Korean language education in businesses. *Culture and Convergence, 45*(6), 89–101.

Zhang, X., Chen, Y., Hu, L., & Wang, Y. (2022). The metaverse in education: Definition, framework, features, potential applications, challenges, and future research topics. *Frontiers in Psychology, 13*, 1016300. https://doi.org/10.3389/fpsyg.2022.1016300

7 Using a YouTube channel as a supplementary language teaching and learning platform

Myounghee Cho

1. Introduction

YouTube is a Web 2.0 tool that allows users to share, view, and comment on videos (Brook, 2011). As an online video repository, it provides extensive information and content. Also, as a social media platform, it allows users to communicate via the Internet. YouTube was launched in 2005, and it has become one of the most popular social media platforms. As of 2019, YouTube was the second most visited website in the world, right behind Google and ahead of Facebook (De Bérail et al., 2019), and in 2021 it reached 38 million channels and 2 billion active users worldwide (Ahmad et al., 2021). YouTube is one of the most popular smartphone applications in Korea (Kim & Kim, 2021), and it is the most popular social media platform in the US, with an average of 91% of Americans aged 18 to 49 using it as of January 2023 (Pew Research Center, 2024). Additionally, YouTube also provides young generations with a "participatory culture" that may affect their development (Chau, 2010, p. 65). By actively engaging in creation, collaboration, and sharing, young individuals benefit from informal mentorship and guidance, and they feel socially connected to peers within the community.

In language education, as an online video repository with extensive information and content, YouTube provides potential benefits in terms of video and audio materials. These benefits include increased exposure to authentic use of language and authentic cultural context (Cho, 2019), as well as the opportunity to enhance multiple language skills, such as listening, pronunciation, vocabulary development, and conversational skills. Studies on the use of YouTube in language classrooms also suggest that it is beneficial for a variety of language learning and teaching activities that promote autonomous and student-centered learning and develop collaboration skills (Brook, 2011; DeWitt et al., 2013; Watkins & Wilkins, 2011).

By enabling users to connect media creation and social networking, YouTube can also serve as a platform for student-generated and student-centered authentic activities. Students can create and share videos and engage in peer feedback for their own YouTube videos or vlogs (Brook, 2011; Orús et al., 2016; Saiful, 2019). Additionally, integrating the practice of viewing, creating, and sharing YouTube videos into language education can also appeal to students, the so-called "digital natives" generation. Thus, YouTube can be used to bridge the gap between

DOI: 10.4324/9781032725307-10

satisfying students' diverse learning needs and meeting the demands of language teaching (Terantino, 2011).

Although there are general concerns involving copyright infringement, privacy, and safety that have made YouTube controversial (Jones & Cuthrell, 2011), its diverse content and organic community interactivity have led to the widespread use of YouTube videos in all educational stages (Pattier, 2021) and across diverse educational sectors (Ranga, 2017).

I have also utilized YouTube for various pedagogical purposes for my Korean as a Foreign Language (KFL) learners at the University of Rochester. Through available YouTube videos and channels, I design teaching materials and class activities and projects. Before class, I play YouTube videos related to Korean language and culture to create a relaxing atmosphere and provide increased exposure to the target culture (Lang, 2015; Cho, 2022). Moreover, I utilize YouTube videos related to class materials to reinforce students' learning (Cho, 2022). Additionally, I design theme-based activities and projects incorporating YouTube videos and channels with specific themes, such as unboxing videos and the *Sebasi Talk* channel, a Korean version of TED Talks or TED-X Talks.

This use of YouTube may seem similar to that of other educators; however, I tried to go one step further and created a YouTube channel to support those students' learning needs that cannot be fully addressed in class and during office hours, mainly due to time constraints. Although there are studies discussing teachers' use of YouTube as a platform to teach language (Raj et al., 2019) and specific YouTube channels to improve listening and pronunciation skills (Indriani, 2021), the literature rarely addresses the figure of the teacher/YouTuber who utilizes a YouTube channel as a supplementary teaching and learning platform alongside a traditional learning management system (LMS). Ranga (2017) used a YouTube channel, although his channel was primarily used as a storage space for customized chemistry course videos. He uploaded the links to the videos on his course LMS. Since the videos were unlisted on YouTube, students could access them only via the links on the LMS. On the contrary, the videos on the YouTube channel discussed in this chapter can be accessed by anybody and in any circumstance, allowing students to watch them for immediate and general learning purposes based on their needs and convenience.

In the next section, I will provide background information on the creation of the channel, its content, and its utilities from both users' and teachers' perspectives. Following this, I will present the challenges I encountered in creating the channel, along with suggestions for educator-creators who are considering starting their own channel.

2. YouTube channel as a supplementary Korean language teaching and learning platform

The channel I created is 제시카의 Vlog (Jessica's Vlog) (see Figure 7.1). Jessica is my avatar, known to my students as their fellow Korean language learner. I used this name for the channel to make it appear friendly to students.

The channel started with two playlists containing grammar tutorials for two elementary-level courses. While it has expanded over time by adding supportive

Using a YouTube channel as a learning platform 117

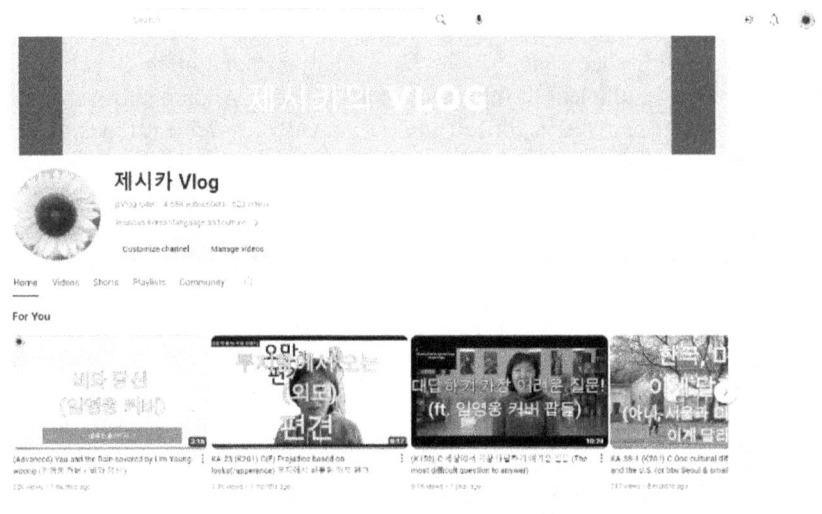

Figure 7.1 Jessica's Vlog – YouTube channel

materials to reflect students' immediate and general learning needs, the channel has evolved into a supplementary teaching and learning platform for both my students and the instructor.

Videos on the channel are recorded in Korean, English, or both languages, according to the purposes of the content. Most videos recorded in Korean provide the option for watching them with Korean captions, English subtitles, or both. The videos are intentionally made short, typically no longer than ten minutes, as students are more engaged and focused when watching short videos (Slemmons et al., 2018). The titles of the playlists and the videos include proficiency levels to help learners select videos appropriate for their course or proficiency level. The playlists are updated with new or revised videos, and the frequency of updates varies for each playlist. However, on average, the channel is updated once a week.

The channel link is provided on the LMS for all courses that I teach, but students are not required to utilize the channel. At the beginning of a semester, I briefly introduce the channel to the students, focusing on its contents and playlists and emphasize that it was created for educational purposes to provide them with additional support, and they are not required to subscribe to it. During the semester, when I make videos useful for supporting my students' ongoing learning, I email the links to them along with a brief description of the content. Students can then decide whether to watch the videos based solely on their individual needs.

2.1 Background of the YouTube channel's creation

In this section, I will explain students' diverse support needs, which motivated me to pursue a platform accessible beyond the confines of the traditional LMS and outline the reasons why I chose YouTube for this purpose.

Students' different types of needs for teacher's assistance

Student needs differ according to individual situations, and often class time and office hours are insufficient to fully address all of them. Additionally, scheduling conflicts sometimes make it difficult to find mutually convenient times between teacher and the individual student. Furthermore, struggling students are those who sometimes hesitate to ask for help, fearing that they will take up too much of the instructor's time. Through the YouTube channel, I wanted to resolve the issues.

Since students' proficiency levels are not clear cut and classes are heterogeneous, some students continue to struggle despite repeated instructions and additional support, while others seek additional and challenging materials to enhance their proficiency at their own pace. The videos can be used as a form of self-directed learning by both types of students. Finally, some students are unable to enroll in the next higher-level course in the following semester and must wait one academic year or more, and these students often express concerns about forgetting what they had learned previously. Along with these students, some others prefer to continue studying Korean on their own after completing their language requirements or graduating from university. The students as well typically access the material on the YouTube channel.

Reasons for choosing YouTube as a platform

I chose YouTube to support students' independent learning for two reasons. First, YouTube is ubiquitous among language learners. Many Korean language learners have mentioned their use of YouTube videos and channels for learning Korean language and culture. For example, they emphasized that even watching entertaining YouTube videos and channels not specifically designed for Korean language learners helps them learn Korean and Korean culture. These observations align with Watkins and Wilkins' (2011) findings, namely that YouTube can facilitate language learning both inside and outside of the classrooms. Second, YouTube channels are often user friendly, in terms of user experience; therefore this suggests that a YouTube channel would make it easier for educators to organize content by themes or playlists, enabling users to easily navigate the content.

2.2 Content of the channel

The channel contains various content on the Korean language and culture, organized into five themes designed to help students with their ongoing learning. The following elaborates on the content theme by theme, explaining the intended purpose of each theme.

Theme 1. Grammar tutorials

This theme has four playlists, titled *K101*, *K102*, *K151*, and *K152* and corresponding respectively to four courses: Elementary Korean 1 and 2 and Intermediate

Korean 1 and 2. The videos are listed in line with the learning progression within each course. Providing grammar tutorial videos was the original theme of the channel. Similarly to Rogerson (2003, p. 163), who said that "even after classes or meetings where I felt I had explained things very well, there were students for whom the answer to the exam was not obvious," instructors often encounter situations where they need to provide students with further explanations or repeat instructions for grammar. These tutorial videos are thus prepared for students' quick reviews or previews of grammar points that they have learned or will learn in class, catering to self-paced, self-directed learners.

Theme 2. Culture

This theme has one playlist titled *Jessica's Fun Experiences in the US*. It is intended to help students gain insight into Korean culture while enhancing their skills in listening and vocabulary. This theme highlights cultural comparisons and differences between the US and Korea that I discovered while living in the US. By moving to the US in my early forties, I witnessed many differences between the two countries from an adult's perspective, particularly regarding living styles and ways of thinking. These differences may differ from those discovered by young Korean students while living and studying in the US and are often different from those generally found in resources designed for Korean language learning. Information now readily crosses international borders through social media, and lifestyles change rapidly; therefore it is not easy to keep the content updated. Nevertheless, students can gain valuable insights into Korean through the understanding of cultural differences.

Theme 3. Jessica's Korean class

This theme has one playlist titled *J's Korean* and contains supplementary teaching and learning materials including texts from Korean literature (e.g., poems and essays), customized videos for in-class teaching, content requested by students (e.g., Korean proverbs and idioms), demonstrations of corrections for incorrect usages of Korean words, expressions and treatment of common errors made by students. Regarding error correction and demonstrations, I use students' speaking and writing samples reflecting their current struggles, with their permission. These videos enable me to provide not only visual and verbal feedback but also meaningful instruction-combined feedback (Hattie & Timperley, 2007) rather than corrections alone. Considering that language learners have a preference to receive individualized and corrective feedback (Brown, 2009; Caruso et al., 2019), these videos are some of the most useful.

Theme 4. Jessica's daily life

The theme has one playlist with the same title. It is intended to provide Korean expressions associated with daily life. Additionally, it aims to bridge the gap between teacher and student. As a teacher, by sharing my daily life and interests with the students, I aim to foster a friend-like interaction and alleviate learning anxiety (Young, 1991). The playlist contains videos showing daily activities such as cooking Korean foods, traveling with my family and friends, and chatting about Korean singers. Additionally, some videos recorded in Korea provide insights into Korean life and culture, such as riding the subway, singing in a *noraebang* (karaoke), and enjoying *chimaek* (chicken and beer).

Theme 5. Conversation samples per grammar point

This theme consists of two playlists designed for two courses: Elementary Korean 2 and Intermediate Korean 1. These playlists contain audio conversation samples to support students' understanding of the usages of grammar points presented in each course within a conversational context. Two native Korean students at my university, hired with the support of the university's teaching center, created one short and one long conversation sample for each grammar point. The description of each video includes the script along with English translations. These conversation samples demonstrate how grammar points are used in a real-world and everyday life context rather than in textbook scripts drafted on purpose (Nunan, 1998). Additionally, these samples can help students gain a deeper understanding of the way Korean university students converse.

2.3 Users and usage patterns of the channel

The channel has approximately 4000 subscribers (as of March 2024). Considering that many students use the channel without subscribing to it, the number of subscribers does not represent the real regular users of the channel. In terms of composition, and based on the subscribers to the channel, comments left on the videos, and comments received from current students during face-to-face interactions and through email, it is possible to estimate that the users consist of three groups: my (current and former) students, general public viewers (mostly Koreans), and other Korean language learners. The following sections illustrate how these different users interact with the channel.

My students

Both the feedback from current students and the number of views of videos on the channel indicate that elementary-level learners are the most frequent users compared to the other groups. The playlist they most frequently visit is *Grammar Tutorials*, followed by *J's Korean* and *Jessica's Daily Life*. Regarding grammar tutorial videos, students watch them to reinforce their understanding, do homework, and prepare for lesson tests and exams. Some students watch them along with the class slides uploaded on the LMS, especially when they miss a class. Some students even watch the videos from previously taken courses to review what they learned. Students' comments align with those reported in Ranga (2017), where he used customized videos, despite the different accessibility. It also appears that students across different proficiency levels watch *J's Korean* for correction demonstrations, focusing on errors they commonly make and incorrect usage of Korean words and expressions. Regarding *Jessica's Daily Life*, students watch the videos for fun, and they enjoy reading the comments added to the videos. Therefore, the use they make of these videos is generally not for learning purposes. The comments left on the videos also indicate that some former students regularly visit and watch the videos from the playlists *J's Korean* and *Jessica's Daily Life*.

Other Korean language learners

It seems other Korean language learners, beyond the students enrolled in the courses I teach, watch the videos related to Korean language learning, such as grammar tutorial videos and videos in the *J's Korean* playlist. This suggests that although the channel was originally created for my own students, it can serve as a supportive learning platform for a diverse group of Korean language learners, including self-directed, web-based, informal learners.

General public viewers

Most of these users are ethnic Koreans and therefore not Korean language learners. Once I attended my favorite Korean singer's concert in LA and subsequently uploaded a review video of the concert to *Jessica's Daily Life*. The video unexpectedly attracted the singer's fans, many of whom have since subscribed to the channel. These unexpected users engage with and actively comment on the videos, mostly on those related to the singer. This group of users also seem to watch videos in other playlists – *Jessica's fun experiences in the US* and *Jessica's Korean* – to learn about life in the US and get used to the English idiomatic expressions presented in the videos. While these users were originally unexpected, their comments serve as a further resource to design class activities.

2.4 Usefulness of the channel as a supplementary teaching and learning platform

The channel has three major benefits when it is used as a supporting and additional teaching platform.

Assistance at students' fingertips

The most useful aspect of the channel is that it enables students to access assistance based on their needs and convenience, freeing them from time conflicts and the burden of requesting meetings. If students know where to find the content they need on the channel, then they can watch the videos at their convenience as often as they want. When students reach out via email for help, I include a link to the relevant video along with a brief comment in my response. This enables students to receive verbal and visual explanations, at the same time helping the instructor saving a considerable amount of time used to write lengthy email explanations. The feedback received from students is consistently positive, and students often express gratitude for sharing the videos. It seems the channel bridges language learning and digital humanities (Blyth & Thoms, 2021), as my students engage with both traditional language learning materials and interact with digital content and online resources. The use of the channel therefore aligns with the broader trend in education, leading towards incorporating technology to enhance learner experience. While some students still prefer to receive help through face-to-face meetings, the number of students visiting face-to-face for support has decreased since the launch of the channel.

Building rapport with my students and adding fun to class

Making the videos on the channel publicly available has unexpectedly attracted an audience beyond the students for whom the videos were originally created, and it increased the number of views and comments. This aspect further added an element of fun to my own classes, since students consistently mention the videos and the number of views of videos they have watched, making this a common topic of conversations in and out of class. In other words, talking about the videos itself has helped in building a good relationship between the students and the teacher, thus fostering teacher's role as a supportive friend and increasing learners' motivation (Dörnyei & Csizér, 1998; Horwitz, 2001; Young, 1991). Considering these kinds of interactions, it is possible to assume that the channel helps in creating low-anxiety learning environments (regarding classroom emotions, see also Fraschini and Tao, Chapter 8).

Storing resources for (supplemental) class materials and activities

The channel also serves as a repository of resources for class materials and activities. To begin with, the channel enables the teacher/administrator to provide supplementary language and culture materials that cannot be addressed in class due to time constraints. This material deals with content such as culture-related explanations, literary texts, and tutorials, all material specifically designed to address students' struggles and meet their requests. Some of the materials hosted on the platform are also used in the classroom, such as conversation samples, customized videos for use in class, and culture videos related to class topics.

The channel also enabled the instructor to design activities focused on real language use. For example, one such activity consisted in encouraging students to learn from native Koreans' language use by analyzing public viewers' comments posted to the videos. Another activity involved engaging students in watching a video and sharing similar experiences by posting their comments in Korean to the videos (see Figure 7.2).

It is important to acknowledge that using YouTube in class raises concerns related to privacy, safety, and potential exposure to inappropriate language and

Using a YouTube channel as a learning platform   123

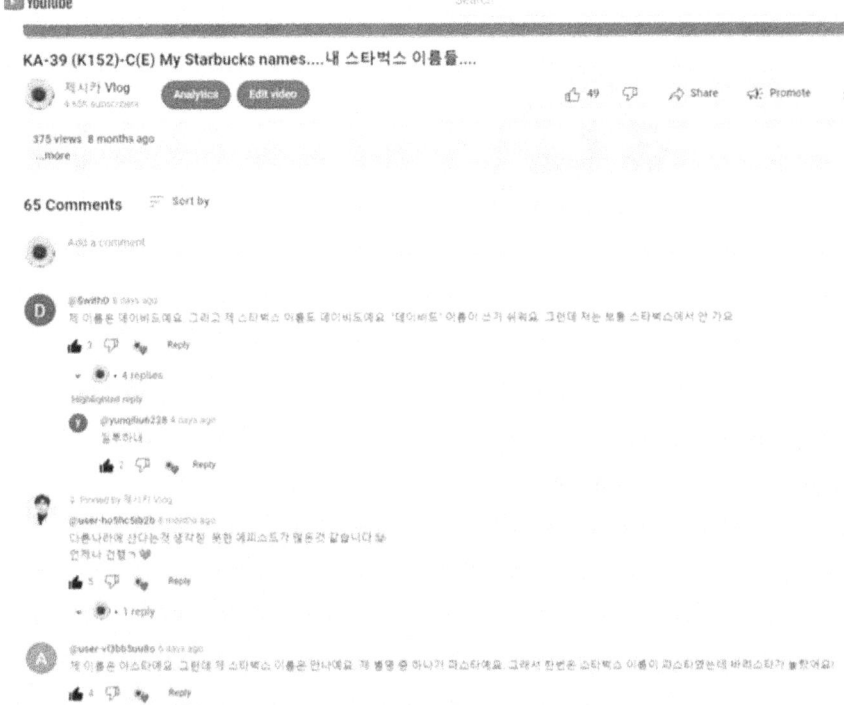

Figure 7.2 Students' activity: commenting on a YouTube video and others' comments on the Jessica's Vlog channel

content (Brook, 2011). However, the channel provided students with a relatively safe environment to engage in language learning activities, encountering less inappropriate language (e.g., slang, curses, etc.) compared to when they engaged in the similar activities using videos and channels they selected on their own.

3. Running a YouTube channel for educational purposes

Any Korean language instructor wishing to open an educational channel on YouTube can do this easily, since anyone with a free Google account is already provided with a blank YouTube channel. Instructors can build their channel by designing and adding content via the YouTube Studio page (see Figure 7.3). Running an educational channel, beyond the benefits described so far, also opens the potential for easily sharing educators' expertise with other learners and teachers.

However, educators wishing to open their own YouTube channel need to bear in mind that the creation and management of such a channel involve several challenges. The following section illustrates some of these challenges along with possible solutions.

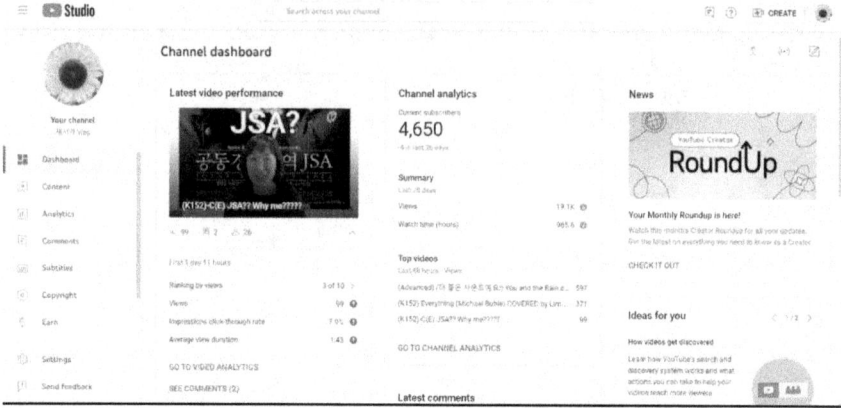

Figure 7.3 YouTube Studio page
Source: (from the Jessica's Vlog channel)

3.1 Challenges and solutions

Making a presence on YouTube and availability of the videos

The biggest challenge when establishing a presence on YouTube, a social media platform viewed by an unspecified public, is to establish a presence. Despite having accounts on other various social media platforms, at first I refrained from posting on most of them since I did not prioritize establishing a presence there.

I initially insisted on making tutorial videos featuring myself, strongly believing that a teacher's presence in the videos would lead to better learning outcomes. This belief was supported by the research conduct by Homer et al. (2008), who found that students with high visual preferences have greater cognitive load in videos without a teacher presence compared to students with low visual preferences, thereby negatively affecting the effectiveness of the videos. This aspect ultimately prompted me to create the channel, establish a presence on YouTube, and make the videos available to the general public. Educators can create videos featuring themselves and customize their visibility, with the possibility to select among private, unlisted, and public modes of visibility (see Figure 7.4).

Educators can restrict the visibility of videos to themselves by setting them to private. To share videos exclusively with their students, they can use the unlisted option and then integrate the links into their LMS, following the approach employed by Ranga (2017) in his courses. In the channel described in this chapter, the videos are set to public to make them available to former students. If videos are unlisted, they remain hidden on the channel, and subscribers do not receive notifications of new videos, making it challenging for both subscribed and general viewers to discover new and past content.

Using a YouTube channel as a learning platform 125

Figure 7.4 Three levels of video visibility
Source: (from the Jessica's Vlog channel)

Video quality and videography

Another personal challenge was the lack of skills in videography, photography, and editing, as video quality can impact the appearance of instructional presentations and how students perceive them (Heribanova et al., 2011). Many studies suggest that poor video quality can decrease attention and negatively affect students' perception and understanding of the content (Lange & Costley, 2020; Molnar, 2017). However, the convention that providing additional support to students through a purposively created YouTube channel does not necessarily require professional creators' knowledge and skills prompted the launch of the channel.

Most of the tutorial videos were created using Zoom and edited through Wondershare Filmora, but the editing involves only basic functions such as cutting, pasting, and adding subtitles. For skilled creators, better quality can be achieved also with common laptops or even with mobile phones.

Time commitment

The creation and maintenance of the channel demand a significant time commitment. Producing YouTube videos involves several steps: preparing script and instructional notes, recording and editing the video, adding captions and subtitles. Typically, it takes about three to five hours to create a video with content equivalent to a five-minute in-class delivery. In addition, teacher-creators must bear in mind the time commitment required to keep the channel updated with new and revised videos, since already uploaded videos need to be revised with fresh looks and updated content, because studies suggest that outdated videos can negatively impact students' engagement and attention (Perko et al., 2008). However, despite the time commitment, the benefits of the channel as an additional teaching and learning platform are worth the investment to maintain and update it. Having multiple playlists with various topics can also increase the time commitment because of the range of themes to be covered. Over the long term, focusing on one or two topics or playlists will make it more feasible to have one's own YouTube channel for teaching purposes.

Enhancing the effectiveness of videos by adding Korean captions and English subtitles

For videos recorded in Korean, originally a full script in the video's description along with brief English translations was provided; however, now the videos include Korean captions, English subtitles, or both so that viewers can choose the viewing modality they prefer. This change stems from comments from users indicating that videos with Korean captions and English subtitles were more helpful in supporting understanding and learning. These comments align with many studies suggesting that captioning enables language learners to connect auditory to visual input (Garza, 1991), thus aiding vocabulary recognition, retention, and overall comprehension of the videos, (Winke et al., 2010). Additionally, videos with both L1 captions and L2 subtitles improve listening comprehension compared to videos with L2 subtitles only (Dizon & Thanyawatpokin, 2021).

Adding captions and subtitles increases the time commitment, but it can be easily done by AI tools or by using auto-generated captions, which are typically available a couple of hours after a video is added to the channel. Nevertheless, since auto-generated captions and subtitles do not always accurately convey the spoken messages and captions in the video, they need to be checked for mistakes.

3.2 Other YouTube channels created by educators and open educational resources

Educators interested in creating a YouTube channel but finding it challenging can refer to YouTube channels created by other educators for insights into the design and maintenance of their own channel. These insights may include aspects of video design and quality, playlists and content organization, and update frequency, among others. Although these channels offer a variety of different materials, they are all intended for learners, educators, and others interested in the field, thus holding great potential as open educational resources (OER).

YouTube videos as open educational resources?

OERs are educational materials allowed to be freely accessible, reused, revised, remixed, and redistributed (Wiley, 2013) for the purpose of providing them at low or no costs to those who otherwise would not have access to them (Mishra, 2017). YouTube videos (and other online materials) allowed for public views are often mistaken for OER. However, within academia, only materials with an open license such as a Creative Commons Attribution license (CC BY) can be regarded and used as OER free from any concerns associated with copyright issues.

Figure 7.5 Applying a CC-BY license to YouTube videos
Source: (from Jessica's Vlog Channel)

Creative Commons is an international non-profit organization that empowers people to grow and sustain commons of shared knowledge and culture. Its license allows others to distribute, remix, adapt, and build upon the material in any medium or format, even commercially, as long as they acknowledge the creator's contribution (Creative Commons, 2024). However, it does not grant permission to use the creator's work in a way that suggests the creator endorsed or approved the user's work. Additionally, if others use the material, they may not be required to license they own works under the same terms (Creative Commons, 2024).

YouTube channels have the potential to be used as open educational resources due to their ease of sharing with public viewers. Additionally, it is simple to apply CC BY licenses to YouTube videos. If educator-creators want to share their materials as OER, they only need to mark their videos with CC BY on the YouTube Studio page (see Figure 7.5). By doing so, they grant others the ability to reuse the same video for educational purposes without any concerns about copyright issues.

4. Discussion and conclusion

This chapter demonstrated the use of a YouTube channel as a supplementary language teaching and learning platform integrated in the teaching routing together with the course LMS. The channel, containing a variety of videos on the Korean language and culture, was initially created to provide students with additional support unavailable during the usual class time or consultation hours. As the channel expanded over time, it turned into a supplementary teaching and learning platform that benefits both students and the instructor.

The most significant benefit of the channel is that it enables students to access assistance based on their needs and convenience. The videos on the channel may not address all types of students' needs and may not be viewed by all of them. Nevertheless, the channel fits its purposes, as demonstrated by the positive comments posted by its users.

The channel was designed on the observation of students' needs, and content is continuously added to satisfy their requests. It should be acknowledged that if the channel had been created with a strict focus on students' voices and together with students' participation, its potential use and content may be now different. Some students have expressed interest toward specific topics, such as Korean idioms and example sentences, more frequently than such content was uploaded to the playlist *J's Korean*. More detailed background knowledge of students' needs, along with their active participation in the production of the videos, may have delivered playlists and contents more effectively tailored to their needs. Nevertheless, the channel serves as an online environment where language learners can engage in real-life activities without encountering undesirable language and negative online behavior.

Creating and maintaining a YouTube channel involves diverse challenges, such as a significant time commitment. Nevertheless, given students' positive feedback; the various benefits of the channel; and its further potential uses that have not yet been explored here, such as uploading student-generated content, it is worth considering having a YouTube channel as a supplementary teaching and learning platform. Additionally, allowing educational materials for public viewing has the potential for easy sharing as OER, leading to the need to explore further the influence and impact of educator-creators' YouTube channels in the evolving landscape of language teaching and learning through digital platforms.

References

Ahmad, P. M., Hikami, I., Zufar, B. N. F., & Syahfrullah, A. (2021). Digital labour: Digital capitalism and the alienation of YouTube content creators. *Journal of Asian Social Science Research, 3*(2), 167–184.

Blyth, C. S., & Thoms, J. J. (Eds.). (2021). *Open education and second language learning and teaching: The rise of a new knowledge ecology*. Multilingual Matters.

Brook, J. (2011). The affordances of YouTube for language learning and teaching. *Hawaii Pacific University TESOL Working Paper Series, 9*(1, 2), 37–56.

Brown, A. V. (2009). Students' and teachers' perceptions of effective foreign language teaching: A comparison of ideals. *The Modern Language Journal, 93*(1), 46–60.

Caruso, M., Fraschini, N., & Kuuse, S. (2019). Online tools for feedback engagement in foreign language learning. *International Journal of Computer-Assisted Language Learning and Teaching, 9*(1), 68–78.

Chau, C. (2010). YouTube as a participatory culture. *New Directions for Youth Development, 128*, 65–74.

Cho, M. (2019). Film-incorporated curriculum: Adding authenticity and versatility to foreign language classrooms. *The Korean Language in America, 23*(1), 99–112.

Cho, M. (2022). Classroom activities for student engagement: 5 Minutes and survey project. In F. Carra-Salsberg, M. Figueredo, & M. Jeon (Eds.), *Curriculum design and praxis in language teaching: A globally informed approach* (pp. 198–208). University of Toronto Press.

Creative Commons. (2024). *Creative commons*. Retrieved May 6, 2024, from https://creativecommons.org/

De Bérail, P., Guillon, M., & Bungener, C. (2019). The relations between YouTube addiction, social anxiety and parasocial relationships with YouTubers: A moderated-mediation model based on a cognitive-behavioral framework. *Computers in Human Behavior, 99*, 190–204.

DeWitt, D., Alias, N., Siraj, S., Yaakub, M. Y., Ayob, J., & Ishak, R. (2013). The potential of Youtube for teaching and learning in the performing arts. *Procedia-Social and Behavioral Sciences, 103*, 1118–1126.

Dizon, G., & Thanyawatpokin, B. (2021). Language learning with Netflix: Exploring the effects of dual subtitles on vocabulary learning and listening comprehension. *Computer Assisted Language Learning*, *22*(3), 52–65.

Dörnyei, Z., & Csizér, K. (1998). Ten commandments for motivating language learners: Results of an empirical study. *Language Teaching Research*, *2*(3), 203–229.

Garza, T. J. (1991). Evaluating the use of captioned video materials in advanced foreign language learning. *Foreign Language Annals*, *24*(3), 239–258.

Hattie, J., & Timperley, H. (2007). The power of feedback. *Review of Educational Research*, *77*(1), 81–112.

Heribanova, P., Polec, J., Ondrušová, S., & Hosťovecký, M. (2011). Intelligibility of cued speech in video. *World Academy of Science, Engineering and Technology*, *79*, 492–496.

Homer, B. D., Plass, J. L., & Blake, L. (2008). The effects of video on cognitive load and social presence in multimedia-learning. *Computers in Human Behavior*, *24*(3), 786–797.

Horwitz, E. K. (2001). Language anxiety and achievement. *Annual Review of Applied Linguistics*, *21*, 112–126.

Indriani, K. S. (2021). Teachers' confidence in teaching English using YouTube channel in early pandemic Covid-19. *Jurnal Kependidikan*, *7*(1), 1–16.

Jones, T., & Cuthrell, K. (2011). YouTube: Educational potentials and pitfalls. *Computers in the Schools*, *28*(1), 75–85.

Kim, S., & Kim, H.-C. (2021). The benefits of YouTube in learning English as a second language: A qualitative investigation of Korean freshman students' experiences and perspectives in the U.S. *Sustainability*, *13*(13), 1–16.

Lang, J. M. (2015). Small changes in teaching: The five minutes before class. *The Chronicle of Higher Education*. www.chronicle.com/article/Small-Changes-in-Teaching-The/234178

Lange, C., & Costley, J. (2020). Improving online video lectures: Learning challenges created by media. *International Journal of Educational Technology in Higher Education*, *17*, 1–18.

Mishra, S. (2017). Open educational resources: Removing barriers from within. *Distance Education*, *38*(3), 369–380.

Molnar, A. (2017). Content type and perceived multimedia quality in mobile learning. *Multimedia Tools and Applications*, *76*(20), 21613–21627.

Nunan, D. (1998). Teaching grammar in context. *ELT Journal*, *52*(2), 101–109. https://doi.org/10.1093/elt/52.2.101

Orús, C., Barlés, M. J., Belanche, D., Casaló, L., Fraj, E., & Gurrea, R. (2016). The effects of learner-generated videos for YouTube on learning outcomes and satisfaction. *Computers & Education*, *95*, 254–269.

Pattier, D. (2021). Teachers and YouTube: The use of video as an educational resource. *Ricerche di Pedagogia e Didattica. Journal of Theories and Research in Education*, *16*(1), 59–77.

Perko, M. A., Chaney, E. H., Chaney, D. J., Gordon, B. C., & Eddy, J. M. (2008). Lessons lived: Development and discovery in health education distance programs. *The Health Education Monograph Series*, *25*(1), 11–17.

Pew Research Center. (2024). *Social media fact sheet*. www.pewinternet.org/fact-sheet/social-media/

Raj, S. A. S., Ann, W. H. T., Subramaniam, P. A., & Yunus, M. M. (2019). Using YouTube as a platform to learn social expression. *Creative Education*, *10*(2), 288–296.

Ranga, J. S. (2017). Customized videos on a YouTube channel: A beyond the classroom teaching and learning platform for general chemistry courses. *Journal of Chemical Education*, *94*(7), 867–872.

Rogerson, B. J. (2003). Effectiveness of a daily class progress assessment technique in introductory chemistry. *Journal of Chemical Education*, *80*(2), 160–164.

Saiful, J. A. (2019). EFL teachers' cognition in the use of YouTube vlog in English language teaching. *Journal of Foreign Language Education and Technology*, *4*(1), 72–91.

Slemmons, K., Anyanwu, K., Hames, J., Grabski, D., Mlsna, J., Simkins, E., & Cook, P. (2018). The impact of video length on learning in a middle-level flipped science setting: Implications for diversity inclusion. *Journal of Science Education and Technology, 27*, 469–479.

Terantino, J. (2011). YouTube for foreign languages: You have to see this video. *Language Learning & Technology, 15*(1), 10–16.

Watkins, J., & Wilkins, M. (2011). Using YouTube in the EFL classroom. *Language Education in Asia, 2*(1), 113–119.

Wiley, D. (2013). *What is open pedagogy? Improving learning.* https://opencontent.org/blog/archives/2975

Winke, P., Gass, S., & Sydorenko, T. (2010). The effects of captioning videos used for foreign language listening activities. *Language Learning & Technology, 14*(1), 65–86.

Young, D. J. (1991). Creating a low-anxiety classroom environment: What does language anxiety research suggest? *The Modern Language Journal, 75*(4), 426–439.

Part III
Moving beyond technology for innovation in Korean language teaching

8 Excitement and confusion

An emotion-based approach to Korean language teaching

Nicola Fraschini and Yu Tao

1. Introduction

Over the past two decades, research on emotions has significantly enriched our comprehension of the intricate relationship among language learners' affective responses, the classroom environment, and the language acquisition process. However, in the context of in-class instruction, much of the scholarly focus has been on examining how emotions impact learners' communicative abilities and their ultimate mastery of the language and, therefore, how emotions affect the goal of learning a foreign language. Regrettably, there has been comparatively less exploration into how emotions contribute to creating new knowledge in second language acquisition and how emotions affect the learning process of a foreign language.

In educational psychology, emotions associated with the acquisition of new knowledge are classified as epistemic emotions; examples include curiosity, epistemic anxiety, excitement, confusion, and frustration (Pekrun et al., 2017). As we have argued elsewhere (Fraschini & Tao, 2023), scrutinising epistemic emotions in the language classroom is essential for understanding how the learning environment elicits emotions that can either facilitate or obstruct the acquisition of an additional language.

Existing studies on Korean language learners reveal that the learning environment highly influences emotions within the language classroom, encompassing factors such as the nature of language learning activities (Fraschini, 2023) and the characteristics of the language teacher (Fraschini & Tao, 2021). In this chapter, we expand the range of epistemic emotions considered in second language acquisition (SLA) research by examining learners' confusion and excitement in relation to teacher behaviour and difficulty of the language learning task. Consequently, our findings have crucial pedagogical implications, affecting teacher behaviour and the design of learning activities and laying the ground for adopting pedagogical strategies and methods that harness the power of emotions to facilitate the language learning process.

2. Literature review

To contextualise our exploration and findings, we shall first provide an overview of the existing scholarly insights into the intricate role of epistemic emotions in

DOI: 10.4324/9781032725307-12

SLA. In particular, we focus on lesser-studied epistemic emotions, namely confusion and excitement. By weaving these epistemic emotions into a broader tapestry that includes intended effort and perceived difficulty, the following review sets the groundwork for a more nuanced understanding of epistemic emotions and their relevance to SLA.

2.1 Epistemic emotions and SLA research

For several decades, the role of emotions in SLA has intrigued researchers. In particular, this area has seen a notable uptick in scholarly attention in the last ten to fifteen years. Back in the seventies, the seminal work of Scovel (1978) paved the way for a series of investigations culminating in the conceptualisation of foreign language anxiety by Horwitz et al. (1986). These efforts later evolved into a more nuanced understanding of the emotional landscape of the language classroom, recently expressed in dynamic and complex terms by Gregersen (2020) and Oxford and Gkonou (2021).

While the vast majority of emotion research in instructed SLA has been focused on anxiety and on how this emotion affects the language learning process, the contributions of research on other emotions should not be overlooked. For example, MacIntyre and Gregersen (2012) were instrumental in integrating positive psychology into SLA research, opening avenues for inquiries into emotions such as enjoyment (Dewaele & MacIntyre, 2014), pride (Fraschini & Tao, 2021), and love (Pavelescu & Petrić, 2018). Further research, expanded to include boredom (Li et al., 2023), has illustrated how emotions are interconnected in learning a foreign language. Recent years have also witnessed the emergence of additional emotion-related constructs, including emotional intelligence (Li et al., 2021), grit (Sudina & Plonsky, 2021; Teimouri et al., 2020), and flow (Dewaele & MacIntyre, 2022a, 2022b).

Despite the growing body of research and the demonstration that emotions affect learning additional languages, a comprehensive understanding of the role of emotions in language classrooms remains elusive. The current understanding of the role of emotions in the language acquisition process is limited due to the complexity and the vast array of emotional experiences that human beings can undergo compared to the relatively limited number of emotions and language teaching settings taken so far into consideration by SLA researchers. Epistemic emotions are a particular category of emotions that has been virtually ignored so far by language learning and teaching researchers, but whose importance for the learning process has already been stressed by research conducted in educational psychology.

Epistemic emotions have been defined as emotions arising from "information-oriented appraisals about the alignment or misalignment between new information and existing beliefs" (Muis et al., 2018, p. 169). In other terms, epistemic emotions are associated with knowledge generation. They are experienced in situations where there is a clash between what is already known or believed and a new piece of information. Epistemic emotions include both positive feelings, like curiosity and enjoyment, as well as negative ones, such as anxiety and confusion (Chevrier et al., 2019). Since epistemic emotions are experienced when new knowledge is discovered or presented (Vogl et al., 2019), they often surface from complex and conflicting understandings (Chevrier et al., 2019).

In SLA, epistemic emotions hold particular relevance. Students' approaches to learning a new language are influenced by their interactions with the teacher, fellow students, and the learning activity. Furthermore, learners approach the study of a new language with their own understanding and belief of how a language should function, grounded in their past experiences. Therefore, the possibility of a clash between new information regarding the target language and previous knowledge and beliefs regarding language structures is high. Regrettably, only a handful of studies within SLA research have delved into the topic of epistemic emotions, primarily focusing on aspects of curiosity (Fraschini & Tao, 2023; Mahmoodzadeh & Khajavy, 2019; Nakamura et al., 2022). Thus, there remains much to explore in this underexamined yet crucial area, and this chapter focuses on two underexplored epistemic emotions in SLA research – confusion and excitement.

2.2 Confusion and excitement

Research in educational psychology has shown how confusion frequently emerges as a dominant emotion within the classroom (Di Leo et al., 2019; Geerling et al., 2020). Confusion occurs when learners cannot make sense of new information, therefore struggling to assimilate new knowledge into their previous one (Nerantzaki et al., 2021). Therefore, the experience of confusion often suggests that the learner perceives the task they are approaching as having low feasibility (Vazard & Audrin, 2021). Our decision to focus on confusion is grounded on the fact that this emotion is particularly relevant for the language learning classroom since it can be affected not only by the nature of the new information presented to the learners but also by the means of how this information is delivered (i.e., on the use more or less extensive of the target language or the learners' dominant language), as can be inferred by the results of Rusk et al. (2016).

D'Mello and Graesser (2012) conceptualise the state of confusion as "cognitive disequilibrium". When unresolved, this disequilibrium can lead to frustration or boredom (Di Leo et al., 2019); however, once addressed, it often gives way to positive emotions like enjoyment, excitement, or surprise (D'Mello & Graesser, 2012). Therefore, perhaps counterintuitively, confusion can also serve a constructive role as it can drive learners to readdress the cognitive imbalance, fostering a deeper comprehension of the subject matter (Chevrier et al., 2019; D'Mello et al., 2014). For example, it has been discovered that confusion, in contrast to frustration, can positively mediate between a learner's knowledge-related beliefs and the production of critical thinking (Muis et al., 2021) and can promote exploratory behaviour (Vogl et al., 2019).

How much a student feels in control of a particular academic activity and the value they put on that activity are among the triggers of epistemic emotions, including confusion (Pekrun et al., 2017). Perceptions of novelty, complexity, or an impasse also contribute to triggering confusion (Muis et al., 2018). Once experienced, confusion affects various aspects of learning, including goal-setting, motivation, cognitive strategies, and, ultimately, learning outcomes (Muis et al., 2018). Nevertheless, studies explicitly focused on confusion in SLA remain scant. Some research suggests that the extended use of a second language in the classroom can create epistemic imbalances, necessitating the use of learners' native language to re-establish an equilibrium (Rusk et al., 2016). Others, like Hong et al. (2023), propose that strategically designed "impasses" can induce productive confusion, thereby enhancing learning.

The other epistemic emotion considered in this chapter is excitement. This emotion is often viewed as an intensified form of enjoyment and interest (Ainley & Hidi, 2014). In the context of SLA, excitement has been less explicitly studied, though its close relative, enjoyment, has often been examined in relation to anxiety (Boudreau et al., 2018; Dewaele & MacIntyre, 2014). Subsequent research has highlighted the significant role of the teacher in eliciting enjoyment (Dewaele et al., 2018, 2022; Thumvichit, 2022), as well as its positive impact on learners' willingness to communicate and academic achievement (Botes et al., 2022). In this chapter we decided to focus on excitement because recent SLA research has demonstrated that this emotion is closely connected to a state of flow (Dewaele & MacIntyre, 2022a), therefore leading to better engagement and attainment of learning outcomes, and also because the experience of a higher level of enjoyment and a longer state of flow are more common in learners of languages other than English (Dewaele & MacIntyre, 2022b), which makes the Korean language classroom the optimal setting to observe this emotion.

The relationship between confusion and excitement or enjoyment has been explored, albeit with mixed findings. Some studies found a weak yet significant correlation between the two emotions (Muis et al., 2021), while others found either no correlation (Trevors et al., 2017) or a negative one (Schubert et al., 2023). Notably, Schubert et al. (2023) reported that confusion did not significantly affect learners' attention or motivation, unlike enjoyment.

In summary, existing studies emphasise the influential role of the teacher and pedagogical choices in shaping learners' experience of epistemic emotions. Notably, there is a call for further research into the triggers of these emotions (Muis et al., 2021) and an acknowledgement that findings concerning confusion's effects are still inconclusive, particularly regarding whether it positively affects knowledge generation (Vogl et al., 2019). This chapter, therefore, aims to enrich our understanding of what triggers epistemic emotions, and what are the effects of epistemic emotions in the Korean language classroom. Based on the empirical findings, we seek to devise emotion-based teaching strategies that enhance learning.

2.3 Perceived difficulty, perception of teacher's behaviours, and intended effort

We have remarked that epistemic emotions arise from the intricate process of assimilating new knowledge into established cognitive frameworks. For example, confusion often signals a learner's struggle to integrate fresh information or complete a particular learning task, highlighting a notable correlation between epistemic emotions and the learner's perception of difficulty. Yet it is crucial to recognise that perceived difficulty does not inevitably stifle learning. On the contrary, when learners encounter tasks with an appropriate level of challenge, the emotional state can shift away from confusion, thereby promoting learning (Lodge et al., 2018).

Similar to confusion, curiosity is also triggered by a dissonance between new and extant information (Muis et al., 2018). Therefore, like confusion, it has garnered significant attention in SLA research, including in discussions centred around perceived difficulty and epistemic emotions. For example, Nakamura et al. (2022) underlined comprehensibility as an essential precursor to curiosity, positing that moderate difficulty can foster curiosity in language learning contexts. However, the impact of excitement on the perception of the difficulty of a language learning activity has not been extensively examined, a gap this chapter intends to fill.

Beyond the language learning activity and its associated perceived difficulty, the teacher is a further element of the language classroom environment that affects learners' emotions. Teacher behaviour is an important variable to consider when gauging learners' affective states. For example, previous research has found that some teacher-related variables are closely linked to learners' enjoyment (Dewaele et al., 2018). In the Korean language classroom, Fraschini and Tao (2021) found that teachers' strictness was not correlated to enjoyment, while friendliness seemed to promote it. Fraschini (2023) showed the considerable effect of teachers' positive feedback and classroom decisions on increasing or decreasing classroom certain emotions. Following Dewaele (2019a) and Fraschini and Tao (2021), we focus on teachers' perceived strictness and friendliness in this chapter.

Within SLA research, intended effort and attainment of language proficiency are often used as reference criteria. This chapter focuses on the intended effort for two main reasons. First, despite all study participants being beginner learners of Korean, not all started the course with the same proficiency. Second, because intended effort has often been used in association with the assessment of learner motivation (Yun et al., 2018), and becomes our metric of preference when considering the strict link between motivation and emotions. Many studies indeed confirm that motivation positively influences intended effort (Taguchi et al., 2009; Teimouri, 2017). Yashima et al. (2017) substantiated the catalytic role of intended effort, demonstrating its correlation with elevated proficiency levels. Al-Hoorie's (2018) meta-analysis further emphasised that motivation and learning experience are substantial predictors of intended effort. This chapter aims to augment the existing body of research by offering additional empirical evidence on the relationship between intended effort and perceived difficulty.

3. Research design and methodology

As shown in the previous section, an expanding corpus of academic literature has shed light on the importance of understanding and utilising emotional landscapes within language classrooms. However, the particular realm of epistemic emotions, notably confusion and excitement, calls for a more nuanced exploration. In the ensuing section, we delineate the foundational research questions and theoretical models that inform our empirical investigation. We also introduce the study's setting, sample, and survey instruments.

3.1 Research questions

The interplay between confusion, excitement, the perceived complexity of language learning tasks, and students' intended efforts is a nuanced relationship that merits further exploration. Existing literature underscores the pivotal role teachers and their pedagogical choices play in shaping these epistemic emotions in the SLA context. However, the impact of students' perceptions of their teachers – whether viewed as strict or friendly – on these emotional experiences remains an underexplored avenue. Given that epistemic emotions such as confusion may signify the low feasibility of a task (Vazard & Audrin, 2021), while epistemic emotions like excitement often correlate with heightened levels of interest and enjoyment (Ainley & Hidi, 2014), a deeper understanding of these emotional triggers holds substantial pedagogical value. In particular, we must seek empirically grounded answers to the following research questions to lay the groundwork for innovative, emotion-focused pedagogy.

RQ1: How does a student's view of their teacher being strict (i.e., perceived teacher strictness) affect how confused or excited they feel in class?
RQ2: How does a student's view of their teacher being friendly (i.e., perceived teacher friendliness) affect how confused or excited they feel in class?
RQ3: How do a student's confusion and excitement impact how difficult they think the learning tasks are (i.e., perceived difficulty)?
RQ4: How does a student's belief about the learning tasks' difficulty (i.e., perceived difficulty) affect how much effort they plan to put in (i.e., intended effort)?

3.2 The setting and the sample

Our study focused on *ab initio* learners enrolled in a 12-week Korean language course at an Australian university. The syllabus design ensured students mastered the Korean script within the first fortnight. From the third week, the course incorporated two weekly tutorials: one centred on grammatical exercises and the other on developing and improving speaking, listening, and reading skills. The data for this study were culled explicitly from these latter tutorials, which were consistent across tutorial groups in terms of teaching materials and learning trajectories.

Having obtained approval from the Human Ethics Research Committee, we administered the survey over six consecutive teaching weeks in the latter half of the semester. Seamlessly integrated into the learning management system, the survey was easily accessible to prospective participants. Regular announcements followed each second language tutorial to encourage participation and were reinforced by weekly reminders. These announcements clarified that participation was voluntary and that students were not obligated to complete all six survey iterations.

To prevent confusion, each weekly survey was closed as soon as the subsequent one became available.

Among the 317 students enrolled in the course, 91 contributed to the survey, resulting in 188 entries. Predominantly appealing to first-year students owing to its introductory nature, the course was most commonly chosen as an elective subject. Two demographic characteristics of the cohort warrant particular attention. First, a significant majority of the participants were female, a trend that resonates with the gender distribution in many other language courses across Australian universities. Second, a notable number of students were either speaking, had studied, or were currently studying an Asian language other than Korean. This diversity reflects the multicultural and multilingual fabric of the contemporary Australian university student population. A comprehensive breakdown of key background variables can be found in Table 8.1.

3.3 Survey instrument

The survey comprises 29 questions to elicit a broad spectrum of data on learners' experiences and perceptions. The first few questions collect demographic and academic background information, including gender, first language, year of enrolment, and the status of the Korean language course within their curriculum as either an elective or a compulsory subject. In addition, a pair of attendance-related questions sought to identify the tutorial group and instructor to contextualise subsequent responses.

The questionnaire also incorporates several scales adapted from established academic works to measure specific aspects of learning. For example, a four-item scale focused on the characteristics of teachers was drawn on metrics from Dewaele (2019a). This scale, previously employed by Fraschini and Tao (2021), assesses, among other aspects, how a learner perceives their teacher's friendliness and strictness. Four additional items delved into the perceived difficulty of the course. These

Table 8.1 Descriptive statistics of valid observations

Variables	Value	Count	Total Number of valid observations
Gender (GD)	*Male*	37	187
	Female	150	
First-year student (FS)	*No*	83	188
	Yes	105	
Speak, have studied, or are studying an Asian language other than Korean (AL)	*No*	81	188
	Yes	108	
Take the course as a compulsory unit (CL)	*No*	43	188
	Yes	145	
Attend the unit online in the week of filling out the survey (OL)	*No*	92	182
	Yes	90	

Notes: Words in parentheses mark respective variables in the SEM diagram (Figure 8.1) and results table (Table 8.2).

were formulated to assess learners' comprehension and application of content from the first tutorial class and their experiences with language activities in the second tutorial (Cronbach's alpha: 0.86). In addition, a six-item scale from Yashima et al. (2017) gauged the intended effort (Cronbach's alpha: 0.79).

Last, the survey included two single-item measures for the two epistemic emotions of interest: confusion and excitement. These measures are adapted from the short version of the Epistemically Related Emotions Scale by Pekrun et al. (2017). Relevant instructions were tailored to fit the context of Korean language learning.

4. Data analysis

Our research questions, aiming to augment the existing literature, scrutinise the causes and outcomes of epistemic emotions. We place a particular emphasis on teacher behaviour, as well as student perceptions of task difficulty and intended efforts. This section will delineate our statistical model and present the analytical findings, establishing a robust empirical basis for ensuing pedagogical discussions. Employing structural equation modelling (SEM), we utilise a flexible and potent statistical framework aptly suited to exploring these intricate research questions.

4.1 The model

SEM provides a comprehensive framework for examining multiple relationships simultaneously, offering an integrated perspective on complex systems. Given the intricate nature of our research questions – which encompass perceptions of teacher behaviour, emotional experiences, and learner attitudes such as perceived difficulty and intended effort – SEM serves as an invaluable tool for unified analysis. The SEM framework employed here controls for various confounding variables, including gender, study stage (first-year student or not), course status (compulsory or elective), prior Asian language exposure, and teaching mode (online or offline). Figure 8.1 presents the model we constructed based on our research questions.

The model demonstrates a solid fit for our empirical data across multiple goodness-of-fit indicators. With a chi-square value of 15.07 and 7 degrees of freedom, it achieves a p-value of 0.04, comfortably below the 0.05 significance level. The root mean square error (RMSEA) (0.08) stands within the ideal 0.05–0.08 range, and the comparative fit index (CFI) value (0.927) exceeds the accepted 0.90 threshold. Overall, these indicators affirm the model's efficacy.

4.2 The empirical findings

As reported in Table 8.2, our empirical findings reveal the multifaceted dynamics between perceived teacher characteristics, student emotional states, and their academic pursuits.

First, our research underscores the pivotal role of perceived teacher friendliness in cultivating student enthusiasm. We have found a significant positive correlation between how friendly a teacher is perceived and a student's excitement.

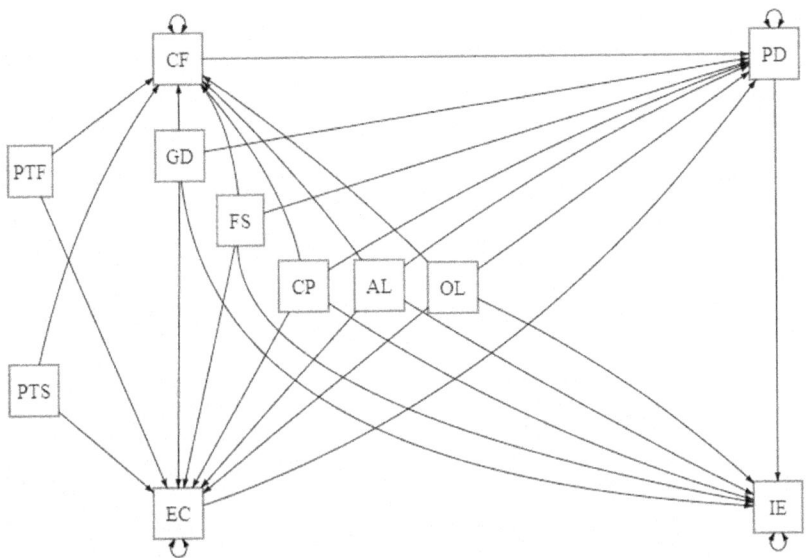

Figure 8.1 The SEM diagram

Notes: Thick frames and lines highlight key analytical variables and regression effects. PTF stands for perceived teacher friendliness. PTS stands for perceived teacher strictness. CF stands for the epistemic emotion of confusion. EC stands for the epistemic emotion of excitement. PD stands for the perceived difficulty of the week's learning. IE stands for the intended efforts that the students reported that they would make to study the Korean language. GD, FS, AL, CP, and OL are confronting variables that could impact relevant key analytical variables, and their meanings are explained in the notes of Table 8.1.

Table 8.2 Statistical results of the SEM

		Coefficient	Std. err.	z	P > z
EC ←					
	PTF	0.2375	0.0710	3.350	0.001***
	PTS	0.0571	0.0776	0.740	0.462
	GD	0.0785	0.0734	1.070	0.284
	FR	−0.0875	0.0817	−1.070	0.284
	AL	−0.1123	0.0785	−1.430	0.152
	CP	0.1064	0.0847	1.260	0.209
	OL	−0.0969	0.0750	−1.290	0.196
	_cons	1.1635	0.7037	1.650	0.098
CF ←					
	PTF	−0.1642	0.0729	−2.250	0.024**
	PTS	−0.0511	0.0780	−0.650	0.513
	GD	0.0436	0.0739	0.590	0.555
	FR	0.0594	0.0823	0.720	0.471
	AL	−0.0282	0.0794	−0.350	0.723
	CP	−0.1953	0.0840	−2.330	0.020**
	OL	0.1395	0.0749	1.860	0.063
	_cons	3.3768	0.6754	5.000	0.000

(*Continued*)

Table 8.2 (Continued)

		Coefficient	Std. err.	z	P > z
PD ←					
	EC	−0.1381	0.0620	−2.230	0.026**
	CF	0.5523	0.0534	10.350	0.000***
	GD	0.0814	0.0613	1.330	0.184
	FR	0.0512	0.0679	0.750	0.451
	AL	0.0293	0.0654	0.450	0.654
	CP	0.0479	0.0718	0.670	0.505
	OL	−0.0222	0.0622	−0.360	0.722
	_cons	4.5554	0.3392	13.430	0.000
IE ←					
	PD	0.1381	0.0723	1.910	0.056*
	GD	0.0876	0.0737	1.190	0.235
	FR	−0.0976	0.0815	−1.200	0.231
	AL	−0.1184	0.0778	−1.520	0.128
	CP	−0.1713	0.0851	−2.010	0.044*
	OL	−0.0422	0.0747	−0.560	0.572
	_cons	3.6391	0.3973	9.160	0.000
	var(e.EC)	0.9112	0.0396		
	var(e.CF)	0.9206	0.0379		
	var(e.PD)	0.6374	0.0559		
	var(e.IE)	0.9289	0.0364		

Notes: For meanings of the variable names, refer to Figure 8.1's notes. Single asterisks (*) indicate coefficients significant at the 10% level. Double asterisks (**) indicate coefficients significant at the 5% level. Triple asterisks (***) indicate coefficients significant at the 1% level.

Additionally, this perceived friendliness inversely correlates with student confusion: the friendlier the teacher, the less befuddled the students are. In contrast, a teacher's strictness shows no significant correlation with either student enthusiasm or confusion.

In the realm of student emotions, both excitement and confusion appear to be significantly linked to how students perceive the difficulty of their learning tasks. Excitement negatively correlates with perceived difficulty. In plain terms, more excited students find the subject matter less challenging. Similarly, confusion shows a positive correlation with perceived difficulty. That is to say, the more confused students are, the more daunting they find their academic tasks.

Last, after controlling for an array of student-specific variables, we found that perceived difficulty is significantly and positively correlated with intended effort to study; however, we adopted a reversed scale. In other words, students who find their learning task less challenging are more inclined to invest their best effort, an encouraging implication for educators striving for high academic achievement.

When considered collectively, our results suggest that perceived teacher friendliness at a higher level can lead to increased student excitement. A heightened excitement, in turn, may reduce students' perception of difficulty, culminating in a rise in their intended efforts. On the other hand, a higher level of teacher strictness does not necessarily heighten students' perception of difficulty or diminish their intended efforts, as it shows no significant impact on either student enthusiasm or confusion.

5. Pedagogical implications

The empirical findings of this research contribute to the nuanced understanding of teacher-learning task-student dynamics in SLA, calling for a deeper reflection of how the teacher affects learners' emotions and how these, in their relationship with the perception of the learning task, affect learners' intended effort. In the following section, we discuss the results in light of previous research on emotions in education and suggest how they can be applied to develop an emotion-based Korean language pedagogy.

5.1 *Do not be afraid of being strict for good reasons*

Teachers play essential roles in not only disseminating knowledge but also nurturing their students' critical thinking skills (Tao & Griffith, 2020). Unfortunately, in many contemporary universities influenced by neoliberal ideologies, students frequently aspire to attain high grades without necessarily putting in sufficient effort (Tao, 2021). This challenge often leaves educators in a quandary, reluctant to impose rigorous standards for fear of alienating their students. From the teacher's perspective, concerns loom that students may leave punitive teaching evaluations or may abandon future semesters courses perceived as overly challenging. Such apprehensions stem from a prevailing academic sentiment suggesting that strict pedagogical methods could dampen student enthusiasm or cause confusion, thus impairing the educational experience.

However, our empirical data contradicts this belief, aligning more coherently with research that establishes no straightforward correlation between a teacher's perceived strictness and students' emotional or academic outcomes. For instance, Dewaele et al. (2019) noted that learners often cease to feel anxious once they realise their teacher is not just strict but also empathetic. Similarly, Poplin et al. (2011) revealed that effective teachers in struggling educational settings frequently view their strictness as indispensable for nurturing effective learning and ensuring safety and respect. In these contexts, students also regard their teachers' strictness as serving broader educational goals.

This decoupling of strictness from student motivation enables educators to foster a pedagogical environment beyond a simple transactional exchange of grades for minimal effort. Instead, it provides a fertile ground for educators to recalibrate their teaching approaches. Numerous studies, also conducted on Korean language learners, including Fraschini (2023), show that a classroom environment where the teacher is fair towards all students and provides clear guidelines promotes positive emotions, leading to engagement and learning. Liberated from the misbelief that strictness stifles engagement or understanding, educators can be strict but fair, knowing that this classroom attitude does not promote overtly negative emotions.

At the policy level, it is common for educational institutions to place undue emphasis on student evaluations when gauging teaching efficacy. Our results show that teachers' strictness does not harm learners' emotions; nevertheless, evaluation scores are among the causes of teachers' anxiety (Fraschini & Park, 2021) because of their connection with performance reviews and contract renewals. Therefore, these metrics push teachers to be permissive and lenient with students. Our findings suggest that universities should reconsider and refine the metrics used to assess teaching excellence to avoid teachers being over-lenient with students. This recalibration should align more closely with evidence-based educational practices (Uttl et al., 2017).

5.2 The importance of friendly teachers in the language classroom

Our research findings underscore the crucial role that social interactions play in shaping educational experiences. We have found a strong positive correlation between the perceived friendliness of the teacher and a student's eagerness to learn. This relationship can potentially reshape classroom management strategies and pedagogical approaches fundamentally. Central to this transformation is the idea that teacher friendliness is instrumental in creating an educational environment that elevates student enthusiasm and minimises confusion and, therefore, is conducive to intent to put effort into learning the language.

Building up a growing body of research that places the emotional climate of educational settings at the forefront (Khajavy et al., 2018; Peng & Woodrow, 2010), a principal implication of our findings is the pressing need for teacher training and professional development programs to place a greater emphasis on the cultivation of interpersonal skills, and to support the development of teachers' emotional intelligence (Dewaele, 2019b). In light of our research, the teacher–student relationship should not be treated as a secondary consideration but as integral to effective pedagogical practice. This resonates with the findings from the literature in educational psychology regarding teachers' influence on learners' emotions and, consequently, final attainment (Frenzel et al., 2009). Therefore, pedagogical training should actively incorporate techniques to enhance perceived friendliness, such as open communication, active listening, and creating an inclusive classroom environment.

Moreover, our findings advocate a pedagogical shift toward a more student-centred approach. Khajavy et al. (2018) found that a positive and supportive classroom environment significantly contributes to lowering negative emotions and increasing learners' willingness to communicate. Furthermore, teachers perceived as friendly create a setting where students feel valued, included, and thus more inclined to engage (Jenkins & Hewitt, 2010). A pedagogical model that capitalises on teacher friendliness can lead to enhanced learning outcomes, as it fosters greater eagerness among students to participate while concurrently reducing confusion.

Finally, our study reveals an inverse correlation between perceived teacher friendliness and student confusion that has profound implications for managing human resources in educational institutions. It suggests that teachers seen as approachable and friendly will likely promote a learning environment able to lower students' cognitive imbalances and resolve confusional states. Consequently, friendliness is not merely a positive attribute but may well be a pedagogical asset, particularly in subjects perceived as challenging, such as Korean language learning.

5.3 The necessity and challenges of emotion-based pedagogical strategies

The profound interplay between student emotions and their perceptions of academic task difficulty offers significant educational implications. Well-established theories like the control-value theory (CVT) emphasise emotions' instrumental role in cognitive processes, particularly academic engagement and performance (Pekrun, 2006). This theory elaborates on how cognitive appraisals, control beliefs, and the subjective values students attach to educational tasks are intricately linked to emotions. Although the CVT has been developed predominantly in studies focused on achievement emotions (i.e., emotions related to the attainment or non-attainment of a goal), research has also shown that control has a significant impact on epistemic emotions (Muis et al., 2018; Pekrun et al., 2017). Our findings further corroborate the role of control appraisal in triggering emotions and, therefore, the need to manage emotions in educational environments like language classrooms.

Our empirical evidence substantiates the pedagogical significance of emotions like excitement, positively correlated with reduced task difficulty perception. Ultimately, the experience of excitement follows a pattern similar to its related enjoyment in fostering learners' intended efforts, as outlined by Botes et al. (2022). Furthermore, excitement, an emotion with positive valence, fosters heightened engagement, improves information retention, and increases intrinsic motivation (Fredrickson, 2001). Such positive effects of excitement have started recently to gain attention thanks to studies that consider the concept of flow in language learning (Dewaele & MacIntyre, 2022a). As such, educators are advised to nurture a stimulating learning environment. Strategies to achieve this include incorporating gamified elements into curricula, presenting students with motivating and achievable goals, designing interactive classroom activities, and demonstrating friendliness to students both within and outside the classroom setting.

In this sense, an emotion-conscious pedagogy, as we put forward in this chapter, should be considered complementary to other approaches suggested in this volume. For example, VR can be used to promote students' excitement and consequently pave the way to a state of flow, despite some episodes which could trigger confusion or frustration (see Kim and Kim, Chapter 5). AI-based chatbots can be implemented promote self-efficacy, an enhanced perception of control, and consequently enjoyment (see Ryu, Chapter 2).

However, the data also reveal that elevated levels of confusion can augment perceptions of academic complexity. In this respect, we noted not only that a difficult task augments confusion, as noted by Vazard and Audrin (2021) but also that an already confused student may perceive a task they are about to approach as more difficult. Though commonly viewed as counterproductive, confusion plays a nuanced role in learning. For example, moderate confusion can stimulate critical thinking and problem-solving abilities (D'Mello et al., 2014). Excessive confusion, conversely, is detrimental, causing frustration, disengagement, and academic failure. Therefore, the pedagogical challenge is balancing the double-edged sword of confusion – alleviating its drawbacks while exploiting its advantages. The detrimental effect of confusion on the perception of the learning activity reinforces the need to be aware of the emotionally significant effects of the teacher's talk on learners' emotions (Fraschini, 2023). A further approach to managing learners' confusion is adopting scaffolding techniques, where educators offer progressive levels of support that recede as students gain proficiency.

Our research further elucidates an intriguing relationship within educational settings: a distinct positive correlation exists between students' perception of task difficulty and their willingness to invest effort in academic endeavours, showing that the more students perceive a task to be difficult, the less they are willing to invest learning efforts. Our results show that teachers' behaviour can positively affect learners' emotions, task perception, and consequently learning efforts, and call for a nuanced pedagogical framework, especially in the context of emotion-focused educational strategies. Once again, scaffolding and the zone of proximal development (ZPD), as conceptualised by Vygotsky (1978), provides invaluable guidance. The ZPD delineates the gap between what students can accomplish independently and what they can achieve with assistance. Pedagogical initiatives should aim to situate learning tasks within this zone, striking a balance that optimises emotional and cognitive engagement for more efficient learning. The adoption of frequent and manageable formative assessments, such as those endorsed by Black and Wiliam (1998) for example, not only can equip instructors with actionable insights into a student's position relative to the ZPD but also can foster students' feeling of accomplishment by breaking down a challenging learning task into manageable smaller components. Emotional cues from these assessments can subsequently guide instructors in calibrating task difficulty, aligning more closely with the emotional dimensions of learning.

6. Conclusion

This chapter considered the effect of teachers' friendliness and strictness on two important classroom emotions, excitement and confusion, and how these emotions affect the perception of the difficulty of a learning task and learners' intended effort. The results confirm the significant impacts that teachers' perceived characteristics have on learners' emotions and foreground the necessity of adopting an emotion-based pedagogy in the Korean language classroom.

A limitation of this study is to consider only two emotions; however, we acknowledge that learners experience a variety of emotions and that emotions in the language classroom are intricately entangled. In order to take into account the complex and dynamic nature of emotions, further studies should observe how other emotions vary depending on teachers' pedagogical choices. Such an understanding of a larger variety of emotions would then give a clearer picture of how to develop an emotion-based language classroom pedagogy.

References

Ainley, M., & Hidi, S. (2014). Interest and enjoyment. In R. Pekrun & L. Linnenbrink-Garcia (Eds.), *International handbook of emotions in education* (pp. 205–227). Routledge.

Al-Hoorie, A. (2018). The L2 motivational self system: A meta-analysis. *Studies in Second Language Learning and Teaching, 8*(4), 721–754.

Black, P., & Wiliam, D. (1998). Assessment and classroom learning. *Assessment in Education: Principles, Policy & Practice, 5*(1), 7–74.

Botes, E., Dewaele, J.-M., & Greiff, S. (2022). Taking stock: A meta-analysis of the effects of foreign language enjoyment. *Studies in Second Language Learning and Teaching, 12*(2), 205–232.

Boudreau, C., MacIntyre, P., & Dewaele, J.-M. (2018). Enjoyment and anxiety in second language communication: An idiodynamic approach. *Studies in Second Language Learning and Teaching, 8*(1), 149–170.

Chevrier, M., Muis, K., Trevors, G., Pekrun, R., & Sinatra, G. (2019). Exploring the antecedents and consequences of epistemic emotions. *Listening and Instruction, 63*, 101209. https://doi.org/10.1016/j.learninstruc.2019.05.006

Dewaele, J.-M. (2019a). The effect of classroom emotions, attitudes toward English, and teacher behaviour on willingness to communicate among English foreign language learners. *Journal of Language and Social Psychology, 38*(4), 523–535.

Dewaele, J.-M. (2019b). The relationship between trait emotional intelligence and experienced ESL/EFL teachers' love of English, attitudes towards their students and institution, self-reported classroom practices, enjoyment and creativity. *Chinese Journal of Applied Linguistics, 41*(4), 468–487.

Dewaele, J.-M., & MacIntyre, P. (2014). The two faces of Janus? Anxiety and enjoyment in the foreign language classroom. *Studies in Second Language Learning and Teaching, 4*(2), 237–274.

Dewaele, J.-M., & MacIntyre, P. (2022a). "You can't start a fire without a spark". Enjoyment, anxiety, and the emergence of flow in foreign language classrooms. *Applied Linguistics Review.* https://doi.org/10.1515/applirev-2021-0123

Dewaele, J.-M., & MacIntyre, P. (2022b). Do flow, enjoyment, and anxiety emerge equally in English foreign language classrooms as in other foreigl language classrooms? *Revista Brasileira de Linguística Aplicada, 22*(1), 156–180. http://dx.doi.org/10.1590/1984-6398202218487

Dewaele, J.-M., Magdalena, A. F., & Saito, K. (2019). The effect of perception of teacher characteristics on Spanish EFL learners' anxiety and enjoyment. *The Modern Language Journal, 103*(2), 412–427.

Dewaele, J.-M., Saito, K., & Halimi, F. (2022). How teacher behaviour shapes foreign language learners' enjoyment, anxiety and attitudes/motivation: A mixed modelling longitudinal investigation. *Language Teaching Research.* https://doi.org/10.1177/13621688221089601

Dewaele, J.-M., Whitney, J., Saito, K., & Dewaele, L. (2018). Foreign language enjoyment and anxiety: The effect of teacher and learner variables. *Language Teaching Research, 22*(6), 676–697.

Di Leo, I., Muis, K., Singh, C., & Psaradellis, C. (2019). Curiosity... confusion? Frustration! The role and sequencing of emotions during mathematics problem solving. *Contemporary Educational Psychology, 58*, 121–137. https://doi.org/10.1016/j.cedpsych.2019.03.001

D'Mello, S., & Graesser, A. (2012). Dynamics of affective states during complex learning. *Learning and Instruction, 22*, 145–157.

D'Mello, S., Lehman, B., Pekrun, R., & Graesser, A. (2014). Confusion can be beneficial for learning. *Learning and Instruction, 29*, 153–170.

Fraschini, N. (2023). Language learners' emotional dynamics: Insights from a Q methodology intensive single-case study. *Language, Culture and Curriculum, 36*(2), 222–239. https://doi.org/10.1080/07908318.2022.2133137

Fraschini, N., & Park, H. (2021). Anxiety in language teachers: Exploring the variety of perceptions with Q methodology. *Foreign Language Annals, 54*(2), 341–364. https://doi.org/10.1111/flan.12527

Fraschini, N., & Tao, Y. (2021). Emotions in online language learning: Exploratory findings from an ab initio Korean course. *Journal of Multilingual and Multicultural Development*, 1–20. https://doi.org/10.1080/01434632.2021.1968875

Fraschini, N., & Tao, Y. (2023). How epistemic anxiety and curiosity link perceived value and intended efforts in the language classroom. *Annual Review of Applied Linguistics, 43*, 23–40. https://doi.org/10.1017/S0267190523000041

Fredrickson, B. L. (2001). The role of positive emotions in positive psychology: The broaden-and-build theory of positive emotions. *American Psychologist, 56*(3), 218–226.

Frenzel, A. C., Goetz, T., Lüdtke, O., Pekrun, R., & Sutton, R. E. (2009). Emotional transmission in the classroom: Exploring the relationship between teacher and student enjoyment. *Journal of Educational Psychology, 101*(3), 705–716.

Geerling, D., Butner, J., Fraughton, T., Sinclair, S., Zachary, J., & Sansone, C. (2020). The dynamic association of interest and confusion: The potential for moderation by utility value and gender. *The Journal of Experimental Education, 88*(3), 407–430. https://doi.org/10.1080/00220973.2018.1561403

Gregersen, T. (2020). Dynamic properties of language anxiety. *Studies in Second Language Learning and Teaching, 10*(1), 67–87.

Hong, J., Lin, C., Tsai, Y., & Tai, K. (2023). Confusion and Chinese character learning. *The Language Learning Journal, 51*(1), 1–17. https://doi.org/10.1080/09571736.2021.1915365

Horwitz, E., Horwitz, M., & Cope, J. (1986). Foreign language classroom anxiety. *The Modern Language Journal, 70*(2), 125–132.

Jenkins, K., & Hewitt, A. (2010). A teacher's vision: A friendly teaching environment that supports growth and learning. *Childhood Education, 86*(5), 316–320.

Khajavy, G. H., MacIntyre, P., & Barabadi, E. (2018). Role of the emotions and classroom environment in willingness to communicate: Applying doubly latent multilevel analysis in second language acquisition research. *Studies in Second Language Acquisition, 40*(3), 605–624.

Li, C., Dewaele, J.-M., & Hu, Y. (2023). Foreign language learning boredom: Conceptualisation and measurement. *Applied Linguistics Review, 14*(2), 223–249.

Li, C., Huang, J., & Li, B. (2021). The predictive effects of classroom environment and trait emotional intelligence on foreign language enjoyment and anxiety. *System, 96*, 102393.

Lodge, J., Kennedy, G., Lockyer, L., Arguel, A., & Pachman, M. (2018). Understanding difficulties and resulting confusion and learning: An integrative review. *Frontiers in Education, 3*(49). https://doi.org/10.3389/feduc.2018.00049

MacIntyre, P., & Gregersen, T. (2012). Emotions that facilitate language learning: The positive-broadening power of imagination. *Studies in Second Language Learning and Teaching, 2*(2), 193–213.

Mahmoodzadeh, M., & Khajavy, G. H. (2019). Towards conceptualising language learning curiosity in SLA: An empirical study. *Journal of Psycholinguistic Research, 48*(2), 333–351.

Muis, K. R., Chevrier, M., Denton, C. A., & Losenno, K. M. (2021). Epistemic emotions and epistemic cognition predict critical thinking about socio-scientific issues. *Frontiers in Education, 6*, 669908. https://doi.org/10.3389/feduc.2021.669908

Muis, K. R., Chevrier, M., & Singh, C. (2018). The role of epistemic emotions in personal epistemology and self-regulated learning. *Educational Psychologist, 53*(3), 165–184. https://doi.org/10.1080/00461520.2017.1421465

Nakamura, S., Reinders, H., & Darasawang, P. (2022). A classroom-based study on the antecedents of epistemic curiosity in L2 learning. *Journal of Psycholinguistic Research, 51*, 293–308.

Nerantzaki, K., Efklides, A., & Metallidou, P. (2021). Epistemic emotions: Cognitive underpinnings and relations with metacognitive feelings. *New Ideas in Psychology*, *63*, 100904. https://doi.org/10.1016/j.newideapsych.2021.100904

Oxford, R., & Gkonou, C. (2021). Working with the complexity of language learners' emotions and emotion regulation strategies. In R. J. Sampson & R. S. Pinner (Eds.), *Complexity perspectives on researching language learner and teacher psychology* (pp. 52–67). Multilingual Matters.

Pavelescu, L. M., & Petrić, B. (2018). Love and enjoyment in context: Four case studies of adolescent EFL learners. *Studies in Second Language Learning and Teaching*, *8*(1), 73–101.

Pekrun, R. (2006). The control-value theory of achievement emotions: Assumptions, corollaries, and implications for educational research and practice. *Educational Psychology Review*, *18*(4), 315–341.

Pekrun, R., Vogl, E., Muis, K., & Sinatra, G. (2017). Measuring emotions during epistemic activities: The epistemically-related Emotion Scales. *Cognition and Emotion*, *31*(6), 1268–1276. https://doi.org/10.1080/02699931.2016.1204989

Peng, J. E., & Woodrow, L. (2010). Willingness to communicate in English: A model in the Chinese EFL classroom context. *Language Learning*, *60*(4), 834–876.

Poplin, M., Rivera, J., Durish, D., Hoff, L., Kawell, S., Pawlak, P., Hinman, I. S., Straus, L., & Veney, C. (2011). She's strict for a good reason: Highly effective teachers in low-performing urban schools. *Phi Delta Kappan*, *92*(5), 39–43. https://doi.org/10.1177/003172171109200509

Rusk, F., Pörn, M., & Sahlström, F. (2016). The management of dynamic epistemic relationships regarding second language knowledge in second language education: Epistemic discrepancies and epistemic (im)balance. *Classroom Discourse*, *7*(2), 184–205. https://doi.org/10.1080/19463014.2016.1171160

Schubert, S., Pekrun, R., & Ufer, S. (2023). The role of epistemic emotions in undergraduate students' proof construction. *ZDM – Mathematics Education*, *55*, 299–314. https://doi.org/10.1007/s11858-022-01413-y

Scovel, T. (1978). The effect of affect on foreign language learning: A review of the anxiety research. *Language Learning*, *28*(1), 129–142.

Sudina, E., & Plonsky, L., (2021). Academic perseverance in foreign language learning: An investigation of language-specific grit and its conceptual correlates. *The Modern Language Journal*, *105*(4), 829–857.

Taguchi, T., Magid, M., & Papi, M. (2009). The L2 motivational self system amongst Chinese, Japanese, and Iranian learners of English: A comparative study. In Z. Dörnyei & E. Ushioda (Eds.), *Motivation, language identity and the L2 self* (pp. 66–97). Multilingual Matters.

Tao, Y. (2021). The understanding and take on the blatant instrumentalism among university students: Reflections from an early-career academic. *Australian Universities' Review*, *63*(2), 62–66.

Tao, Y., & Griffith, E. (2020). Making critical thinking skills training explicit, engaging, and effective through live debates on current political issues: A pilot pedagogical experiment. *PS: Political Science & Politics*, *53*(1), 155–160.

Teimouri, Y. (2017). L2 selves, emotions, and motivated behaviors. *Studies in Second Language Acquisition*, *39*, 681–709.

Teimouri, Y., Plonsky, L., & Tabandeh, F. (2020). L2 grit: Passion and perseverance for second language learning. *Language Teaching Research*, *26*(5), 893–918.

Thumvichit, A. (2022). Unfolding the subjectivity of foreign language enjoyment in online classes: A Q methodology study. *Journal of Multilingual and Multicultural Development*. https://doi.org/10.1080/01434632.2022.2050917

Trevors, G., Muis, K., Pekrun, R., Sinatra, G., & Muijselaar, M. (2017). Exploring the relations between epistemic beliefs, emotions, and learning from texts. *Contemporary Educational Psychology*, *48*, 116–132.

Uttl, B., White, C. A., & Gonzalez, D. W. (2017). Meta-analysis of faculty's teaching effectiveness: Student evaluation of teaching ratings and student learning are not related. *Studies in Educational Evaluation, 54*, 22–42.

Vazard, J., & Audrin, C. (2021). The noetic feeling of confusion. *Philosophical Psychology, 35*(5), 757–770. https://doi.org/10.1080/09515089.2021.2016675

Vogl, E., Pekrun, R., Murayama, K., Loderer, K., & Schubert, S. (2019). Surprise, curiosity, and confusion promote knowledge exploration: Evidence for robust effects of epistemic emotions. *Frontiers in Psychology, 10*. www.frontiersin.org/articles/10.3389/fpsyg.2019.02474

Vygotsky, L. S. (1978). *Mind in society: Development of higher psychological processes*. Harvard University Press.

Yashima, T., Nishida, R., & Mizumoto, A. (2017). Influence of learner beliefs and gender on the motivating power of L2 selves. *The Modern Language Journal, 101*(4), 691–711.

Yun, S., Hiver, P., & Al-Hoorie, A. (2018). Academic buoyancy: Exploring learners' everyday resilience in the language classroom. *Studies in Second Language Acquisition, 40*, 805–830.

9 Multimodal approaches to Korean language teaching

Lucien Brown

1. Introduction

Communication does not take place merely in spoken or written words and grammar. Whenever we speak, we produce manual gestures and other bodily visual practices (Ford et al., 2012) such as head nods, smiles and shifts in gaze, all of which have communicative functions (see Andries et al., 2023). We also modulate the pitch, loudness and other qualities of vocal production to produce meaning (see Freeman, 2014, 2015, 2019), and use various non-verbal speech sounds (also known as "sound objects"; see Reber, 2012) such as sighs, hisses, clicks and lip smacks that rarely appear in dictionaries and occupy a liminal space on the edge of language (Dingemanse, 2020). Written texts, particularly in computer mediated communication, increasingly contain visual elements such as emojis, stickers, GIFs, memes and selfies (Highfield & Leaver, 2016; Konrad et al., 2020), while many text types such as advertisements, online news and comics use a combination of written words and visuals to convey meanings. The use of images in these texts is patterned and systematic to the extent that it can be said to possess its own "visual grammar" (Cohn, 2013; Kress & Van Leeuwen, 2001). All of the evidence therefore tells us that communication is an embodied, multimodal and multisensory phenomenon.

Some aspects of multimodal communication may be shared across languages and cultures, such as associations between head nodding and agreement and between sighs and frustration, as well as some of the conventions of visual narratives such as comics (see Cohn, 2013). However, other aspects of multimodal communication are no doubt culture and/or language specific. For example, whereas in some cultures pointing gestures are performed predominantly with the index finger, in other cultures they may be performed by the chin (Chatino indigenous group in Mexico; see Mesh et al., 2023), the lips (Northern Kampa Arawaks of Peru; see Mihas, 2023) or the nose (e.g., Yupno Valley of Papua New Guinea; see Cooperrider et al., 2018). Meanwhile, Cohn (2010, p. 192) demonstrates that the visual language of Japanese manga has its own specific characteristics such as depicting sex "through metaphoric crashing surf or blossoming flowers" or denoting lust via bloody noses and sexual thoughts by lengthening the area between the nose and lips. Korean multimodal communication also has its own special characteristics, as I shall explore in Section 2.4.

DOI: 10.4324/9781032725307-13

Despite the inherent multimodality of all modes of communication, the vast majority of L2 language teaching practices still focus on the written or spoken word (Royce, 2007). The tendency for language teaching to disregard visual (as well as acoustic) aspects of communication no doubt relates back to the traditions of 20th-century linguistics, which was dominated by the study of verbal language (see Vigliocco et al., 2014). But recent years have witnessed a multimodal turn across many areas of linguistics, buoyed by the development of systemic functional linguistics (see Eggins, 2004), multimodal discourse analysis (Kress & Van Leeuwen, 2001) and multimodal conversation analysis (Mondada, 2019). This has been accompanied by burgeoning interest in shifting language teaching towards multimodal perspectives, particularly via the multiliteracies framework (see Paesani et al., 2015) and Royce's (2007) concept of "multimodal communicative competence" (see Section 2 for details).

The time is therefore ripe to begin imagining what a multimodal pedagogy for the Korean language might look like. As a stepping stone towards this, the current chapter provides an overview of shifts towards multimodality that have occurred in linguistics, language teaching and the study of the Korean language (Section 2). Then, in Section 3, I set out three distinct examples for teaching different aspects of Korean from a multimodal perspective. Finally, I conclude in Section 4 with some reflections for the future.

2. Multimodality and language teaching

I use this section to sketch out a view on language and communication that is inherently multimodal (Section 2.1) and outline how this can be applied to the idea of communicative competence (Section 2.2) and classroom teaching (Section 2.3). I conclude the section by overviewing some salient multimodal features of Korean (Section 2.4).

2.1 From texts and talk to multimodality

I take the stance in this chapter that language and communication are fundamentally multimodal, albeit to various extents and in different ways. In order to move towards a view of language as a multimodal achievement, proponents of multimodal communicative competence (notably Royce, 2007) and pedagogies of multiliteracies (Paesani et al., 2015; The New London Group, 1996) look towards the principles of systemic functional linguistics.

Founded by Michael Halliday (see Halliday & Matthiessen, 2013), systemic functional linguistics sees language as a social semiotic system that orders the world according to categories that are meaningful to language users (see Eggins, 2004). These categories might differ cross-linguistically. For example, whereas Korean makes a distinction between verbs used for tight-fit (끼다 *kkida*) and loose-fit (넣다 *neota*) containment relations, English can use the same verb for both (*put*) (Choi, 2006). And whereas English sibship terms (*brother, sister*) only differentiate the gender of the sibling, Korean kinship terms (형 *hyeong*, 오빠 *oppa*,

누나 *nuna*, 언니 *eonni*, 동생 *dongsaeng*, 형님 *hyeongnim*, etc.) additionally index the gender of the person related to the sibling and relative age, as well as honorification (see Brown & Park, 2020, p. 85). These conventions of language usage are often culturally grounded in that they reflect parameters that are important in the communities where the language is spoken, such as age, gender and politeness in the case of Korean kinship terms. From this perspective, language usage is about making meaningful choices, and although these choices often follow convention, they can also be made creatively and even subversively, such as female students referring to older male students as 형 *hyeong* 'older brother of a man' (M. Kim, 2022) or gay men addressing each other as 언니 *eonni* 'older sister of a woman' (Brown & Park, 2020, p. 86).

As pointed out by Royce (2007, p. 367), this view of language can be readily extended to the inclusion of multimodal elements. Indeed, the very description of language as a social semiotic system positions it alongside other human signifying practices, including signs, symbols, gestures and images. Just as grammatical and lexical choices represent meaningful distinctions to language users, the same can be said of multimodal features. For instance, English speakers can gesture forward and to the right to clarify that the ambiguous expression "Next Wednesday's meeting has been moved forward two days" refers to moving the meeting to Friday (rather than Monday, as may be indicated by moving the hand backwards and to the left) (Winter & Duffy, 2020). In Korean, speakers pass an object to a status superior or adult stranger using two hands, whereas just one hand is used towards children and intimates of similar or younger age, with this distinction marking similar social meanings to the use of honorifics (Brown & Winter, 2019). Looking at multimodal texts, post-2000 Korean soju ads use various visual modalities to mark qualities related to "softness," including images of female models with gentle personas and soft colour palettes of green and blue, contrasting with the "hard" semiotics of 1980s ads (see Harkness, 2013 and Section 2.4 for full details). Given the ways in which various different modalities use meaningful contrasts in ways somewhat akin to language, starting with the work of Gunther Kress and Theo van Leeuwen (Kress & Van Leeuwen, 2001), scholars have constructed new "grammars" for other semiotic modes such as colour (Kress & Van Leeuwen, 2002), visual design (Kress & Van Leeuwen, 2020) and visual narratives (Cohn, 2013).

It should go without saying that nobody here is claiming that semiotic modes such as gestures, colours and visual designs are as specified or as developed for communication as spoken or written language. But nonetheless they share something with language in the ways in which they operate as semiotic systems, and indeed they are often synchronised with spoken or written language or accompanied by it, with various multimodal cues interacting with and enriching the spoken or written content. Also, these multimodal features are to varying extents specific to certain language and cultures, including the examples of Korean two-handed gestures and the semiotics of soju adverts mentioned previously. It therefore appears logical to claim that developing and exhibiting knowledge of multimodal aspects of communication should be seen as part of the repertoire that second language learners need to acquire.

2.2 Multimodal communicative competence

Recent decades have witnessed a steady evolution and expansion of how we view the goals of language teaching. First of all, with the genesis of "communicative competence" (Canale, 1983; Canale & Swain, 1980; Hymes, 1972) came the recognition that learners required more than merely "linguistic competence" (i.e., grammar, vocabulary, pronunciation, spelling). They also needed "sociolinguistic competence" (defined as the ability to use and understand language appropriately in various contexts) as well as "discourse competence" and "strategic competence". In addition, it soon became recognised that "cultural competence" (Byram, 1997) and then "intercultural competence" (Byram et al., 2002) were indispensable aspects of second language learning. From the work on cultural competence in language learning came the earliest recognition that notions of language competence also needed to recognise multimodal features of communication. Claire Kramsch (Kramsch, 2006, 2011; Kramsch & Whiteside, 2008) contended that in the digitally interconnected global age, language learners must possess the ability to understand and control the intricate symbolic aspects of language, termed "symbolic competence." Importantly, she emphasised that "symbolic competence" should encompass not only spoken communication but also proficiency in written, visual and electronic modes of expression.

Building on this, Royce (2007) proposed the notion of "multimodal communicative competence," which he observes is becoming more important than ever given changes in communication channels that have happened in recent years. He contended that a systemic functional view of language could be extended to cover the "grammar of the visual" and "explain the multimodal competencies needed for second-language contexts" (p. 367). This "multimodal competence" is described in terms of the ability to interpret visual as well as verbal meanings as they are activated in the cultural context in which they are situated. Rather than an ability to understand different modalities in isolation, it involves the knowledge and skills to understand how different modalities come together in part–whole and class–subclass relationships to intersemiotically produce meaning (p. 375).[1]

The concept of multimodal communicative competence focuses mostly on visual literacy, in other words, training learners to read and produce multimodal texts. Royce (2007, p. 366), following the New London Group (1996) and Lo Bianco (2005), also identified a need for learners to develop a metalanguage to facilitate their ability to describe and analyse visual images, as stressed within multiliteracy approaches to language education (see following section). So far, to the best of my knowledge, there has not been any explicit discussion of multimodal aspects of face-to-face communication such as gestures and voice quality within the remit of communicative competence. However, given their communicative functions and their cultural specificity, there is every reason to believe that learners also need to develop proficiency in embodied and vocal aspects of language as essential elements of second language competence.

2.3 Previous studies on multimodal teaching

Preceding the emergence of Royce's (2007) concept of communicative competence, the New London Group (1996) already recognised the importance of multimodal literacies within their call for the adoption of a pedagogy of multiliteracies. The call for second language classes to adopt multiliteracies came off the back of observations, including by the Modern Language Association (Geisler et al., 2007), that second language classes in the university settings were losing their relevance due to the way that they focused merely on the acquisition of linguistic skills. This meant that language classes were becoming distanced from the critical study of literature and other content that was taking place elsewhere in the arts and humanities, and indeed was seen as the raison d'être for these disciplines. The New London Group (1996) therefore called for multiliteracies to be adopted in order to bring critical literacy into the language classroom and therefore reinvigorate the place of language learning within the arts and humanities.

Multiliteracies is a pedagogy focused on training learners to critically engage with target language texts, including the ideological meanings contained within them. The "multi-" in "multiliteracies" has various interlocking meanings, including the inclusion of multiple discourses and genres, while foregrounding multilingualism and multiculturalism (see Kalantzis et al., 2016; Kress, 2009). It also emphasises the multiple ways that texts can be read and understood, with multiliteracies encouraging learners to draw their own interpretations of the texts that they read, becoming active "designers of meaning" (The New London Group, 1996, p. 74). Also, and crucially to the current chapter, multiliteracies recognised that critical literacy in the digital age had to focus on "multiple" modes of representation much broader than language alone (The New London Group, 1996). In multiliteracy classrooms, students are engaged in uncovering "the new meanings created by the co-influences of multiple modes when language is just one of the resources available" (Kumagai et al., 2015, p. 136) via the critical reading of authentic texts and the pursuit of their own creative literacy practices (see Suh & Jung, 2020 for an account of multiliteracies in the Korean language context).

Various studies have explored the effectiveness of multiliteracies pedagogies across a wide range of languages, including a number of studies that have focused specifically on the development of multimodal communicative competence. Coccetta (2018), for instance, reported on the implementation of a 30-hour module teaching multimodal literacy within an English course at a university in Italy, which involved students analysing and discussing the multimodal characteristics of a Lego instruction manual and a pedagogical science animation on the cell cycle. Meanwhile, in a study that looked at second language learners as multimodal text producers, Danzak (2011) reported on a project whereby ESL learners in the United States represented their own families' immigration stories using the genre of the graphic novel.

Recently a small number of studies in the context of Korean language learning have experimented with using multiliteracy techniques for teaching multimodal aspects of Korean. Lee-Smith (2016) used Korean TV public service announcements to develop standards-based pedagogical techniques based on multiliteracies. Brown et al. (2015) used various media materials to teach a class on the topic of "foreigners" in South Korea to advanced-level learners, which included discussion of how visual elements including physical appearance and dress became contested features of ethno-national identity in South Korea. Meanwhile, Kim and Omerbašić (2017) explored how adolescent global fans of Korean popular culture use multimodal literacies to engage with Korean dramas and express imagined identities in transnational mediascapes.

There is also one previous study, Yoon and Brown (2017), that has looked specifically at teaching multimodal components of spoken Korean. This study discussed the creation and execution of an 80-minute lesson aimed at instructing various aspects of Korean politeness through a multiliteracy approach. The lesson utilised excerpts from Korean dramas and a government-issued guidebook for foreigners in Korea. Examination of the ensuing classroom interactions revealed that students gained insights into nonverbal elements associated with politeness in the materials and effectively navigated their own identities in relation to the content. Additionally, during a concluding task that involved rewriting the government guidebook, students demonstrated the ability to employ both text and visual elements, such as drawings and diagrams, to elucidate intricate aspects of multimodal politeness and impoliteness.

2.4 Multimodal features of Korean

I conclude this section with a brief overview of previous research in Korean linguistics and social semiotics that have shed light on important aspects of multimodality in the Korean language and South Korean society. The findings of these studies may be useful to educators looking to include multimodal features into their Korean language teaching.

Studies looking at motion events (e.g., the ball rolled down the hill) have revealed some key characteristics for how these are encoded in Korean via speech and gesture and how this differs from some other languages, including English (Choi & Lantolf, 2008; Park, 2020, 2022). Whereas English encodes the manner of motion on the main verb (e.g., roll, slide, bounce), Korean often uses ideophones or mimetic words (e.g., 떼굴떼굴 *ttegulttegul* for a rolling motion) and/or gestures for encoding manner, although it can also be done via an auxiliary verb. When gestures alone are used to encode manner, they tend to be synchronised with the path or ground component (e.g., a rolling gesture would occur synchronised with 들어 *deureo* 'enter' and/or 상자에 *sangja-e* 'into the box' in the sentence 공이 상자에 들어 갔다 *gong-i sangja-e deureo gatda* 'the ball went into the box'). These cross-linguistic differences in how motion events are encoded in speech and gesture continue to be challenging even for advanced learners (Choi & Lantolf, 2008) and sequential bilinguals (Park, 2020).

A recent wave of research has looked at gestural and embodied aspects of Korean politeness (Brown, Hübscher, et al., 2023; Brown, Kim, et al., 2023; Brown & Winter, 2019), as well as vocal attributes (Brown et al., 2014; Idemaru et al., 2019, 2020; Winter & Grawunder, 2012). When interacting politely with a status superior, Korean speakers use a lower-pitched, quieter and clearer voice. They also use fewer manual and facial gestures, as well as adaptors (i.e., touches to their own body) and haptics (i.e., touches to the body of the interlocutor), and they adopt more erect but constrained body positions while orienting the body towards the status superior and maintaining eye gaze on them. When manual gestures are used, they tend to be less expressive, with speakers using fewer manner gestures and fewer character-oriented gestures (i.e., instances where the gesturer assumes the role of the character performing the action, with their hands directly representing the hands of the character).

The literature also touches on gender-related aspects of gesture and embodiment which seem to take on rather culture-specific meanings in the Korean context. Several studies have made reference to vocal and embodied aspects of 애교 *aegyo*, performances of embodied cuteness enacted primarily by women (Brown, 2013a, 2017; Crosby, 2023; Jang, 2021; Puzar & Hong, 2018; Strong, 2013). *Aegyo* is characterised by a falsetto voice, nasalised delivery and frequent use of elongation, as well as affrication and/j/-insertion (e.g., pronouncing 했어 *haesseo* 'I did it' as [해쪄 *haejjyeo*] – see Jang, 2021). It is also accompanied by various childlike embodied behaviours such as head tilts, cupping the face in the hands (i.e., what is known in Korean as 꽃받침 *kkotbatchim* 'flower's sepal'), clasping the hands in front of the body, pouting the lips and batting the eyelids.

Korean computer mediated communication is also known to feature its own distinctive range of multimodal features, consisting of various computer-mediated communication (CMC) cues. These cues are important for second language learners of Korean to master, given that Togans et al. (2021) found that Koreans and other East Asians use more CMC cues than Americans and also display a greater propensity to vary their use of cues depending on the context. Korean uses a range of CMC cues that are not necessarily familiar to speakers of other languages, particularly those outside the East Asian cultural sphere. Korean speakers often use vertical emoticons to represent emotions, which focus on the shape of the eye (e.g., "^_^"), whereas English speakers more frequently use horizontal emoticons that focus on the mouth (e.g., ":)") (Sun et al., 2023). In addition to emoticons, Korean also uses graphic metaphor and metonymy via Hangul to mark emotions (see Harkness, 2015), including ㅋ and ㅎ for laughing, and ㅠ for crying (see Kang et al., 2022). Finally, the Kakao Talk messaging app, which is used ubiquitously in South Korea, has its own sets of emojis, including widely used humanoid emoji stickers. Sun et al. (2023) found that American undergraduate students struggled to identify the communicative functions of Kakao Talk emoji stickers, such as those shown in Figure 9.1.

Korean visual media texts have their own special characteristics, with several previous studies looking at Korean advertising. Harkness (2013) looked at how soju adverts from the 2000s use a multimodal language to depict soju as being "soft" and fun for everyone to drink, including by using a colour palette of blues and greens and female models with gentle bodily images. This contrasted with soju adverts in the 1980s, which featured reds and browns, tough-looking men and an overall depiction of a harsh and serious drinking experience. Harkness also discussed how post-2000 soju ads feature the sound 캬 *kya* being produced after downing soju shots – a softer sound object in place of the harsher 크 *ku*.

Several studies have explored the multimodal features of Korean urban landscapes. J. Lee (2022) explored how transnational Korean linguistic landscapes both

Figure 9.1 Kakao Talk emoji stickers

in South Korea and in overseas Koreatowns represent Koreanness through various linguistic and multimodal channels including 태극 *taegeuk* icons (the yin-yang design used in the centre of the South Korean flag), colours (red), names of previous dynasties on the Korean peninsula (고려 *Goryeo*, 신라 *Silla*) and multimodal references to disputed geographic locations (such as Dokdo, a disputed group of islets located between Korea and Japan). Tokens of other cultures are also present, such as shop and café names that evoke Italianness and Frenchness. Meanwhile, T. Kim (2021a) explores the multimodality of the (Korean) Chinese migrant neighbourhood in Daerim-dong, Seoul, which features Chinese-language signs and prominent use of red.

Recently studies have also investigated how embodied practices have become the locus of political debate and tensions. T. Kim (2021b) and Milak (2022) both explored the semiotics of face mask wearing during the COVID-19 pandemic and previously under the fine-dust crisis. Whereas T. Kim (2021b) argued that the mask became politicised as a sign of the threat of China (which was the geographic source of both the fine dust and COVID-19) and the government's responsibility for the crisis, Milak (2022) discussed how the mask came to "embody the tension between government oversight and civil liberties." Meanwhile, Chesnut et al. (2021) investigated how signs encouraging people to mask during the COVID-19 pandemic fluctuated between the semantics of fear and the semantics of cuteness. Investigating another sensationalised and politicised controversy, Brown (2023) looked at how representations of a precision grip hand gesture denoting small size in advertising materials became a locus for anti-feminist discourses, with misogynist online communities and the conservative press treating the gesture as a misandrist emblem that needed to be controlled.

Multimodal approaches to Korean language teaching 159

3. Bringing multimodality into the Korean classroom

Until now pedagogical manuals and handbooks for Korean second language acquisition (Byon & Pyun, 2022; Y. Y. Cho, 2020) have not directly addressed the need to include multimodal elements in Korean language teaching. To address this gap, in the current section, I map out three examples of multimodal pedagogical techniques for teaching Korean, all of which build directly off the research outlined in the previous section. Rather than being applied directly, as described here, these models can be adapted or transferred to other domains to suit the specifics of each Korean language class.

3.1 Multimodal discourse analysis: Soju ads

This teaching idea involves developing a multiliteracy-oriented lesson plan using the model provided by Paesani et al. (2015) and soju ads analysed by Harkness (2013). The lesson plan would be appropriate for learners with high intermediate proficiency or higher. The goals of the lesson plan are to develop students' multimodal competence in understanding Korean adverts and how they depict gender. The materials could also lead into further discussion of Korean alcohol culture and/or gender in South Korean society. Following Paesani et al. (2015), the lesson features five different stages: pre-reading, initial reading, detailed reading, critical reading and knowledge application. The materials for the lesson include two televised soju adverts from the Harkness (2013) that are freely available on YouTube: An ad for Bohae soju containing the slogan 사나이라면 묻지를 마라 *sanairamyeon mutji-reul mara* "If you're a man don't ask" (Bohae Liquor, 1982)[2] and an ad for Chum Churum with the slogan 흔들어라 *heundeureora* "Give it a shake" (Lotte Chilsung Beverage Co, 2008)[3] A selection of still shots from these ads are shown in Figure 9.2 to provide an overview of their aesthetics and to contextualise the activities.

2a: Bohae Soju advertisement containing the slogan 사나이라면 묻지를 마라 *sanairamyeon mutji-reul mara* "If you're a man don't ask" (Bohae Liquor, 1982)

2b: Chum Churum advertisement with the slogan 흔들어라 *heundeureora* "Give it a shake" (Lotte Chilsung Beverage Co, 2008)

Figure 9.2 Still shots from the two main ads

In the first stage of the lesson plan, which, following the conventions of Paesani et al. (2015), is known as pre-reading, students are shown a number of printed soju ads from the post-2000 period.[4] Students are asked questions such as the following:

1. What products are these adverts for?
2. Do you know any of the brands in these ads? Do you buy any of these brands yourself?
3. Which of these adverts do you think is the best?
4. What do the ads have in common? You can think of the slogans, colours, backgrounds, choice of model, what the model is doing, etc.?
5. We are going to analyse two television soju adverts in more detail. One is from 2008 and the other is from 1982. What do you expect to see in the adverts? How do you think they will be different?

Patterns that students might notice in the ads include the use of female models, the prevalence of greens, blues and whites, and the appearance of the word 부드럽다 *budeureopda* 'soft' (as well as 깨끗하다 *kkaekkeutada* 'clean, fresh') in the slogans.

In the second stage, initial reading, students watch the two main television adverts for Bohae soju (1982) and Chum Churum (2008). The goal at this stage is for learners to identify the overall narratives and mood of the adverts. Guiding questions would include the following:

1. Where are the ads set?
2. What are the people in the ads doing?
3. What overall impression or feeling do the ads give?

Students may notice that the 1982 Bohae ad codes soju drinking as a male experience and gives the overall impression that drinking soju is a rough and serious activity. In contrast, the 2008 Chum Churum ad positions soju drinking as a fun experience that can be enjoyed everywhere and by everyone, including by women.

Next is the detailed reading stage, which involves students taking a deep dive into the materials and analysing them in detail. Here students might be asked to take notes on the different modalities featured in the ads that come together to mark a "hard" drinking experience in the Bohae ad and a "soft" drinking experience in the Chum Churum one:

1. Slogan
2. Spoken content
3. Sound of the voice
4. Kinesics
5. Music
6. Colours
7. Physical appearance and clothing of models

This stage could be done as a type of jigsaw activity, with half of the students assigned to the Bohae ad and half to the Chum Churum commercial.

In the fourth stage, critical reading, students should be encouraged to critically interrogate the textual choices that they uncovered in the previous stage. Questions that could lead such discussions would include the following:

1. Why do the ads use the slogans/music/colours that they do?
2. Do you think that soju really is "soft" and "clean", as claimed by the 2000s soju ads? Why do the companies market soju in this way?
3. Why have the ads changed between the 1980s and the 2000s? What does this tell us about (1) soju consumption and/or (2) gender in South Korea?
4. Does soju have to become "softer" and be marketed in a "softer" way in order for women to consume it?

These open-ended questions may be difficult for students with lower proficiency levels. In such cases, it might be preferable to choose just one question and to assign it as a written activity.

The final step is called knowledge application, and this typically involves activities in which students need to apply their knowledge to new contexts and/or the creation of new texts. I would like to suggest two possible activities here, with the second being best suited for a homework task. The first activity would be to apply students' observations on soju ads to advertisements for other products such as ramyeon, soft drinks and cosmetics that depict women and men in "soft" and "hard" ways, respectively, and/or which subvert these aesthetics. Some suggested commercials that could be used include 2012 adverts for 남자라면 *Namja Ramyeon* starring Ryu Seung-ryong,[5] various ads since around 2017 for Sprite[6] and commercials for the male cosmetics company MIP.[7] Of note here is the fact that adverts for ramyeon and soft drinks frequently include the ㅋ and 캬 sound objects identified by Harkness (2013) as markers of softness and hardness, respectively, which provide one further avenue via which students could explore the ads. As a second idea for a knowledge application activity, I recommend that students create their own soju adverts, with the option of following the conventions of extant soju ads or subverting them. The ads could be produced in various formats, including written ads, videos or in-class skits.

3.2 Multimodal politeness: honorifics and embodiment

In a previous paper co-authored with Sue Yoon (Yoon & Brown, 2017), we explored multiliteracy techniques for teaching multimodal aspects of Korean politeness. Specifically, we devised and trialled an 80-minute lesson that employed clips from Korean TV dramas and a section on politeness from a government-produced guidebook for overseas residents in Korea. Our lesson plan involved students critically analysing and discussing multimodal features of politeness in the drama scripts and critiquing the descriptions of politeness in the guidebook. For the final knowledge application activity, students rewrote the guidebook section, creating their own multimodal text combining written content and drawings explaining multimodal features of politeness. Elsewhere, I have written on techniques for using multimedia materials for teaching non-honorific language (Brown, 2013b).

Here, I would like to focus instead on how multimodal elements of honorifics can be taught at lower levels. Here an assumption is that learners need to be taught different levels of speech from beginner level as an essential part of communicative competence in the Korean context, an argument that I made previously (Brown, 2010). My position here is that introducing multimodal aspects of the ways in which Korean speakers perform politeness to status superiors can help learners to see connections with how politeness is performed in their extant languages and cultures and thereby de-exoticise and demystify honorifics and deference.

When learners are introduced to Korean honorifics for the first time, this often occurs via complex grammatical descriptions and/or via elaborate descriptions of Korean culture and its Confucian heritage, which are often stereotyped or even exotified. My suggestion here is that the teaching of honorifics and associated cultural norms can instead begin by showing learners images featuring the performance of multimodal politeness, which can easily be sourced from Korean media, as in the examples in Figure 9.3. The lesson can start with learners being shown images such as those in Figure 9.3 (short video clips can be used instead) and being asked questions such as the following:

1. Who is the elder/status superior?
2. How do you know? What are the status inferiors doing?

These questions can be asked and answered in a mixture of Korean and the local language, and basic metalexemes such as 윗사람 *witsaram* 'elder, senior' can be introduced. If learners have already been taught words for body parts, then these can be reviewed and expressions for bodily behaviours can be introduced (e.g., cross legs, give with one/two hands, bow).

After this discussion, the teacher can provide learners with a table of basic embodied behaviours that occur and do not occur when interacting with elders (see Table 9.1). Rather than providing the table in its final form, learners can be given a blank table and asked to match each item to the correct column.

Only after completing these activities will students be introduced to verbal aspects of honorifics. This introduction can be linked to images such as those in Figure 9.4, where 4a and 4b show similar situations. The teacher can be asked to provide the verbal content, and at this stage it can be introduced that whereas you would use the honorific leave-taking expression 안녕히 계세요 *annyeonghi gyeseyo* to your boss while bowing (4a), to an intimate co-worker you might say 안녕 *annyeong* and wave (4b). Similarly, where you might offer a coffee to a status superior by saying 커피 한 잔 드세요 *keopi han jan deuseyo* while extending the cup with two hands or with one hand across the stomach, with an intimate you

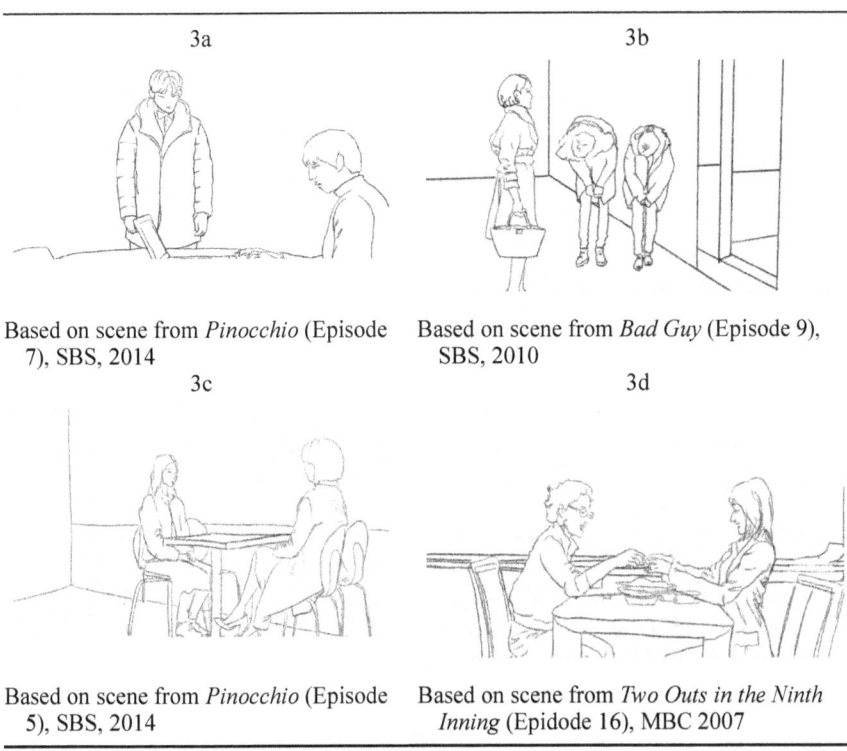

Based on scene from *Pinocchio* (Episode 7), SBS, 2014

Based on scene from *Bad Guy* (Episode 9), SBS, 2010

Based on scene from *Pinocchio* (Episode 5), SBS, 2014

Based on scene from *Two Outs in the Ninth Inning* (Epidode 16), MBC 2007

Figure 9.3 Drawings based on scenes from Korean dramas showing multimodal politeness

Table 9.1 Table of appropriate embodied behaviours

Embodied behaviours usually appropriate for interactions with elders:	*Embodied behaviours usually not appropriate for interactions with elders:*
Bowing	Waving
Passing items with two hands	Passing items with one hand
Sitting up straight with knees together	Sitting slouched with legs splayed or crossed
Clasping your hands in front of your body	Putting your hands on your hips
-	Touching the other person on their shoulder

might say 커피 한 잔 마셔 *keopi han jan masyeo* and offer the cup with one hand, and so forth

This approach to introducing honorifics comes with a number of important advantages. First of all, learners will find that some of the embodied differences are recognisable to them because they are somewhat universal and shared to some extent in other cultures, even if they are performed more rigorously in Korean. This allows learners to appreciate that expressing deference to elders and varying how you interact depending on the identity of the addressee is not a social practice that

4a   4b

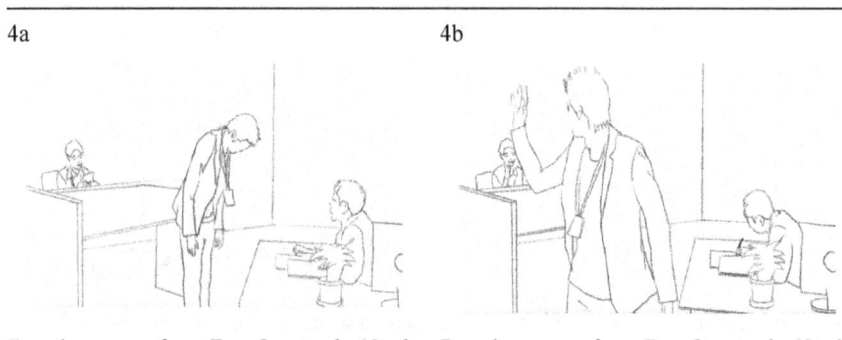

Based on scene from *Two Outs in the Ninth*   Based on scene from *Two Outs in the Ninth*
Inning (Epidode 2), MBC 2007   *Inning* (Epidode 2), MBC 2007

Figure 9.4 Example images that can be used for introducing verbal aspects of politeness

is unique to Korean but something that also exists to some extent in other cultures. Learners might also find the embodied behaviours recognisable because they have been exposed to them via Korean television and popular culture, which provides another avenue of connection to learners' existing knowledge. A second advantage is that this approach embeds the introduction of honorific language within embodied social action, thereby providing learners with a holistic and situated understanding of honorifics from the start. Third and finally, teaching embodied aspects of honorifics from the start is advantageous since learners are able to directly apply this knowledge when they visit Korea or interact with Korean people, no matter how basic their level of spoken Korean might be. This is important since, as demonstrated by Lo (2009), whereas Koreans may dismiss infelicities in the use of honorifics merely as grammatical errors, use of inappropriate embodied behaviours is judged more harshly and is seen more closely as an index of a speaker's deficient morality. Language learners who display embodied politeness are therefore more likely to be judged favourably by Korean speakers.

3.3 *Multimodal ethnographic project work*

In this third example, I propose that learners at all levels of competence can be assigned projects involving multimodal ethnography (Dicks et al., 2006) in order to enhance their multimodal competences and to increase their critical understanding of Korean culture. Using projects for exploring culture is known to be effective due to its student-centred nature, which allows for learners to explore their own ideas about culture and discover their own versions of Korea (see Byon, 2007 for previous examples of project work in the Korean L2 context; Jung & Lee, 2018).

The basic idea here is that learners are tasked with projects that involve them going out into global Korean communities and collecting images of what they see and then subjecting these images to analysis. The ethnography can take place either physically (i.e., through visiting Korean communities) or digitally (i.e., via Internet-based digital technologies, including Google Images and Google Maps). With digital ethnography, learners can explore aspects of Korean communities in South Korea or anywhere on the globe without the necessity of any kind of physical visit (see Berti, 2020). Possible topics for ethnography are various, particularly with digital ethnography, but might include food, shopping, transportation systems, holidays, food, fashion and traditional culture.

Here I would like to introduce a multimodal ethnographic project that could be used in upper-intermediate or advanced-level Korean classes. The project would involve exploring urban spaces in overseas Korean communities, which could be urban spaces local to the students or, via digital ethnography, any other urban spaces that are known to have vibrant Korean communities. Students would search either physically or digitally for photographs of these urban spaces, making collections of images of restaurants, storefronts, menus, signage and so forth. Images collected by individual students or groups of students would then be pooled with the class and subjected to analysis.

Although potentially several different frames of analysis could be applied, my idea here is that the materials can be analysed in relation to the notion of "Koreanness," in other words, for how notions of Korean identity or Korean culture are created and contested in the artefacts captured by the images. As demonstrated by Lee (2020, 2022), in Korean communities around the globe, Korean culture is represented, reinvented and contested in public spaces in numerous ways, including via translingual practices and various semiotics. Students would analyse the materials for linguistic, visual and other semiotic markers of Korean identity, as well as markers that assigned local or other identities.

As one quick example of the kind of materials that students might analyse, consider the images in Figure 9.5 of Korean storefronts in suburban Melbourne that I collected via Google Street View (see S. Kim & Chesnut, 2020 for investigation of the use of Google Street View for language teaching). These storefronts are all multilingual, with J Mart featuring Chinese alongside English and Korean and KT Mart featuring both Chinese and Japanese (not clearly shown in the image), and they also display various visual features such as contrasting fonts, smartphone–style icons (J Mart and KT Mart), adverts (East Mart, Little Korea) and logos. One interesting pattern is that all four supermarkets represent themselves in English (as well as Chinese and Japanese) as Asian rather than specifically Korean supermarkets, with Little Korea using the term "Asian Groceries" and the three others all mentioning Chinese and Japanese products on their signage. J Mart describes itself as a Korean and Japanese supermarket in the English signage but also adds Chinese to the Chinese sign. At the same time, all four make references to their Korean identities, although these references are sometimes subtle and would be clearly visible only to those with linguistic and cultural knowledge of Korea. East Mart describes itself in Korean as a Korean grocers, whereas Korean products are never mentioned in the English signage (which mentions only Japanese and Chinese). Little Korea uses a picture of an earthenware pot inscribed with "Asian groceries"

5a. J Mart, Boronia
Image credit: Google Streetview

5b. East Mart, Mount Waverley
Image credit: Google Streetview

5c. Little Korea, Oakleigh
Image credit: Google Streetview

5d. KT Mart, Mitcham
Image credit: Google Streetview

Figure 9.5 Korean storefronts in suburban Melbourne

as its logo, whereas this pot would be recognisable to Korean patrons as a jar for making kimchi. Meanwhile, the colours and/or logos of J Mart and KT Mart make multimodal references to well-known brand names in Korea, and the name format *X*-Mart follows a conventional naming practice for supermarkets in South Korea and overseas Korean communities. In sum, these storefronts show a variety of ways in which Korean supermarkets in Melbourne try to present an image of being an Asian rather than exclusively Korean supermarket to the wider community while at the same time displaying their Koreanness clearly to Korean shoppers. These are the kinds of patterns that students can be trained to identify through this project work and which can be interrogated in class via further discussion.

Student projects could be presented in various formats, including printed portfolios, in-class presentations or video presentations. Importantly, the requirements for the presentation should mandate exploration of the reasons why Koreanness is presented in the way that it is in these urban spaces. Students should be asked to interrogate why certain symbols become markers of Koreanness and the reasons why Korean businesses sometimes choose not to explicitly articulate Korean identities. The presentation of the project should also feature opportunities for students to reflect on what they have learned and how their understanding of Korean communities and cultures has developed or changed over the course of the data collection and analysis.

4. Conclusion

In this chapter I have presented a mandate for adopting multimodal pedagogies in Korean language classrooms, based on the observation that communication is inherently multimodal and the argument that multimodal aspects of communicative competence are increasingly important in contemporary society. To get to know a language and a culture is not merely about understanding spoken and written words but, increasingly, relies on an understanding of various semiotic cues, including the sound of the voice and the use of gestures and other bodily visual practices, as well as various visual semiotic practices. Going forward, the undeniable multimodal and embodied nature of communication needs to be reflected more clearly in Korean language teaching, given that the majority of pedagogical practices are still rather monomodal and disembodied.

This chapter has come with obvious limitations. In this format, I was only able to present quite brief and sketchy overviews of three pedagogical ideas for teaching Korean in a multimodal format, and these only covered a small number of the possible multimodal features of Korean that could be taught. The ideas themselves were also limited by the relative lack of previous research on multimodal teaching beyond the framework of multiliteracies, particularly in the Korean context. Future studies will need to explore more detailed pedagogies for the multimodal teaching of Korean, including areas not covered in the current chapter, such as speech-synchronised gestures and emojis.

I conclude by calling for Korean language educators to include room for multimodality in their design of curricula, teaching materials and textbooks and also to consider embodied and multimodal features in their research designs. A multimodal turn is needed in the ways in which we think about language in the context of L2 teaching, and this turn should be reflected across all areas of Korean language pedagogy and the academic study of Korean pedagogical practices.

Acknowledgements

This work was supported by the Core University Program for Korean Studies through the Ministry of Education of the Republic of Korea and Korean Studies Promotion Service of the Academy of Korean Studies (AKS-2023-OLU-2250001).

Notes

1 Beyond the context of second language learning, other scholars have talked of the ability to understand multimodal texts and digital media by terms such as "multimodal competence" (Kress, 2003), "digital literacy" (Jones & Hafner, 2021) and "media literacy" (Scheibe & Rogow, 2011).
2 www.youtube.com/watch?v=AthSQRiKpUI [accessed April 2024]
3 www.youtube.com/watch?v=vyp_VTdaZX8 [accessed April 2024]

4 Soju adverts for the leading brands can be accessed from company websites including the following: Jinro (www.hitejinro.com/socialmedia/library.asp), Bohae (www.bohae.co.kr/bbs/board.php?bo_table=tl_gallery_print) and Choongbuk (www.cbsoju.com/board/go).
5 The best of which can be viewed here: www.youtube.com/watch?v=4kIlYK5lIOk [accessed April 2024]
6 One example is here: www.youtube.com/watch?v=ybNFC-dNKU4 [accessed April 2024]
7 Examples include the following: www.youtube.com/watch?v=rB6W65TBHjY [accessed April 2024]

References

Andries, F., Meissl, K., de Vries, C., Feyaerts, K., Oben, B., Sambre, P., Vermeerbergen, M., & Brône, G. (2023). Multimodal stance-taking in interaction: A systematic literature review. *Frontiers in Communication, 8*, 1187977.

Berti, M. (2020). Digital ethnography for culture teaching in the foreign language classroom. *Intercultural Communication Education, 3*(1), 44–54.

Bohae Liquor (Director). (1982). *30 보해 BOHAE white liquor*. www.youtube.com/watch?v=AthSQRiKpUI

Brown, L. (2010). Questions of appropriateness and authenticity in the representation of Korean honorifics in textbooks for second language learners. *Language, Culture and Curriculum, 23*(1), 35–50.

Brown, L. (2013a). "Oppa, hold my purse": A sociocultural study of identity and indexicality in the perception and use of oppa' older brother' by second language learners. *Korean Language in America, 18*(1), 1–22.

Brown, L. (2013b). Teaching 'casual' and/or 'impolite' language through multimedia: The case of non-honorific panmal speech styles in Korean. *Language, Culture and Curriculum, 26*(1), 1–18.

Brown, L. (2017). "Nwuna's body is so sexy": Pop culture and the chronotopic formulations of kinship terms in Korean. *Discourse, Context & Media, 15*, 1–10.

Brown, L. (2023). "The denigration of Korean men's genitals": Precision grip gestures and the multimodal construction of "taking offence" in media discourse surrounding anti-feminism in South Korea. *Journal of Language Aggression and Conflict, 12*(2), 234–262.

Brown, L., Hübscher, I., Kim, H., & Winter, B. (2023). Indexing social distance through bodily visual practices in two languages. In A. Jucker, I. Hübscher, & L. Brown (Eds.), *Multimodal im/politeness: Signed, spoken, written* (pp. 131–161). John Benjamins Publishing.

Brown, L., Iwasaki, N., & Lee, K. (2015). Implementing multiliteracies in the Korean classroom through visual media. In Y. Kumagai, A. López-Sánchez, & S. Wu (Eds.), *Multiliteracies in world language education* (pp. 158–181). Routledge.

Brown, L., Kim, H., Hübscher, I., & Winter, B. (2023). Gestures are modulated by social context: A study of multimodal politeness across two cultures. *Gesture, 21*(2/3), 167–200.

Brown, L., & Park, M. Y. (2020). Culture in language learning and teaching. In Y. Y. Cho (Ed.), *Teaching Korean as a foreign language: Theories and practices* (pp. 81–108). Routledge.

Brown, L., & Winter, B. (2019). Multimodal indexicality in Korean: "Doing deference" and "performing intimacy" through nonverbal behavior. *Journal of Politeness Research, 15*(1), 25–54.

Brown, L., Winter, B., Idemaru, K., & Grawunder, S. (2014). Phonetics and politeness: Perceiving Korean honorific and non-honorific speech through phonetic cues. *Journal of Pragmatics, 66*, 45–60.

Byon, A. S. (2007). The use of culture portfolio project in a Korean culture classroom: Evaluating stereotypes and enhancing cross-cultural awareness. *Language, Culture and Curriculum, 20*(1), 1–19.

Byon, A. S., & Pyun, D. O. (2022). *The Routledge handbook of Korean as a second language*. Routledge.

Byram, M. (1997). *Teaching and assessing intercultural communicative competence*. Multilingual Matters.

Byram, M., Gribkova, B., & Starkey, H. (2002). *Developing the intercultural dimension in language teaching: A practical introduction for teachers*. Council of Europe.

Canale, M. (1983). From communicative competence to communicative language pedagogy. In J. C. Richards & R. W. Schmidt (Eds.), *Language and communication* (pp. 2–27). Longman.

Canale, M., & Swain, M. (1980). Theoretical bases of com-municative approaches to second language teaching and testing. *Applied Linguistics, 1*(1), 1–47.

Chesnut, M., Curran, N. M., & Kim, S. (2021). Cuteness and fear in the COVID-19 linguistic landscape of South Korea. *The Linguistic Landscape of COVID-19*. www.covidsigns.net/post/michael-chesnut-et-al-cuteness-and-fear-in-the-covid-19-linguistic-landscape-of-south-korea

Cho, Y. Y. (2020). *Teaching Korean as a foreign language: Theories and practices*. Routledge.

Choi, S. (2006). Influence of language-specific input on spatial cognition: Categories of containment. *First Language, 26*(2), 207–232.

Choi, S., & Lantolf, J. P. (2008). Representation and embodiment of meaning in L2 communication: Motion events in the speech and gesture of advanced L2 Korean and L2 English speakers. *Studies in Second Language Acquisition, 30*(2). https://doi.org/10.1017/S0272263108080315

Coccetta, F. (2018). Developing university students' multimodal communicative competence: Field research into multimodal text studies in English. *System, 77*, 19–27.

Cohn, N. (2010). Japanese visual language: The structure of manga. In T. Johnson-Woods (Ed.), *Manga: An anthology of global and cultural perspectives* (pp. 187–203). Bloomsbury Publishing.

Cohn, N. (2013). *The visual language of comics: Introduction to the structure and cognition of sequential images*. A&C Black.

Cooperrider, K., Slotta, J., & Núñez, R. (2018). The preference for pointing with the hand is not universal. *Cognitive Science, 42*(4), 1375–1390.

Crosby, D. M. (2023). *Oppa-Ng Gamsahamnita-Ng~~~: The phonetics of nasal cuteness in Korean Aegyo* [PhD Thesis, University of South Carolina].

Danzak, R. L. (2011). Defining identities through multiliteracies: EL teens narrate their immigration experiences as graphic stories. *Journal of Adolescent & Adult Literacy, 55*(3), 187–196.

Dicks, B., Soyinka, B., & Coffey, A. (2006). Multimodal ethnography. *Qualitative Research, 6*(1), 77–96.

Dingemanse, M. (2020). Between sound and speech: Liminal signs in interaction. *Research on Language and Social Interaction, 53*(1), 188–196.

Eggins, S. (2004). *Introduction to systemic functional linguistics*. A & C Black.

Ford, C. E., Thompson, S. A., & Drake, V. (2012). Bodily-visual practices and turn continuation. *Discourse Processes, 49*(3–4), 192–212.

Freeman, V. (2014). Hyperarticulation as a signal of stance. *Journal of Phonetics, 45*, 1–11.

Freeman, V. (2015). *The phonetics of stance-taking* [PhD Thesis, University of Washington]. https://digital.lib.washington.edu/researchworks/handle/1773/34001

Freeman, V. (2019). Prosodic features of stances in conversation. *Laboratory Phonology, 10*(1).

Geisler, M., Kramsch, C., McGinnis, S., Patrikis, P., Pratt, M. L., Ryding, K., & Saussy, H. (2007). Foreign languages and higher education: New structures for a changed world: MLA ad hoc committee on foreign languages. *Profession*, 234–245.

Halliday, M. A. K., & Matthiessen, C. M. (2013). *Halliday's introduction to functional grammar*. Routledge.

Harkness, N. (2013). Softer soju in South Korea. *Anthropological Theory*, *13*(1–2), 12–30.

Harkness, N. (2015). Linguistic emblems of South Korean society. In L. Brown & J. Yeon (Eds.), *The handbook of Korean linguistics* (pp. 492–508). Wiley.

Highfield, T., & Leaver, T. (2016). Instagrammatics and digital methods: Studying visual social media, from selfies and GIFs to memes and emoji. *Communication Research and Practice*, *2*(1), 47–62.

Hymes, D. (1972). On communicative competence. In J. B. Pride & J. Holmes (Eds.), *Sociolinguistics; Selected readings* (pp. 269–293). Penguin.

Idemaru, K., Winter, B., & Brown, L. (2019). Cross-cultural multimodal politeness: The phonetics of Japanese deferential speech in comparison to Korean. *Intercultural Pragmatics*, *16*(5), 517–555.

Idemaru, K., Winter, B., Brown, L., & Oh, G. E. (2020). Loudness trumps pitch in politeness judgments: Evidence from Korean deferential speech. *Language and Speech*, *63*(1), 123–148.

Jang, H. (2021). How cute do I sound to you? Gender and age effects in the use and evaluation of Korean baby-talk register, Aegyo. *Language Sciences*, *83*, 101289.

Jones, R. H., & Hafner, C. A. (2021). *Understanding digital literacies: A practical introduction*. Routledge.

Jung, J.-Y., & Lee, E. (2018). Citizen sociolinguistics: Making connections in the foreign language classroom. *The Korean Language in America*, *22*(1), 1–24.

Kalantzis, M., Cope, B., Chan, E., & Dalley-Trim, L. (2016). *Literacies*. Cambridge University Press.

Kang, C., Hong, J.-O., Chang, W., Suk, H.-J., & Hong, H. (2022). Korean emoticons: Understanding how subtle emotional differences are evoked online. In *Companion Publication of the 2022 Conference on Computer Supported Cooperative Work and Social Computing* (pp. 121–125).

Kim, G. M., & Omerbašić, D. (2017). Multimodal literacies: Imagining lives through Korean dramas. *Journal of Adolescent & Adult Literacy*, *60*(5), 557–566.

Kim, M. (2022). Performing gender in Korean: Language, gender, and social change. In S. Cho & J. Whitman (Eds.), *The Cambridge handbook of Korean linguistics* (pp. 689–716). Cambridge University Press.

Kim, S., & Chesnut, M. (2020). Teaching with virtual linguistic landscapes: Developing translingual and transcultural competence. In D. Malinowski, H. H. Maxim, & S. Dubreil (Eds.), *Language teaching in the linguistic landscape* (Vol. 49, pp. 69–92). Springer International Publishing.

Kim, T.-S. (2021a). Center and margin on the margin: A study of the multilayered (Korean) Chinese migrant neighborhood in Daerim-dong, South Korea. *Geoforum*, *120*, 165–175.

Kim, T.-S. (2021b). Mythologizing the face mask: How protective covers became political during the fine-dust and COVID-19 crises in South Korea. *International Journal of Media & Cultural Politics*, *17*(2), 97–117.

Konrad, A., Herring, S. C., & Choi, D. (2020). Sticker and emoji use in Facebook Messenger: Implications for graphicon change. *Journal of Computer-Mediated Communication*, *25*(3), 217–235.

Kramsch, C. (2006). From communicative competence to symbolic competence. *The Modern Language Journal*, *90*(2), 249–252.

Kramsch, C. (2011). The symbolic dimensions of the intercultural. *Language Teaching*, *44*(3), 354–367.

Kramsch, C., & Whiteside, A. (2008). Language ecology in multilingual settings. Towards a theory of symbolic competence. *Applied Linguistics, 29*(4), 645–671.

Kress, G. (2003). *Literacy in the new media age*. Routledge.

Kress, G. (2009). Comments on Cope and Kalantzis. *Pedagogies: An International Journal, 4*(3), 205–212.

Kress, G., & Van Leeuwen, T. (2001). *Multimodal discourse: The modes and media of contemporary communication*. Arnold.

Kress, G., & Van Leeuwen, T. (2002). Colour as a semiotic mode: Notes for a grammar of colour. *Visual Communication, 1*(3), 343–368.

Kress, G., & Van Leeuwen, T. (2020). *Reading images: The grammar of visual design*. Routledge.

Kumagai, Y., Konoeda, K., & Nishimata, M. (2015). Fostering multimodal literacies in the Japanese language classroom. In Y. Kumagai, A. López-Sánchez, & S. Wu (Eds.), *Multiliteracies in world language education* (pp. 135–157). Routledge.

Lee, J. W. (2020). On the possibilities of 'Korea'in the linguistic landscape. In I. Theodoropoulou & J. Tovar (Eds.), *Research companion to language and country branding* (pp. 259–278). Routledge.

Lee, J. W. (2022). *Locating translingualism*. Cambridge University Press.

Lee-Smith, A. (2016). Pedagogy of multiliteracies for Korean language learners: Developing standards-based (the 5Cs) teaching-learning materials using TV public service announcements. *Journal of Korean Language Education, 27*(2), 143–192.

Lo, A. (2009). Lessons about respect and affect in a Korean heritage language school. *Linguistics and Education, 20*(3), 217–234.

Lo Bianco, J. (2005). Multiliteracies and multilingualism. In B. Cope & M. Kalantzis (Eds.), *Multiliteracies: Literacy learning and the design of social futures* (pp. 89–102). Routledge.

Lotte Chilsung Beverage Co (Director). (2008). 처음처럼 *[Chum Churum] soju*. www.youtube.com/watch?v=vyp_VTdaZX8

Mesh, K., Cruz, E., & Gullberg, M. (2023). When attentional and politeness demands clash: The case of mutual gaze avoidance and chin pointing in Quiahije Chatino. *Journal of Nonverbal Behavior, 47*(2), 211–243.

Mihas, E. (2023). Interactional functions of lip funneling gestures: A case study of Northern Kampa Arawaks of Peru. *Gesture, 16*(3), 432–479.

Milak, E. (2022). (Un)masking Seoul: The mask as a static and dynamic semiotic device for renegotiating space. *Linguistic Landscape. An International Journal, 8*(2–3), 233–247.

Mondada, L. (2019). Contemporary issues in conversation analysis: Embodiment and materiality, multimodality and multisensoriality in social interaction. *Journal of Pragmatics, 145*, 47–62.

The New London Group. (1996). A pedagogy of multiliteracies: Designing social futures. *Harvard Educational Review, 66*(1), 60–93.

Paesani, K., Allen, H. W., & Dupuy, B. (2015). *Multiliteracies framework for collegiate foreign language teaching*. Pearson.

Park, H. I. (2020). How do Korean – English bilinguals speak and think about motion events? Evidence from verbal and non-verbal tasks. *Bilingualism: Language and Cognition, 23*(3), 483–499.

Park, H. I. (2022). The role of language in expressing agentivity in caused motion events: A cross-linguistic investigation. *Frontiers in Psychology, 13*, 878277.

Puzar, A., & Hong, Y. (2018). Korean cuties: Understanding performed winsomeness (Aegyo) in South Korea. *The Asia Pacific Journal of Anthropology, 19*(4), 333–349.

Reber, E. (2012). *Affectivity in interaction: Sound objects in English*. John Benjamins Publishing.

Royce, T. (2007). Multimodal communicative competence in second language contexts. In T. Royce & W. Bowcher (Eds.), *New directions in the analysis of multimodal discourse* (pp. 361–390). Routledge.

Scheibe, C., & Rogow, F. (2011). *The teacher's guide to media literacy: Critical thinking in a multimedia world*. Corwin Press.

Strong, S. (2013). Too cute for words: An investigation of the Aegyo speech style and its pertinence to identity, gender, and sexuality within South Korea. *Washington University Undergraduate Research Digest*, *8*(2). https://openscholarship.wustl.edu/wushta_spr2013/114/

Suh, J., & Jung, J.-Y. (2020). Literacy and multiliteracies in Korean language learning and teaching. In Y. Y. Cho (Ed.), *Teaching Korean as a foreign language: Theories and practices*. Routledge.

Sun, J., Lasser, S., & Lee, S. K. (2023). Understanding emojis: Cultural influences in interpretation and choice of emojis. *Journal of International and Intercultural Communication*, *16*(3), 242–261. https://doi.org/10.1080/17513057.2022.2036790

Togans, L. J., Holtgraves, T., Kwon, G., & Zelaya, T. E. M. (2021). Digitally saving face: An experimental investigation of cross-cultural differences in the use of emoticons and emoji. *Journal of Pragmatics*, *186*, 277–288.

Vigliocco, G., Perniss, P., & Vinson, D. (2014). Language as a multimodal phenomenon: Implications for language learning, processing and evolution. *Philosophical Transactions of the Royal Society B: Biological Sciences*, *369*(1651), 20130292.

Winter, B., & Duffy, S. E. (2020). Can co-speech gestures alone carry the mental time line? *Journal of Experimental Psychology: Learning, Memory, and Cognition*, *46*(9), 1768.

Winter, B., & Grawunder, S. (2012). The phonetic profile of Korean formal and informal speech registers. *Journal of Phonetics*, *40*(6), 808–815.

Yoon, S. Y., & Brown, L. (2017). A multiliteracies approach to teaching Korean multimodal (im) politeness. *The Korean Language in America*, *21*(2), 154–185.

10 Transformative learning through critical pedagogy in Korean language education

Young-mee Yu Cho and Hee Chung Chun

1. Introduction

The student profile of the foreign language classroom in the third decade of the 21st century in the United States is characterized by what Vertovec (2007) dubbed "super-diversity." This concept describes the changing population configurations due to unprecedented global migration of people of diverse national, ethnic, and linguistic backgrounds. Vertovec (2007, p. 1024) argues that we arrive at the state of super-diversity "by a dynamic interplay of variables among an increased number of new, small and scattered, multiple-origin, transnationally connected, socio-economically differentiated and legally stratified immigrants who have arrived over the last decade."

Emerging superdiversity in Korean as a foreign language (KFL) classroom is an even more recent phenomenon. Due to large Korean heritage language communities in North America, the educational challenges of the mixed group of heritage and non-heritage learners have been an issue from the 1980s when KFL instruction started to expand. In addition to the layer of heritage/non-heritage division, we witness an additional dimension of superdiversity in the non-heritage learners.

Korean immigration to the US started in earnest after the Immigration Act of 1965 that abolished the discriminatory policies of immigration on the basis of national origin, race, and ancestry. Many collegiate KFL programs were created to the demands of the second-generation Korean American students who reached the college age in the mid-1980s. The trend has changed in the 21st century when the Korean Wave hit North America. Within the context of foreign language education in the US, the past two decades have seen the most dramatic expansion in KFL programs, particularly, at the university level.

A noteworthy change is the demographic shift in the learner profile. In contrast to the first stage of KFL instruction, non-heritage students and international students from diverse cultures and linguistic backgrounds have been increasing fastest. The curriculum had to be revised from a mixed class of heritage/non-heritage learners to non-heritage 'super-diverse' learners. The American Association of Teachers of Korean (AATK) survey on 106 universities that was conducted in 2021 and made available on the AATK homepage shows that in most universities the percentage of heritage students is less than 20 percent, and the percentage is even lower in the beginning level.

KFL programs currently are dealing with an ever-widening spectrum of the learner population in terms of its linguistic and cultural diversity as well as an increasing gap of proficiency development within the superdiverse classroom, especially in advanced learning where the curriculum is open ended both in themes/topics and grammar. We argue that in order to sustain student motivation through multi-year foreign language learning in the face of diverse proficiencies, interests, and needs, we need to transcend the confines of general academic goals and develop socially responsible transformative learning by adopting critical pedagogy. In Section 3 of this chapter, we will demonstrate the multifaceted benefits of CP-inspired curricula and task-based translation projects. We are able to observe how the students' experiences contribute to improving their language and translation skills and enriching their overall language proficiency in both their native language and the target language. Additionally, they also reflect on the empowerment process inherent in active community engagement.

2. Critical pedagogy: literature review

Critical pedagogy, also known as pedagogy of critical consciousness (PCC), is a philosophy of education that encourages the students to be critical towards their reality and to bring their own knowledge and experience into learning that is often conducted in interactive collaboration. Its starting point is the learner's life-situations in schools and community, and its educational goal is the raising of consciousness and the overcoming of obstacles. Critical pedagogy as a new educational philosophy was first articulated by Brazilian scholar Paulo Freire in his foundational book, *Pedagogy of the Oppressed* (1968/1970). He believed that education should not be separated from real life and that the act of teaching and learning is an act towards enhancing social justice. Freire's ideas were enthusiastically adopted by McLaren (1989), Giroux (1992, 2011), and Luke and Gore (1992) as pedagogical practices of implementing "social visions" (Simon, 1992) in confronting political and economic inequities in contemporary societies. Critical pedagogy is about teaching students to think critically and question the received views of the dominant class in a society that the education system tends to propagate. If students were given a traditional history narrative in a textbook, they are encouraged to conduct their own research and investigate alternative narratives, with the aim of acting upon their beliefs.

Applying critical pedagogy as a guiding philosophy in second language education is relatively recent. However, it has gained momentum since the early 2000s (Norton, 2000; Corson, 2001; Cummins, 2001; Pennycook, 2001; Crooks, 2013, 2021; Norton & Toohey, 2012). There are now hands-on attempts to apply critical pedagogy to language education (Cervantes-Soon et al., 2017; Lee, 2022). This pedagogy naturally transcends the confines of general goals of foreign language education and develops socially responsible transformative learning as it directly addresses learner's local communities brings about changes in personal and public spheres. As foreign language education is no longer narrowly focused on the top-down, step-by-step development of communicative language skills in the classroom, a meaningful alternative is offered to enhance learner agency and teacher effectiveness by examining the students' needs and goals and acknowledging the fluid and uniquely individualistic practices of multilingual learners.

Although not directly couched in critical pedagogy, there has emerged an increased interest in community-conscious learning, which shares similar goals of critical pedagogy. These attempts are based on highlighting the Communities Goals in the 5Cs specified in *Standards in Korean Language Learning* (Korean National Standards Task Force, 2012; The National Standards Collaborative Board, 2015). While all five Cs in *National Standards* are equally important and should be properly integrated into any standards-based curriculum, the last three Cs (Comparisons, Connections, and Communities) have not been explored as extensively as Communication and Cultures. Because its reach transcends the physical confines of the classroom, often Communities is treated as an afterthought/appendage in the curriculum proper, even dubbed "the lost C" (Cutshall, 2012). However, we can define its goal as developing the learner's ability to "communicate and interact with cultural competence in order to participate in multilingual communities at home and around the world" (Korean National Standards Task Force, 2012, p. 549). Then, we can break away from stereotypical practices of Communities and reconceptualize the last C as an integral part of KFL education by implementing the subgoals: (1) use the language to interact and collaborate in their community and the globalized world and (2) set goals and reflect on their progress in using languages for enjoyment, enrichment, and advancement.

While Communities was narrowly defined as local Korean communities or study-abroad experiences before the advent of the 21st-century multimodal technology, today's "communities" include many possibilities, reaching beyond the classroom into the entire university (Lee-Smith, 2018), local Korean American communities (Lee & Choi, 2021), and global Korean-speaking communities (Suh, 2019), both physical and virtual. Social networking services and online resources have enabled crossing geographical and political boundaries to pursue mutual interests and common goals. Because virtual communities are created for communication and interaction, they offer truly interactive opportunities and student-initiated modes of learning to pursue personal/academic interests through chatting/blogging/media-creation/research and other social engagement. Service learning, implemented at advanced levels, is hailed as one of the most effective approaches in fostering social/institutional changes by empowering students and contributing to community development (MacGregor-Mendoza & Moreno, 2016; Sohn & Kim, 2022). Service learning can be defined as a form of experiential learning by which students apply academic knowledge to address community needs. For example, it can be a course where bilingual students translate and interpret for the community or engage with compiling oral histories with minority group members. Within a community-based approach, we expect not only the improvement of linguistic/intercultural proficiency and the growing critical awareness of civic responsibility but the transformation of learning into a meaningful, lived experience in personal and public spheres.

3. Implementing critical pedagogy in the KSL curriculum

3.1 Community-conscious learning opportunities at Rutgers

The establishment and expansion of Rutgers University's Korean program are intimately intertwined with the institution's geographical location. Situated in New Jersey, Rutgers benefits from the proximity to a significant Korean American population, particularly notable in Bergen County, acknowledged for its substantial concentration of Korean Americans (US Census Bureau, 2021). Furthermore, within the state of New Jersey, Korean ranks as the fifth most spoken non-English language at home, as reported by the N.J. Department of Health (n.d.). Over recent decades, Rutgers has established a comprehensive Korean language program distinguished by its multifaceted curriculum and concurrent Korean studies offerings, consistently drawing an annual enrollment of approximately 700 students (Cho & Chun, 2023). Along with the program expansion, student expectations transcended the confines of conventional Korean language instruction, focusing on the development of communicative skills of the language. Students needed justification and motivation for continuing language study when there is no language requirement for graduation. Both heritage and non-heritage students in Korean minor and major program wish to see the relevance of taking three or four years of Korean in their own social context and identity. Consequently, Rutgers extended its pedagogical repertoire to address a diverse array of Korean courses for specific purpose, encompassing language elective courses such as Business Korean, Korean Literature, and Korean translation courses.

The two programs to be introduced in the following section, the Rutgers Korean-English Translation and Interpreting Certificate (KETI) program and the Rutgers-Ewha Study Abroad (RESA) program, are the outcomes of this expansion. The two programs aim to equip students with the linguistic and cultural knowledge so students can make meaningful local and global contributions. The KETI program's mission is to meet the need for Korean translation/interpreting in the New Jersey, a state that currently has the fourth largest Korean population in the US. It is the first academic program that trains professionals to serve in courts, hospitals, schools, and service agencies. RESA is a summer faculty-led study abroad program that offers a diverse group of Rutgers students the opportunity to deepen their language skills and cultural understanding through internships, service learning, and guided research.

Rutgers Korean-English Translation and Interpreting Certificate program

The Korean-English Translation and Interpretation Certificate program was introduced to address evolving demands of intermediate and advanced learners of Korean, affording them pragmatic exposure and professional prospects in using the language. The KETI program's primary objective resides in reorienting learners' motivations, especially those of heritage learners, beyond immediate communicative necessities, towards broader societally impactful contributions engendered by linguistic and cultural expertise. This 12-credit program, one of the first in the discipline in the US, is independent of the Korean major and Korean minor and open to both undergraduate and graduate students as well as to the outside community.

To complete the KETI program, students must either complete elementary and intermediate Korean language courses, which span four semesters, or demonstrate an equivalent level of proficiency through the placement test. Starting with the introductory course, Korean Translations: Intro to Practical Translation and Translation Theories, they fulfil a total of 12 credits by taking Korean Media Translation, Korea in Translations: Literature and Film, Korean Interpreting, Korean Translation/Interpreting Internship, and/or Computer Assisted Translation.

As illustrated in Figure 10.1, the introductory course, interpreting course, and internship course are designated as mandatory courses for certification. Specifically, the latter two courses are categorized as capstone courses, recommended to take during the final stages of their certification. Within each class, students are exposed to practical translation and interpreting activities and projects that are inspired by authentic source materials spanning diverse genres (e.g., legal and medical documents, various media format, literary works, etc.). In addition, it is worth noting that the final products of these tasks are distributed through platforms such as YouTube and Wikipedia, building a connection to the wider community of Korean language users.

Although each course in the certificate program contributes to students' development of community consciousness, two capstone courses are specifically built to promote students' engagement with the community. The internship course (a 15-week, 1.5-credit practicum class) as a whole are offered in collaboration with various institutions, including government agencies, civic organizations, and cultural facilities in the local community. Students are matched with these organizations where they engage in tasks assigned by onsite supervisors and utilize the language, cultural knowledge, and translation and interpreting skills they have acquired in the classroom. The course requires students to invest at least three hours each week in completing the tasks which varied significantly based on the

Required Courses (3 credits)	• Korean Translations: Intro to Practical Translation and Translation Theories (prerequisite: Intermediate Korean or equivalent)
▼	
Electives (4.5–6 credits)	• Korean Media Translation • Korea in Translations: Literature and Film • Computer Assisted Translation (summer online course)
▼	
Korean/English Placement Test	
▼	
Capstone Courses (4.5 credits)	• Korean Interpreting • Korean Translation/Interpreting Internship

Figure 10.1 Pathway to KETI certificate

institution and the community served. For instance, a student working with an organization advocating for consumer rights in Korea sought translations of their advice pieces, including detailed case studies of rights violations and step-by-step solutions. They translated from Korean to English to benefit foreigners residing in Korea. A legal services center for low-income families at the local court requested the student intern translate informational flyers and brochures into Korean, providing guidance for Korean American victims of domestic and dating violence.

One of the two capstone courses, Korean Interpreting covers three types of interpreting: sight translation, consecutive interpreting, and simultaneous interpreting in both directions (into English and into Korean). Through role-playing, various settings are simulated: interpreting in a conference, informal meeting, telephone call, hospital, courtroom settings, and others. Students engage in group practices and training, as well as evaluating each other's performance. Each student works at their respective level, with a partner at a similar level to maximize skill learning. As a performance-based course, assignments include writing and recording of exercise scenarios as well as improving linguistic proficiency.

The launching in 2020 of KETI program, one of the first academic curriculum in the US, provides bilingual students with opportunities to local problems within a globalizing intercultural framework. Students interested in Korean language, culture, and translation greatly benefit from real-life learning experience. While engaging in translating for the Korean-American community, students learn to understand the issues surrounding language and power in ethnic minorities and to reflect on the social structures by dealing with different accents/dialects and the problem of legitimacy. Critical pedagogy enables the students to critique and question the dominant power structures and to take action, however small, to bring about a change: they provide Korean translations for the Patients' Bill of Rights, a series of free legal service guidelines for domestic violence, brochures of museum exhibitions, and others.

Rutgers-Ewha Study Abroad program

The Rutgers-Ewha Study Abroad program is a new faculty-led summer study abroad program that was launched in 2022 to offer a diverse group of students an opportunity to expand and deepen their language skills and to better understand Korean culture and history through an innovative curriculum. The program also provides firsthand intercultural engagement through internships, service learning, and on-site visits to museums, archives, and memorials. These experiences in and out of the classroom not only help students cultivate intercultural communicative competence but create deeper curricula connections across the Korean language and culture program. Out-of-classroom activities offer frequent contact with native Korean language speakers, while curated visits to important cultural sites ensure that intercultural encounters go beyond touristic impressions by bringing history to life. The four-week program strengthens the students' performance in Asia-related coursework upon their return, as they have gone from gaining "passive" cultural awareness through print or other educational media to "actively" interact with contemporary Korean culture in motion.

Participants in the program are obligated to enroll in a three-credit course under Topics in 21st-Century Korea. This course cultivates socio-historically grounded understanding of Korea while affording students firsthand exposure to the language and culture of the country. In addition, students have the option to select between two tracks: the Korean language track and the guided research/internship track. In the language track, students take a language class led by Ewha faculty, enabling them to enhance their language proficiency while interacting with peers from diverse cultural/linguistic backgrounds. On the other hand, the guided research/internship track allows students to enroll in either one or both of 1.5-credit courses. The guided research course encourages students to delve into various aspect of Korean history, media, cuisine, arts, and contemporary issues in South and North Korea, as well as the language, and conduct their own research in these areas. Additionally, students on this track have an opportunity to engage in internships, applying their linguistic and cultural knowledge within an immersive environment to gain valuable professional experience. The faculty advisor monitors their progress based on students' weekly online journal as well as the evaluative report from the service organization.

3.2 Students' perception on critical pedagogy

This chapter examined the KFL curriculum inspired by critical pedagogy through students' self-report. Findings are based on two sets of data collected from students with experience of Korean classes at Rutgers: (1) self-reflection essays from KETI and RESA programs ($n = 60$) and (2) in-depth interviews on learners' experience of learning Korean for career pursuits through the KETI program ($n = 10$). The data are rich in information about the learners' sociolinguistic acquisition, metalinguistic insights, and awareness of social justice. A content analysis revealed that students' own perception of learning Korean extends beyond the acquisition of language and cultural competencies. Some students reported that critical pedagogy had an immediate influence on their professional career choices, which was a serendipitous development resulting from their learning experience and the acquired skill sets that gradually modified their initial career goals.

Data and participants

The first set of data is self-reflection essays collected from students who participated in the KETI program and RESA program. In particular, those who were part of internship course for both programs and "community interpreting" project in the Korean Interpreting class provided valuable insights regarding impact of critical pedagogy and overall learning experience of the Korean language. A total of 60 journal entries, final essays, and reflection papers were collected after students worked for the institutions and tasks illustrated in Table 10.1. The journal entries, final essays, and reflection papers are all integral parts of assessment in the KETI and RESA curriculum. For these essays, students were required to engage in reflective exercises, documenting their experiences and lessons learned throughout the

Table 10.1 Institutions and tasks

KETI internship (29 students)	RESA internship (15 students)
• Legal services center for low-income families: Translating informational flyers/brochures designed to assist victims of domestic/dating violence (E→K). • NGO for Korean-American voters: Translating newsletters about the legislative process/outcomes protecting Korean-American rights (E→K) • Art museum: Translating an exhibition catalog (K→E) • Korean National Library: Translating introductions to overseas children's books, a list of Korean classics, and an exhibition archive • NGO for consumer rights: Translating an advice piece on consumers' rights (K→E) • Korean Economic institute: Translating a Korean ambassador's memoir (E→K)	• Institution promoting cultural exchange of Korea: Collecting data and researching on foreign culture/customs • NGO: Collecting and analyzing data on civil movement around the globe • Art foundation: Assisting promotion of Korean folk culture • Alternative schools for N. Korean refugees: Teaching English • Performing Art Institution: Promoting contemporary performing arts of Korea (and translation K→E)

semester. They were instructed to freely describe their struggles, insights, and feelings on several aspects of the tasks – linguistic, cultural, academic, and personal growth.

The second dataset was obtained through in-depth interviews conducted with KETI alumni. We directed the questions to the first cohort of the KETI program, particularly focusing on those who had either graduated or were in the process of graduating within a semester. Approximately 15 students were identified and asked to be interviewed, and 10 students responded to the request. The interview questions, as seen in (1), were designed to elicit their insights and perceptions regarding the interplay between their Korean language learning experiences and their career pursuits. Due to limited availability of students, the interview was conducted via written format, and follow-up questions were asked either via email or during a zoom meeting.

(1) Interview questions

a. Briefly tell us who you are and about your experience with the Rutgers Korean program.
b. When did you start learning Korean? What motivated it?
c. [For heritage students] Please explain your exposure to Korean before you took college-level Korean courses. How would you characterize your formal Korean language education in college?
d. What are your career goals? What needs to be done to be successful in your career? How is success in your career related to or dependent on Korean language learning?

e. When you first decided to learn Korean, did you think that learning Korean would provide you with more job opportunities and be useful in your future career? When and how did you connect Korean language learning with your career goals?
f. Was learning the Korean language transformative in your life and education?
g. How would you characterize your experience of learning Korean at Rutgers University? Do you think the RU Korean curriculum has helped you to apply course concepts in a way that may serve you in your future career endeavors?
h. Public outreach through real-life engagement generates a level of confidence. Does your experience coincide with the above statement?
i. Can you think of other ways that can forge personal connections to Korean language learning outside of school context?

As outlined by Zhang and Wildemuth (2017), for content analysis, we identified individual themes as the units of analysis and developed a coding scheme. Four main ideas emerged – that critical pedagogy and Korean language learning experience (1) facilitate academic growth, (2) promote (local/global) community engagement, (3) expand students' life experiences and opportunities, and (4) enhance learner agency.

4. Findings

Facilitate academic growth

First and foremost, students reported that the curriculum facilitated their academic growth in four major areas: (1) Korean language competence, (2) translation/interpreting skills and strategies, (3) relevant background knowledge (*Connections* goal of 5Cs), and (4) English competence.

In students' essays, translation projects were frequently cited as instrumental in expanding and diversifying their vocabulary. The experience of struggling through linguistic gaps and finding solutions to complete translation tasks appeared to significantly contribute to each student's lexical enrichment. Students who translated for consumer rights organizations, art museums, or Korean-American voters' rights groups noted that they gained substantial field-specific lexical knowledge resulting from their translation work. They emphasized the struggles with and acquisition of unfamiliar words as one of the most memorable aspects of their tasks.

Moreover, students highlighted the importance of understanding Sino-Korean words and the advantages of recognizing *Hanja*, Chinese characters, while learning Korean. One student, Daisy, mentioned that "through the use of *Hanja* and other root Korean characters, I may be able to decipher the meaning of other words." It was clear that these projects encouraged students to explore the appropriate use of Sino-Korean words and increased their awareness of their significance within the Korean language.

Additionally, it was evident that these projects enabled students to gain insights into socio-linguistic aspects of the Korean language. They learned to differentiate between formal and informal speech styles, compare spoken and written language in Korean, and adapt their language use based on context and register. This awareness was particularly pronounced among heritage learners like Janice, who "learned many things that I wouldn't have learned from home or other places such as Korean school."

Students also mentioned that they were able to improve translation/interpreting skills and strategies, including the use of machine translators and CAT programs. They found CAT tools, in particular, to be invaluable, ranging from free machine translators like Papago and Google to more advanced translation-specific tools such as OmegaT. They also described how translators should specialize and become "an expert in a certain area of translation, because they can continue to hone their skills and create good, accurate translations" (Chole).

Chole's comment connects to another common note on the importance of background knowledge, which is not only relevant to translation tasks but also to the process of language learning. To successfully complete their projects, students had to invest substantial time and effort in gathering resources related to Korean culture, history, and society and US politics, criminology, or finance, which then enabled them to fully comprehend the original text and select the most appropriate expressions based on it. Moreover, many students recognized that their learning extended beyond language acquisition. As Sarah mentioned, "it . . . expanded my understanding of literature. . . . Learning a new language allows one to also understand that region's deep history and culture."

Some students, such as Janet, in the following, even mentioned that the curriculum had an impact on their native language (L1) use, emphasizing the simultaneous learning of Korean and English.

> I could also feel myself improving in English itself because I'd have to write a lot of creative and well-written sentences to match their Korean counterparts. I found myself quite fascinated by what I learned. . . . The decisions I make help me produce a good translation from my own interpretation of the text and my existing skill-set.

In summary, students' reports illustrated the multifaceted benefits of a PCC-inspired curriculum and translation projects, in particular in their academic growth. These experiences contributed to improving their language and translation skills, the integration of language learning with background knowledge, and enriching their overall language proficiency in both their native language and the target language.

Promote (local/global) community engagement

Students frequently described their understanding of community consciousness and engagement. To begin with, students clearly optimized the learning process as an opportunity to broaden their perspectives. Emily, for example, mentioned that the experience gave her "different insights about different parts of the world, which is more than learning and gaining experiences in translation." John also described that his "way of thinking about and interacting with the world is heavily influenced from what I learned in the . . . classes I have taken with the Korean department."

The experience not only encouraged students to consider their individual responsibilities in completing assigned tasks but also fostered a sense of collective responsibility as a member of the community. Students left a number of comments on stress and pressure they felt about task completion and personal growth they experienced while dealing with those stress and pressure. Jenny "learn[ed] the discipline of time management," and Ella "learned to become a more responsible communicator." Joy, a political science major, expressed her realization about her role as a Korean-speaking member of a Korean American community when she was looking into issues related to Korean-Americans' rights. She stated that "it was extremely relevant to having political discussions especially in my hometown in Bergen County, which has a high population of Korean-American citizens." Students had a chance to contextualize their work and to reflect on their contributions by translating for a particular audience, whether they worked for local agencies or institutions in Korea. The internship courses are by nature totally engaged with agencies outside of school, and the instructor provides guidelines by requiring journal writing, reflection essays, and final papers; the course evaluation also reflects the student performance assessment from the agency.

Expand students' life experiences and opportunities

There were various comments discussing connections between the language learning experiences and the students' own life experiences. Their comments were sometimes directly related to their life as a learner and those of improving their language proficiency. Most of the students described their experiences where they voluntarily or involuntarily used Korean in a real-life setting outside of the classroom environment. For example, Joy, who had a part-time job within the Korean American community in NJ, "ha[s] encountered various clients and bosses in various jobs who also speak Korean, and who appreciate my proficiency in the language." Adam, who is a Korean American student, also shared his experience at a local church.

> I attend a Korean-American church and have been asked to translate between conversations a number of times. My father is a pastor of a Korean church in Korea, and I have translated slogans and sermon titles for him.

Brian and Jean, who studied abroad in Korea or traveled to the country after graduation, also shared their thoughts on language use outside of the classroom. Even if the situation may not be as pleasant as it could be when compared to those in classroom settings, they admitted that it was more meaningful engagement with the language.

> I would say that my willingness to engage with languages in public situations has given me more confidence – especially after having lived in a country in which English was not the primary language of communication.
>
> (Brian)

when you are in a situation where you have to force yourself to learn the language, unlike in a school setting, it definitely stick with you more and that experience will help you gain a deeper understanding of the language itself.

(Jean)

Notably, students began identifying themselves as lifelong learners of Korean and expressed a commitment to engage in activities that would continue fostering their language development after graduation. Even without any formal Korean language education, they expressed a genuine intention to invest time and effort in ongoing language learning. This commitment was rooted in their belief that learning the language had been transformative and still held a significant place in their lives, as exemplified by Jean's statement: "I . . . do believe that learning the language was transformative as it still plays an important role in my life."

Furthermore, the language learning process itself had a profound impact on their peer relationships due to its collaborative nature. John highlighted how it facilitated "develop[ment of] stronger bonds" among students. Additionally, the interdisciplinary nature of these peer relationships was emphasized, as "students often add Korean as a supplement to their studies, interacting with them almost always seemed like an interdisciplinary exercise, being exposed to their differing expertise and perspectives."

Moreover, students shared a diverse range of comments regarding their decisions to learn Korean for their career pursuit. Nearly all students acknowledged that learning Korean had influenced their career path, whether directly or indirectly. The impact was evident in the experiences of students like Joy and Helen, who initially did not perceive a strong connection between their majors and language learning but later noticed shifts in their career-related aspirations.

> While this may not initially seem relevant to Korean, it has actually allowed me to understand politics on a global scale, since I am able to watch and read Korean news. . . . My success in my career is not necessarily entirely dependent on Korean language learning, but it has broadened my research interests.
>
> (Joy, who aspires to become a professor of political science)

> I learned a lot about translation during my internship . . . especially as my interest in working in the healthcare field in the future correlated to translating these health-related documents. I now have a stronger awareness of the value of using formal language, cultural differences, and the difficulties associated with translating specific terminology.
>
> (Helen)

Several students highlighted that their knowledge of Korean played a crucial role in securing their positions. For instance, Sam, working in the cybersecurity field, cited his "ability to understand and translate a foreign language – namely, Korean" as a competitive advantage that set him apart from other candidates. Another KETI program alumnus, John, attributed his job offer in the national security industry to his expertise in the Korean language and culture. He emphasized that "[b]eing well versed in the Korean language as well as understanding the . . . history and customs" not only provided financial incentives but also expanded the scope of missions he could be assigned to.

Additionally, students with aspirations to teach English in Korea, become pastors in Korea, or work in media industry in the US firmly believed that their knowledge of the Korean language and culture had already opened or would open new career opportunities for them.

Enhance learner agency

Student comments and reflections also discussed the impact of PCC in their experience as students and learners. Because it was a minimally controlled environment when compared to traditional classrooms, many students experienced initial anxiety when they were to perform their language. However, students such as Laura, in the following, were also able to heighten their motivation and regain a sense of achievement through the internship opportunities.

> While I was very intimidated, once I began to work on it, I realized that I am much more capable than I had believed. Therefore, through this internship, I both worked on developing my weak skills and gained some confidence as a Korean-English translator.

Students also appreciated the student-initiated, collaborative learning process that the curriculum emphasized. Students checked each other's translations, left comments or feedback, and made changes based on their collective discussion. This involved interaction between peers, between students and instructor, and between the internship agency and students. Students were the ones who initiated the process and took the lead in collaboration. In the process, they learned the value of collaboration, as Yasmin discussed in her essay: "asking for help did not mean it was cheating, but it was a better way to ask different perspectives on how it could be better translated."

The curriculum inevitably entailed differentiated learning components, as each student worked for a different agency and was engaging with different projects. Students seemed to learn that each individual learns through different process and "that everyone works at their own pace" (Phoebe) and appreciated the freedom to choose the field and contents that were relevant to them, as illustrated in the following comments:

> I think this genre suits me well . . . this book had a certain literary voice that was fun to work with and the actual content interest[s] me quite a lot.
> (Janet)

> As a political science major, I often have the opportunity to debate, speak on, and write about political issues in English. But because this space is

not offered to me in Korean, I believe that my language skills need much improvement when it comes to discussing politics. . . . this process allowed me to have a deeper understanding and more detailed insight into politics through a Korean perspective.

(James)

I chose the New Brunswick Community Interpreter Project . . . since I will be going into a career involving healthcare administration. Being able to translate documents for Korean-speaking patients is something I can add to my resume.

(Eunice)

As detailed earlier, the open-ended nature of internship projects granted students autonomy and fostered learner agency, enabling them to take an active role in their learning experience. Students had the freedom to determine what and how they wanted to learn and how to apply their knowledge beyond the classroom, nurturing a strong sense of ownership throughout the process. Utilizing collaborative decision-making process among peers, tasks were distributed in a manner that catered to individual students' language proficiency, strengths, and weaknesses. These student-driven projects allowed individuals like Ella to redefine their identities, as she aptly expressed in her essay: "I gained deeper insights, a wider spectrum, grew as a student, as a translator, and as a person." The multifaceted experience not only honed students' language skills but also equipped them for future endeavors outside of academic settings. Learner agency was both the process and outcome of these internship projects, profoundly contributing to the successful and transformative impact of the internship program.

5. Conclusion

In the previous sections, we have shown that it is possible to embed critical pedagogy in a KFL curriculum with two examples of the Korean program at Rutgers University. Critical pedagogy encourages teachers and learners to understand and overcome the social structures in which people are dominated and oppressed. The unequal structure also exists in the classroom, where the teacher imparts knowledge top-down to students whose voices and experiences are often not heard. We can change the imbalance by not treating students an empty vessels but giving them as much agency as possible. Even in intermediate level of study, they can choose their own learning materials based on their needs and academic and personal interests. For instance, students were asked to choose their own "short videos," known as "Shorts," for audio-visual literary enhancement. There were as many "Shorts" as the number of students in class; the topics included pets, sports, environmental issues, language, fashion, racial stereotyping, and K-Wave. When their lived experiences are valued in the classroom, the student gets motivated to learn, the teacher becomes a co-learner in the endeavor of education, and together they take action for a positive change (such as writing a letter to the New Jersey Motor Commission to point out a grave mistranslation in the DUI document).

Amidst a growing body of KFL practices through the lens of critical pedagogy that directly addresses the learners' life situations, we report the implementation of the Korean-English Translation-Interpreting Certificate Program and Rutgers-Ewha Study Abroad Program at Rutgers University as a case to illustrate transformative learning in KFL. The survey data are rich with learners' sociolinguistic acquisition, metalinguistic insights, and awareness of social justice, as well as teachers' observations of transformative learning. In sum, we are able to identify four areas of transformation: (1) facilitate academic growth of both Korean and English competency, (2) promote (local/global) community engagement, (3) expand students' life experiences and opportunities, and (4) enhance learner agency.

A content-analysis reveals that students' own perceptions of learning Korean go beyond the acquisition of language and cultural competences. Participants unanimously stated that learning Korean helped them becoming global citizens and lifelong learners. Some students reported that critical pedagogy had immediate influences on their professional careers (academic pursuit in graduate programs, employment in Korea, training as translators), a serendipitous development brought on by the learning experience itself and the acquired skill sets that gradually changed their initial career goals.

In conclusion, what clearly emerges from our analysis is that critical pedagogy produces transformative learning in KFL, whether it helps solve local problems within a globalized intercultural framework (community projects, K-12 teacher training) or opens a door to reach local communities (service learning) and global Korean-speaking communities (multimodal collaboration). Critical pedagogy transcends conventional educational practices that limit learning to the classroom and provides alternatives that address real-life issues and enhance learner agency and teacher effectiveness.

References

Cervantes-Soon, C. G., Dorner, L., Palmer, D., Heiman, D., Schwerdtfeger, R., & Choi, J. (2017). Combating inequalities in two-way language immersion programs: Toward critical consciousness in bilingual education spaces. *Review of Research in Education*, *41*(1), 403–427. https://doi.org/10.3102/0091732X17690120

Cho, Y., & Chun, H. (2023). Innovative strategies for stabilizing enrollment in Korean as a foreign language (KFL) education. In E. H. Uebel, F. A. Kronenberg, & S. Sterling (Eds.), *Language program vitality in the United States: From surviving to thriving in higher education* (pp. 251–265). Springer.

Corson, D. (2001). *Language diversity and education*. Lawrence Erlbaum Associates.

Crooks, G. (2013). *Critical ELT in action*. Routledge.

Crooks, G. (2021). Critical language pedagogy: An introduction to principles and values. *ELT Journal*, *75*, 247–255.

Cummins, J. (2001). *Language, power, and pedagogy: Bilingual children in the crossfire*. Multilingual Matters.

Cutshall, S. (2012, November). More than a decade of standards: Integrating "communities" in your language instruction. *The Language Educator*, 32–37.

Freire, P. (1968/1970). *Pedagogy of the oppressed.* Continuum Books. (Original work published in 1968)
Giroux, H. (1992). *Border-crossings: Cultural workers and the politics of education.* Routledge.
Giroux, H. (2011). *On critical pedagogy.* Bloomsbury Academic.
Korean National Standards Task Force. (2012). *Standards for Korean language learning.* ACTFL Publications.
Lee, H., & Choi, B. (2021). A geolocative linguistic landscape project in Korean as foreign language education. In D. Malinowski, H. Maxim, & S. Dubreil (Eds.), *Language teaching in the linguistic landscape* (pp. 183–204). Springer. https://doi.org/10.1007/978-3-030-55761-4_9
Lee, J. (2022, November 10). *Developing critical consciousness: Applying lessons learned from a community-university partnership program to Korean language classroom.* Talk at PSU Lecture Series.
Lee-Smith, A. (2018). Linking language learning with community: A community-based learning project for advanced Korean courses. *The Korean Language in America, 22*(2), 167–189. https://doi.org/10.5325/korelangamer.22.2.0167
Luke, C., & Gore, J. (1992). *Feminism and critical pedagogy.* Routledge.
MacGregor-Mendoza, P., & Moreno, G. (2016). Connecting Spanish heritage language students with the community through service-learning. *Heritage Language Journal, 14*(3), 405–433. https://doi.org/10.46538/hlj.13.3.6
McLaren, P. (1989). *Life in schools: An introduction to critical pedagogy in the foundations of education.* Longman.
The National Standards Collaborative Board. (2015). *World-readiness standards for learning languages* (4th ed.). The National Standards Collaborative Board.
N.J. Department of Health. (n.d.). *Language access.* N.J. Health. www.nj.gov/health/ommh/resources/language-access/
Norton, B. (2000). *Identity and language learning: Gender, ethnicity, and educational change.* Pearson Education.
Norton, B., & Toohey, K. (2012). *Critical pedagogy and language learning.* Cambridge University Press.
Pennycook, A. (2001). *Critical applied linguistics: A critical introduction.* Lawrence Earlbaum Associates.
Simon, R. (1992). *Teaching against the grain: Texts for a pedagogy of possibility.* Bergin & Garvey.
Sohn, S., & Kim, S. (2022). Community in service learning in Korean. In A. Byon & D. Pyun (Eds.), *The Routledge handbook of Korean as a second language* (pp. 235–254). Routledge.
Suh, J. (2019, October 25). *Telecollaboration-based project.* Presentation at 2019 Language Consortium Workshop: Project-based Language Teaching and Learning.
US Census Bureau. (2021). Total Asian alone or in any combination population (the total groups tallied). *2021 American Community Survey One Year Estimates Detailed Tables.* https://data.census.gov/cedsci/table?q=B02018&g=0400000US06,34,36,48
Vertovec, S. (2007). Super-diversity and its implications. *Ethnic and Racial Studies, 30*(6), 1024–1054. https://doi.org/10.1080/01419870701599465
Zhang, Y., & Wildemuth, B. M. (2017). Qualitative analysis of content. In B. M. Wildemuth (Ed.), *Applications of social research methods to applications to question in information and library science* (2nd ed., pp. 318–329). Brooks/Cole.

Additional resources

This section presents additional resources that the reader can use to explore further some of the topics covered in the book. The resources are grouped around the main topics dealt with in the book and include commented references to further reading or links to online websites or repositories.

AI and other applications of large language models

- Forum on generative artificial intelligence organized by the National Research Foundation of Korea.
  This forum, which took place on 16 November 2023, dealt mainly with ethical issues related to use AI in educational settings. It is available as video at the YouTube channel of the National Research Foundation of Korea, www.youtube.com/watch?v=JFRbaIJBup0.
- WRTN.
  WRTN is an AI-powered chatbot developed in Korea and suitable to be used with and for material in Korean language. The application allows the user to develop ad hoc apps to automize tasks; for example, it is possible to easily create a WRTN-based app to generate examples for Korean grammar items suited for different level of learners. It is available at wrtn.ai.
- Chocarro, R., Cortinas, M., & Marcos-Matás, G. (2023). Teachers' attitudes towards chatbots in education: A technology acceptance model approach considering the effect of social language, bot proactiveness, and users' characteristics. *Educational Studies*, *49*(2), 295–313.
  This paper investigates the factors influencing teachers' acceptance of chatbots by examining the dimensions of the technology acceptance model, including conversational design as well as teachers' age and digital skills.
- AI and education on Wikidocs.
  This set of web documents offers a comprehensive overview of recent advancements in the AI industry, with a particular focus on 56 examples of AI applications in education. It additionally explores research on AI-powered learning methods and their potential impact on educational outcomes. The following links redirect to the page dedicated to the Sejong Institute AI Korean tutor: https://wikidocs.net/128387, while the home page of the section on AI and education is available at https://wikidocs.net/book/5807.

Virtual reality

- Center for Languages and Intercultural Communication (CLIC) VR Learning Lab at Rice University.
  This website collects VR videos for Korean, Chinese, and Japanese learners. The videos for Korean learners are recorded in real settings and present topics such as ordering food, talking at a coffee shop, touring a university campus, and many others. It is available at https://clicvr.rice.edu/category/korean/.
- Virtua traveleR.
  Virtua traveleR presents 360-degree video recorded in Korea. Available via YouTube, it contains playlists with walking videos, drone view videos, and also video recorded in the Gyongi region outside Seoul. It is available at www.youtube.com/channel/UCYcQaGZEDVrShFCgmsY6YAw
- Korea Walker.
  Korea Walker offers a set of videos on Korea, not just VR walking videos but also driving and cycling. Younger students may be interested in the K-pop video playlist. Not all videos are recorded in 360-degree mode. It is available at www.youtube.com/channel/UCiFvmyR0BD9xphJ98nr4qpQ
- Fisheye Taxi.
  Fisheye Taxi offers 360-degree videos to explore Korea. The videos can be broadly grouped into two types, those recorded from the perspective of a car driver and those recorded while hiking in the mountains. It is available at www.youtube.com/channel/UCv8jCKlFRANyYoCG8xMCNiA.
- Korea360.
  This YouTube channel provides learners with 360-degree videos focused on Korean modern and traditional markets, parks, and several of Seoul's tourist hot-spots. It is available at www.youtube.com/channel/UCIpxOEkaVowj3T_2P1FMzBQ.

Metaverse

- Sejong Institute metaverse.
  The metaverse of the Sejong Institute, designed to facilitate online Korean language learning and described in detail in Chapter 6, is available at https://zep.us/@ksif.
- Gather Town.
  This metaverse, also mentioned in Chapter 6, allows the instructor to easily create private metaverses to be used as educational spaces. It is easy to use.

YouTube channels for educators

- Prof. Yoon's Korean Language Class.
  This channel has 170,000 subscribers as of June 2024 and provides language teaching resources for self-study aimed at beginners and intermediate students. Some videos follow the KLEAR textbook series and the Sejong Institute textbooks. Videos deal with listening/reading, grammar, and conversation, and

channels are organized around textbook series and learner proficiency. It is available at https://www.youtube.com/@ProfYoonsKoreanLanguageClass
- Hallyu like that.
This channel has 2,300 subscribers as of June 2024, and it is run by an ethnomusicologist and a filmmaker. The channel includes commentaries on Korean popular culture, mainly pop music, and podcasts. The channel can be of interest to students with a passion for Korean popular culture. Some of the channels are dedicated to young fans of the most popular girl groups and boy bands. It is available at https://www.youtube.com/@hallyulikethat
- Eat Pray Anime.
This channel, with 2,440 subscribers as of June 2024, does not deal with Korean language or Korean culture but is about Japanese anime, which is analyzed from the perspective of culture and religion. This channel, although not related to Korea, is introduced here as a fine example of an educational YouTube channel dealing with (popular) culture. It is available at https://www.youtube.com/@EatPrayAnime

Emotions in language learning

- *Annual Review of Applied Linguistics*, volume 43, 2023.
The 2023 issue of ARAL explores the topic of anxiety in language learning, and it is of great interest to all teachers concerned about learners' wellbeing. This special issue also contains papers dealing with other emotions beyond anxiety, such as curiosity, enjoyment, boredom, and some emotion-related concepts, such as willingness to communicate and classroom silence.
- Williams, M., Mercer, S., & Ryan, S. (2016). *Exploring psychology in language learning and teaching*. Oxford University Press.
This handbook is an introductory resource for language teachers to understand learners' psychology. This book deals with, among others, students' emotions and includes practical discussions on how to consider learners' psychology in everyday teaching.
- Mercer, S., & Gregersen, T. (2020). *Teacher wellbeing*. Oxford University Press.
Teachers' emotions are as important as students' emotions. This book is a practical guide on how language teachers can make the most out of the principles of positive psychology to reach better personal wellbeing, which will, ultimately, benefit learners as well.

Multimodal teaching and learning

- Paesani, K., Allen, H. W., & Dupuy, B. (2015). *Multiliteracies framework for collegiate foreign language teaching*. Pearson.
This book introduces multiliteracy pedagogy and contains excellent examples of how it can be applied in university language classrooms.

- Kress, G., & Van Leeuwen, T. (2020). *Reading images: The grammar of visual design.* Routledge.
  This book provides an accessible and comprehensive introduction to the idea of visual grammar.

Critical pedagogy

- Lee, H., & Choi, B. (2020). A geolocative linguistic landscape project in Korean as foreign language education. In D. Malinowski, H. Maxim, & S. Dubreil (Eds.), *Language teaching in the linguistic landscape.* Educational linguistics, Vol. 49. Springer.
  This study showcases community-conscious activities in KFL classrooms using linguistic landscape (LL) in combination with digital storytelling. The project's student-led, inquiry-based approach positively influenced students' understanding of language, culture, and local multilingualism.
- Norton, B., & Toohey, K. (2012). *Critical pedagogy and language learning.* Cambridge University Press.
  This collected volume is both a theoretical and practical guide, covering important topics such as critical multiculturalism, gender and language learning, and popular culture. It demonstrates the role of applying critical pedagogies in language education in recognizing existing social relations and transforming them towards greater equity in schools and communities. It is also very useful for teacher education and for developing critical testing.

Index

Note: Page numbers in *italics* indicate a figure and page numbers in **bold** indicate a table on the corresponding page.

5 Cs 175, 181

AATK (American Association of Teachers of Korean) 173
academic growth 181–182, 187
aegyo 157
affective filter 101
affective responses 82, 87, 133
agency 41, 175, 181, 183, 185–187
AI (artificial intelligence) 2–5, 13; and academic writing in Korean 13–18, 20–25; additional resources on 189; integration in language learning 21–22, 28, 56, 65; *see also* chatbots; GAI
anti-feminism 158
anxiety: in affective filter 101; and AI 24; and chatbots 4–5, 14, 38–40, 42; and enjoyment 136; epistemic 133–134; of teachers 144; and VR 82, 87, 90; and YouTube videos 120, 122
assistance for students 118, 121–122, 128
AT (user attention) 31, 35–37, 42
attitude, in TAM2 32, 36–37
Australian universities 138, **139**
autonomous learning 49, 65, 115
avatars 7; in metaverses 100–102; in YouTube videos 116; in ZEP 105–106, 109
axial coding 85

background knowledge 128, 181–182
Bard 5, 46–48, 50, 52–54, 56
Bergen County, NJ 176, 183
BI (behavioural intention) 31–32, 35–37, 42
Bing 5, 46–48, 50, 53, 55–56

bodily movements 7
body language 86
boredom 134–135, 191
Brown, Lucien 7

capstone courses 177–178
captions, in Korean 117, 126
CAT (computer-assisted translation) 182
Center for Academic Innovation, University of Michigan 83
chatbot builders 30, 65
chatbots 3, 5–6; additional resources on 189; challenges of using 39–42; future research directions on 42–43; in language learning 14–15, 28–30, 32–39, **35–36**; response creativity 38, 42; in smart learning environments 65; summaries from 20; and TAM 31–32; in ZEP 107, 110; *see also* ChatGPT; Sejong AI Tutor
ChatGPT 13; comparative research on 47; error correction by 5–6, 47, 50–56, 64, 66; and Korean writing 16–21, 23–24, 46–47; in KSL 15; and language learning 48–49, 65–66; *see also* ChatGPT-3.5; ChatGPT-4
ChatGPT-3.5: error correction by 5–6, 50, 52–56, 66–71; literature review on 47–48
ChatGPT-4, error correction by 5, 47, 50–54, 56
Cho, Myunghee 7
Chomsky, Noam 46
Chun, Hee Chung 8
classroom environment 133, 143–144, 183
Claude 51

Index

Cleverbot 47
CLIC (Center for Languages and Intercultural Communication) 91, 190
CLOVA Note 16
CLOVA X 5, 46, 50, 52–54, 56
CMC (computer-mediated communication), Korean 157
cognitive disequilibrium 135, 145
cognitive load 124
cognitive processes 24, 145
cognitive skills, low-order 109
cognitive strategies 24, 136
collaborative learning 108, 185–186
colour, as semiotic mode 153
communication skills: and AI 32; and VR 82, 87
communicative competence, multimodal 7, 152, 154–155, 162, 167
community-conscious learning 175–179
community engagement 174, 181–183, 187
computer-mediated composition 13
confusion: and difficulty perception 145–146; as epistemic emotion 7, 133–138; and perceived teacher behaviour 140–144, 146
content knowledge 17–18, 24
contextual knowledge 17–19
conversation practice, and chatbots 34
conversation samples 120, 122
COVID-19 pandemic: and language teaching 2; and masks 158; and metaverses 100, 102, 110; and VR 79
Creative Commons 126–127
creativity, chatbots and 14, 39–40, 42
critical pedagogy 4, 8, 174, 186–187; additional resources on 192; and Korean as a Second Language 176–181; literature review 174–175; students' perception of 179–186
critical reading 155, 159, 161
critical thinking 23–24, 135
Crystallize 81
cultural competence 154, 175, 187
cultural differences 86–87, 89, 119, 184
cultural knowledge 89, 165, 176–177, 179
cultural understanding 32, 85–87, 176
curiosity: as epistemic emotion 133–135, 137; in intercultural competence 89
cuteness, embodied 157
CVT (control-value theory) 145

data privacy 38, 42
DeepL Translate 47

deference 162–163
detailed reading 159–160
difficulty, perceived 134, 136–142, 145–146
digital environments 7, 103, 111
digital ethnography 165
digital technology 13–15
discourse analysis, multimodal 152, 159–161
disengagement 40, 146
Duolingo 2

e-books 106
educational psychology 133–135, 144
embodied behaviours, appropriate 157–158, 161–164, **163**
emojis 7, 151, 157–158, *158*, 167
emoticons 157
emotional experiences 134, 138, 140
emotional intelligence 134, 144
emotional landscapes 134, 137, 144
emotion-based pedagogy 138, 145–146, 191
emotions 4, 133; and metaverses 101; *see also* epistemic emotions
engagement, and chatbots 28–30, 38–40, 42
English language education: chatbots in 32; LLMs in 47–48, 56; multimodality in 155
English subtitles 117, 126
enjoyment: as epistemic emotion 134–137; in intercultural competence 89
enthusiasm, as epistemic emotion 140, 142–144
Epistemically Related Emotions Scale 140
epistemic emotions 5, 7, 133; literature review on 133–137; and perceptions of teacher behaviour 138–146, **139**
error correction 5, 17, 38; by chatbot and human raters **69**; by LLMs 46, 49–57, 66–71; in YouTube videos 119, 121
error detection 6, 67–68, 70–71
ethnography, multimodal 8, 164–165
excitement: and difficulty perception 145; as epistemic emotion 7, 133–138; and perceived teacher behaviour 140–142, 146; and VR 145
experience web 84

Facebook 101, 115
face masks 158

feedback: instruction-combined 119; peer 115; personalized 40, 42, 70–71
feedback mechanism, in chatbots 38–39
flexibility, and chatbots 38, 40, 42
flow, state of 134, 136, 145
foreign language education: and critical pedagogy 173–174; and LLMs 46, 48
formality 19, 70
Fraschini, Nicola 7
Freire, Paulo 174
friendliness, perceived teacher 7, 137–142, 144–146
frustration 4–5; as cognitive emotion 133, 135; and confusion 145–146; using chatbots 39, 42; using VR 82, 87, 90

GAI (generative artificial intelligence) 13, 46, 48–49, 64–67, 69–71, 189
gamification 101, 107–109, 145
GBL (game-based learning) 107
GEC (grammar error correction) *see* grammar correction, by LLMs
gender: and Korean language learning 139; and politeness 152–153; in soju adverts 159–160
Generation Z 101
Genie K 30
gestures 7, 151, 153–154, 156–157, 167
GIFs 151
Google Bard *see* Bard
Google Translate 19, 47, 182
grammar correction, by LLMs 5, 46, 49–56, **52**, 64–71, 73–76
grammar of the visual 154
grit 134

Halliday, Michael 152
hallucination phenomenon 54–55
Hanbat National University 16
Hangul 25n5, 105, 138, 157
Hanja 181
hardware limitations 88, 90
high-context society 23
HiVR (high-immersion VR) 6, 79–80; literature review 80–83; videos for Korean learners 83–92
honorifics 67, 153, 161–164
House of Languages 81

ImmerseMe 81, 112
impasses 135–136
Imprudence 101
informal learners 121

information retrieval, ChatGPT and 18, 47, 51
initial reading 159–160
intended effort 134, 136–138, 140–143, 145–146
interactive elements 39, 87
intercultural competence 81–82, 89, 154, 178
intercultural framework 8, 178, 187
international students 5; use of AI by 13, 15, 18–20, 22–25
internships 8, 176–179, 183–186
interpreting 178–179
intertextuality 17–18, 20
intuitive interfaces 37, 41

Japanese manga 151
Jessica's Vlog 116–123, *117*, *123*
Jung, Narae 5

Kahoot 108, 110
Kakao Talk 157, *158*
KAP (Korean for academic purposes) 15, 17, 20, 22–23
K-dramas 60, 86, 156, 163; politeness in *163*
KETI (Korean-English Translation and Interpreting Certificate) 176–180, *177*, 184, 187; internships **180**
KFL (Korean as a Foreign Language) *see* Korean language education
KIIP (Korea Immigration and Integration Program) 102
Kim Jiyoung 6
Kim Kukjin 6
Kim Soyeon 6
kinship terms 152–153
knowledge application 159, 161
knowledge generation *see* new knowledge, acquiring
Korea 25n4; as high-context society 23; *see also* South Korea
Korean accents, non-standard 39
Korean Americans 173, 175–176, 178, 180–181, 183
Korean communities 164–166, 175
Korean culture: background knowledge on 182; and honorifics 162; learning via metaverse 102, 107, 111; learning via VR 83, 86–87, 89, 91; and multimodal literacy 156, 164–165; popular 156, 191; YouTube videos on 118–120, 122

Korean grammar, complexities of 6, 70–71; *see also* grammar correction
Korean heritage students 86, 173, 176, 182
Korean identity, semiotic markers of 165, *166*
Korean language: multimodal aspects of 7, 155–158; number of learners 1–2; *see also* error correction; KAP
Korean language education: AI and digital technology in 13–16, 64–66; and chatbots 14–15, 28–30, 32, **35–36**, 37–43; and ChatGPT 48–49; critical pedagogy and 8, 175–181, 184, 187; epistemic emotions in 136–139; learner profile of 173–174; in metaverses 103–112; multimodal and embodied aspects of 159–167; and particles 52; and pedagogical innovations 2–8; using YouTube 116–123, 127–128; VR in 80–81, 83–85, 87–92
Korean language proficiency 20, 22–24, 28, 65–66; *see also* TOPIK
Korean language teachers 5, 7, 15, **15**, 23
Korean multimodal communication 151
Koreanness, multimodal representation of 158, 165–166
Korean politeness 156–157, 161–162, 164
Korean script *see* Hangul
Korean society, information on 18
Korean speaking, chatbots and 28–29, 33–34, 38–39, 42–43
Korean text: error correction in 5, 46–47, 49–56, **52**; samples of 59–63
Korean universities: specialized 25n4; use of AI in 16, 20, 22–25
Korean writing: AI in 5–6, 13–15, 17–24; LLM feedback on 49, 55–56; *see also* Hangul; Hanja
Korea University 22
K-pop 1
Kramsch, Claire 154
Krashen, Stephen 101
Kress, Gunther 153
Kuki 47

language classrooms 7; epistemic emotions in 133–135; friendly teachers in 144–145; HiVR in 83; student profile of 173; YouTube in 115
language learning: AI in 21–22, 56, 66, 71; chatbots in 28, 30–31, 37, 39–40, 42; HiVR in 79–82, 88–91; LLMs in 49; metaverses in 101–103; *see also* SLA

language system knowledge 17, 21–22, 24–25
learner identity 105
learning assessment 105, 109
learning environments: and chatbots 14, 38; metaverses as 102, 108–109, 111
learning experience 5, 8; and AI-generated writings 21; and chatbots 28, 34, 37–39, 42–43, 49; and critical pedagogy 178–179, 186; and intended effort 137; and learner perspectives 14; and VR 79, 82, 84, 91
learning journeys 20, 41
learning materials 119, 122, 186; AI-powered 14
learning objectives: chatbots and 34, 41; and VR 83–84; in ZEP 106–109
Lee, Inhye 5
life experiences 181, 183–185, 187
lifelong learners 184, 187
listening comprehension 87, 126
listening skills 82, 90
literacy: digital 167n1; multimodal 155–156; visual 154; *see also* multiliteracies approach
LiVR (Low-immersion VR) 80
Llama 51
LLMs (large language models) 2–3, 5–6, 46–47, *50*; correcting Korean text 49–57, **52**, 64–71; literature review 47–49, 65–66; writing feedback from 55–56
LMS (learning management system) 116–117, 120, 124, 127, 138
long-term interest 29, 40

machine translation *see* translation, AI for
media literacy 167n1
Melbourne, Koreanness in 165, *166*
memes 151
Meta (formerly Facebook) 88, 101
metacognitive abilities 19
metalexemes 162
metalinguistic insights 8, 179, 187
Meta Quest VR headsets 79–80
metaverses 2, 4, 6–7, 100–103; additional resources on 190; in education 105; Google searches for 111; pedagogical implications 110; *see also* ZEP
Ministry of Education of the Republic of Korea 22
Modern Language Association 1, 155
Mondly VR 81, 112

motion events 156
motion sickness 88–90
motivation 5, 8; in affective filter 101; and chatbots 28, 30, 39, 41; and epistemic emotions 136–137; intrinsic 145; and perceived teacher behaviour 143; and VR 82
multiculturalism 155
multilingualism 155
multiliteracies approach 7–8, 152, 154–156, 161, 167
multimodal communication 151–152
multimodal competence 154, 159, 164, 167n1
multimodal features of language 152–154, 156–157, 159, 162, 167
multimodal teaching 2, 4, 7–8, 152; additional resources on 191–192; of Korean politeness 161–167; previous studies on 154–156

narratives, visual 151, 153
natural language generation 42
Naver 50, 104
neoliberalism 143
New Jersey 176
new knowledge, acquiring 91, 133–136
New London Group 154–155
NLP (natural language processing) 46, 49, 64
non-verbal communication 4, 86–87, 89
NPCs (non-playable characters) 106

Oculus headsets 79–80, 84, 88
OER (open educational resources) 126–128
online resources 122, 175
OpenAI 6, 46–47, 50, 64
open coding 85
open-ended questions 35, 84–85, 161
OpenSim 101
outlines, AI used for 20

Papago 182
participatory culture 115
particles 52, 68
PBC (perceived behaviour control) 32, 35–37, 42
PCC *see* critical pedagogy
pedagogical innovations 2–4
pedagogy of critical consciousness *see* critical pedagogy
peer relationships 184

Perplexity AI 5, 46, 50–56
personal growth 180, 183
PEU (perceived ease of use) 14, 31–32, 35–37, 41–42
PI (personal innovativeness) 32, 35–37, 42
plagiarism 5, 13, 16, 18–19, 21–25, 46
pointing gestures 151
politeness 86; multimodal 8, 156, 161–164, *163, 164*
positive psychology 134
practical skills, chatbot-learned 41
pre-reading 160
prompts, specificity of 54, 56
PU (perceived usefulness) 14, 31–32, 35–38, 42

rapport with students 122
real-life scenarios 39, 51
remote learning, screen-based 105, 109
RESA (Rutgers-Ewha Study Abroad) program 176, 178–180, 187; internships **180**
research participants, teachers **15**
role-playing 34, 49, 109–110, 178
Rutgers University 176, 179–181, 186–187
Ryu, Na-Young 5
Ryu Seung-ryong 161

scaffolding 146
SE *see* self-efficacy
Sebasi Talk 116
Second Life 81–82, 101
Sejong AI Tutor 14, 29–30, 32–35, *33*, 38–40, 42
Sejong Institute 2, 6–7, 25n5, 32; AI Teacher chatbot (*see* Sejong AI Tutor); language proficiency tests 23; metaverse of (*see* ZEP)
self-confidence 101
self-directed learning 6–7, 38, 118, 121
self-efficacy 32, 35–37, 41–42, 145
selfies 151
SEM (structural equation monitoring) 139–141, **141–142**, *141*
semiotic modes 153
Seoul: Chinese migrant neighbourhood in 158; representation in VR 83–85; representation in ZEP 107
Seoul National University of Science and Technology 22
service learning 175–176, 178, 187
short videos 117, 186

SLA (second language acquisition): and emotions 101, 133–137, 143; and meaningful interactions 109
slang 39, 123
Snow Crash 100
social connection 29, 40
social justice 5, 8, 174, 179, 187
social networking 115, 175
social visions 174
sociocultural communication 19
sociolinguistic acquisition 8, 179, 187
soju, advertisements for 153, 157, 159–161, *159*, 168n1
sound objects 151, 161
sound recognition technology *see* speech recognition
South Korea: gender in 161; international students in 15–24, 81; media materials from 155–156; VR videos about 86
speaking skills 39, 90
speech recognition 5, 30, 38–42; in VR 84, 87–88, 90
spelling correction, LLMs and 5, 46, 49, 51–54, **53**, 56, 68–69
Standards in Korean Language Learning 175
stickers 151, 157, *158*
strictness, perceived teacher 7, 137–139, 141–144, 146
student-centred learning 115
student-centred pedagogy 144
student perceptions: of chatbots 28, 30, 34–36, **35–36**, 38, 41–42; of task difficulty 140
Study Korea 300K Project 22
subject-predicate congruence 6, 68–71
summarizing, AI used for 20
Sungkyunkwan University 16, 100
superdiversity 8, 173–174
supermarkets, Korean 165–166
symbolic competence 154
systemic functional linguistics 152–153

TAM (technology acceptance model) 14, 28–31, *31*, 189
TAM2 14, 28, 32, 34–35, 41
Tao, Yu 7
teacher behaviour, perceptions of 133, 136–138, 140
teacher-learning task-student dynamics 143
technical glitches 88, 90
TEUIDA 30, 90

time commitment, to YouTube channels 125–126, 128
TOPIK (Test of Proficiency in Korean) **16**, 22–23, 25n1; evaluation criteria 67, 71n2; writing assignments for 64, 66–68, 70–71
transformative learning 8, 174, 187
translation: AI for 13–14, 19–25, 48, 65, 182; and critical pedagogy 174, 177–178, 181–182, 184–185, 187; multilingual 14, 47, 49; of VR videos 87; *see also* KETI
Trigo Maldonado, Álvaro 6
tutorial videos 7, 118–121, 124–125

United States: Korean immigration to 173; language teaching in 32, 155; *see also* Korean Americans
Uptale 84, 88, 90
urban spaces, Koreanness in 165, *166*
US, in TAM framework *see* usability
usability 32, 35–38, 42, 82
user-centred design principles 37, 41
user experiences 32, 42, 118

van Leeuwen, Theo 153
verbal tense 68–71
video games 88, 101
virtual classrooms 105–106
virtual communities 175
visual design 153
visual grammar 151
visual language 151
visual preferences 124
visual texts 8, 157
voice recognition *see* speech recognition
VR (virtual reality) 2, 4, 79; additional resources on 190; and epistemic emotions 145; headsets 84, 88–91, 112; images *96–99*; for Korean language learning 83–92; and metaverses 103; *see also* HiVR (high-immersion VR)
Vygotsky, Lev 108, 146

Webex 103
Wikipedia 177
writing ability, categories of 17
writing assistance, AI-powered 5
writing practice 21
writing process knowledge 17, 19, 24

written texts, visual components of 7–8, 151
WTC (willingness to communicate) 30

Yoon, Sue 161
YouTube 4, 7, 115–116; 360° videos 81; additional resources on 190–191; CC-BY license on *127*; comments on *123*; educational channels on 123–127; and KETI 177; language learning on 118–123; soju adverts on 159; video visibility on 124, *125*; *see also* Jessica's Vlog

YouTube Studio page 123–124, *124*, 127
Yu Cho, Young-mee 8
Yu Tao 7

ZEP (Zettaverse Expansion Platform) 7, 101–104, 110–112, 190; assessment in 109–110; core characteristics **104**; embedded games in *107*; identity and time in 105–106; interaction and learning objectives in 106–109; special Sollal event *108*
Zoom 16, 104, 125, 180
ZPD (zone of proximal development) 146

For Product Safety Concerns and Information please contact our EU
representative GPSR@taylorandfrancis.com
Taylor & Francis Verlag GmbH, Kaufingerstraße 24, 80331 München, Germany

www.ingramcontent.com/pod-product-compliance
Lightning Source LLC
Chambersburg PA
CBHW050535300426
44113CB00012B/2110